The EVERYTHING®
Tex-Mex Cookbook

Dear Reader,

The first time I tasted Tex-Mex food as a child I immediately fell in love with the cuisine. It was take-out food from a fast food chain store—nothing fancy. But there was something about the flavors and textures that inspired in me a life-long obsession. If I could, I'd put fresh herbs and refried beans into everything!

When I was growing up, my family would vacation for several weeks each winter in Texas, New Mexico, Arizona, and California. In fact, in 1973 we spent a month touring Texas and Mexico in a motor home! I remember eating so many spectacular foods on that trip, including my first tamales and a Tex-Mex shrimp boil on Marco Island with shrimp fresh from the Gulf of Mexico.

My parents also owned a vacation home in Green Valley, Arizona for many years, and we spent a lot of time there. We visited the many Tex-Mex restaurants in that area every day and enjoyed the food, especially Los Amigos' chimichangas. I also vividly remember the first time I had deep fried ice cream: the smooth and sweet ice cream surrounded by the crisp hot coating, all smoth-ered in chocolate sauce, was a delight.

Tex-Mex food can be sophisticated or comforting; it can be spicy and full of complex flavors, and it is always delicious. I think one of the things I like most about Tex-Mex food is that it uses both processed cheese food and fresh corn, canned refried beans and fresh cilantro. You can find a Tex-Mex recipe to suit any mood or occasion, which I think makes this food some of the best in the world.

I hope that you enjoy these recipes and make Tex-Mex meals a part of your life.

Linda Larsen

The EVERYTHING® Series

Editorial

Publishing Director	Gary M. Krebs
Associate Managing Editor	Laura M. Daly
Associate Copy Chief	Brett Palana-Shanahan
Acquisitions Editor	Kate Burgo
Development Editor	Katie McDonough
Associate Production Editor	Casey Ebert

Production

Director of Manufacturing	Susan Beale
Associate Director of Production	Michelle Roy Kelly
Cover Design	Paul Beatrice
	Erick DaCosta
	Matt LeBlanc
Design and Layout	Colleen Cunningham
	Holly Curtis
	Sorae Lee
Series Cover Artist	Barry Littmann

Visit the entire Everything® Series at *www.everything.com*

THE
EVERYTHING®
TEX-MEX
COOKBOOK

300 flavorful recipes to spice up your mealtimes!

Linda Larsen

Adams Media

Avon, Massachusetts

To my parents, Marlene and Duane, for their love of spicy food and
for introducing me to Tex-Mex foods in the first place.

An Everything® Series Book.
Everything® and everything.com® are registered trademarks of F+W Publications, Inc.

Published by Adams Media, an F+W Publications Company
57 Littlefield Street, Avon, MA 02322. U.S.A.
www.adamsmedia.com

ISBN: 1-59337-580-8
Printed in the United States of America.

J   I   H   G   F   E   D   C   B   A

Library of Congress Cataloging-in-Publication Data
Larsen, Linda.
The everything Tex-Mex cookbook : 300 flavorful recipes to spice up your mealtimes! / Linda Larsen.
p.   cm.—(An everything series book)
ISBN 1-59337-580-8
1. Mexican American cookery. I.Title. II. Series: Everything series.

TX715.2.S69L37 2006
641.5979—dc22
2005026083

This publication is designed to provide accurate and authoritative information with regard to the subject
matter covered. It is sold with the understanding that the publisher is not engaged in rendering legal,
accounting, or other professional advice. If legal advice or other expert assistance is required, the ser-
vices of a competent professional person should be sought.

    —From a *Declaration of Principles* jointly adopted by a Committee of the
American Bar Association and a Committee of Publishers and Associations

Many of the designations used by manufacturers and sellers to distinguish their products are claimed as
trademarks. Where those designations appear in this book and Adams Media was aware of a trademark
claim, the designations have been printed with initial capital letters.

Cover photographs © Banana Stock, Corbis, Ingram Publishing, and PhotoDisc.

This book is available at quantity discounts for bulk purchases.
For information, please call 1-800-872-5627.

Contents

Acknowledgments

Thanks to my husband, Doug, for his help and encouragement during this endeavor. Thanks also to my agent, Barb Doyen, for her clear head and calm nature. My editor, Kate Burgo, deserves thanks for her patience and belief in me. And thanks to my father-in-law and his wife, T.E. and Dagmar, for supporting me.

Introduction

Did you know that Tex-Mex cooking is the oldest regional cuisine in America? You would think that such a time-honored cuisine would have clear-cut recipes and menus and be easy to define. But it's hard to say exactly what Tex-Mex cooking is. There are as many definitions as there are dishes!

Generally, Tex-Mex cooking consists of recipes and foods native to Mexico, updated with the foods and customs of the state of Texas and, as the cuisine expanded, France, Spain, and the rest of America. These recipes range from Frito Pie to Caramel Flan, from Barbecued Brisket to Ceviche, and the foods include everything from processed cheese food to fresh herbs, shrimp, lard, chiles, and tortilla chips.

Tex-Mex cooking is scorned by many sophisticated cooks and restaurants, but it can be a delicious and inventive style of cooking. Of course, ingredients such as yellow cheese, raw onion, and refried beans can be used judiciously and well, or can be overdone. The food can be complex and subtle or truly searing and obvious, depending on the taste and mood of the cook.

Of all the Tex-Mex, Texas, and Mexican cookbooks on the market, very few have included some commonly used appliances: the crockpot and the indoor dual-contact grill. Since these tools save time and money and produce high quality foods, they have been incorporated into the book. Crockpot Ranch Casserole made in the crockpot is creamy and rich and is ready when you get home. Texas Toast Grilled Sandwiches and Cheese Quesadillas are crisp, golden, and perfectly done when made in a dual-contact grill.

If you are following a special diet, whether low-fat, low-carb, or South Beach, Tex-Mex cooking can fit into your lifestyle. If you are eating low-carb, most of the meat and vegetable dishes are made for your diet. For low-fat devotees, the vegetarian, side dish, and salad recipes are all good choices. The special foods of Tex-Mex cooking, especially chiles and sauces, are excellent choices to add flavor and variety to any diet and many recipes. And the most commonly used ingredients, corn and chiles, are very high in vitamin content, especially vitamins A and C.

Sauces are very important in Tex-Mex cooking. Once you have mastered Enchilada Sauce, Chili Gravy, and different types of salsas, you will be able to make most dishes in this cuisine. Read the chapter on sauces carefully, as they are the finishing touch to many recipes in the book.

As in all cooking, you choose the level of seasoning and spices. If your family isn't fond of spicy hot food, omit the chile peppers in these recipes or substitute milder peppers for the hotter varieties. Use parsley instead of cilantro for a milder taste, and choose ground black pepper over red pepper flakes for less heat. You can also increase the heat level. Learn about the heat and flavors of chile peppers and spices and you will always be able to control the taste of the food you serve.

This book will teach you about the foods, cooking techniques, and tastes of Tex-Mex cooking. You'll learn about calcabacita, nopales, burritos, pasilla chiles, quesadillas, enchiladas, tacos, epazote, churros, chalupas, frijoles, gorditas, and more, expanding your knowledge of the world along with your kitchen repertoire. There's no better way to travel without leaving your home than to learn a new cuisine.

Chapter One

Tex-Mex Basics

The phrase "Tex-Mex" was first mentioned in the media in 1973 as a style of food combining Mexican and Texan cuisines popular in the southern part of the United States. To food snobs, the term meant fast food served to the undiscerning masses. The foods and recipes evolved and the cuisine borrowed ingredients from other cultures as it grew. This cuisine, built upon the foods and recipes of the ancient Aztec and Mayan Indians, is now much more than fast food: it's the most popular ethnic cuisine in the world!

Origins of Tex-Mex

Mexican cooking is an ancient cuisine that stretches back thousands of years. It is a combination of native Indian and Spanish foods and recipes brought to the country by the Conquistadors. There's even a bit of French, Austrian, and Italian influence! Before Spain invaded Mexico, there was no wheat, cattle, pigs, butter, rice, almonds, or walnuts in the cuisine. That means before the Conquistadors, Mexican cooking did not use pork, beef, cheese, or rice, but was based on corn, tomatoes, squash, beans, game, and pumpkins. The food was very healthy and mostly vegetarian. The Spanish invasion greatly expanded the Mexican cuisine, which even used indigenous animals like the armadillo and iguana.

FACT

The transcontinental railroad, or more specifically the Texas Mexican Railway, was a huge undertaking in the 1800s that helped create the Tex-Mex cuisine. As the railroad pushed west, ranchers and cowhands had more ingredients to work with, including flour, meats, and sweeteners that were not as available in Mexico.

This cuisine came to the United States in the 1800s, when Spaniards and Mexicans arrived in Texas to work on the ranches and settle in the cities. These immigrants found Indians eating regional foods and crops such as rabbits, deer, pumpkins, and cactus. The huge ranches of western Texas added beef products to the cuisine, along with recipes and entire meals cooked over a fire: campfire cooking, smoking, and barbecue. This was simple food made of available and inexpensive, sometimes free, ingredients.

As Tex-Mex cooking spread across the country, chili was introduced at the Chicago World's Fair in 1893, and tamales became a popular street food in Chicago during the Depression. During this time the term itself was considered something of an insult, mocking Mexican dishes that were "Americanized" with lots of cheese, instant rice, and cheap cuts of meat. Even today it's easy to find food advertised as "Tex-Mex" characterized by large combination platters of overcooked food covered in yellow cheese and all tasting the same.

A Cuisine Is Born

As other cultures discovered Tex-Mex cooking, it lost its junk-food status. The French, Brazilians, and even countries in the Middle East adopted the flavors and textures and added their own twists.

What didn't change is that the most important foods in Tex-Mex cooking are tomatoes, beef, beans, chiles, and corn. In fact, corn is so deeply embedded in the culture that many of the names for foods made of corn come directly from the Aztec language—for example, *tamal* (tamale) and *tlaxcalli* (tortilla). Tex-Mex cooking is an Americanized form of Mexican cooking, but with its own twists added from other cultures. Ingredients combined with an eye for color, texture, and flavors, based on regional tastes, are what Tex-Mex food is all about.

There are many different variations of Tex-Mex cooking that incorporate food combinations of other ethnicities, like French-Mex, Cal-Mex, New Mex-Mex, Nuevo-Mex, and Lou-Mex. Tex-Mex cooking, which embraces them all, differs from Mexican food in that it uses more acceptable combinations and more common ingredients. These include canned condensed soups, pro-

cessed cheeses, fried tortilla chips, and canned tomatoes and chiles, which are not used in Mexican cooking.

Pickled chile peppers, especially jalapeños, are commonly used in Tex-Mex cooking, and the plain beefsteak tomato is very popular. Peppers from California, including the Anaheim, along with root vegetables from the South such as sweet potatoes, have made their way into the Tex-Mex cuisine.

Nachos, which are a combination of fried tortillas, sauce, and melted cheese, is a quintessential Tex-Mex food not found in the Mexican cuisine. Chips and dip are not served as an appetizer in Mexico. Flour gravies are an important part of Tex-Mex cooking, made with the drippings created when meat is browned. In Mexico, sauces are almost always made of tomatoes and chiles and are more complicated than Tex-Mex sauces.

The food is simpler than most Mexican cooking, while some classic Mexican dishes are remade in the Tex-Mex mold by using prepared sauces, chili powders, and purchased convenience foods such as taco shells, premade tortillas, and even precooked meats. Flour tortillas are more Tex-Mex than Mexican, and fajitas, especially those eaten in flour tortillas, are an American addition to the cuisine. And margaritas, those popular happy-hour beverages, are not served in Mexico.

QUESTION?

Is it chile or chili?
That final vowel makes a difference! *Chile* refers to the fresh, canned, or dried hot green or red pepper, while *chili* refers to the classic Tex-Mex soupy stew made of beef, tomatoes, and ground chiles, and to the powder made of a blend of chiles and other ingredients.

There are differences too between the types of food eaten by West Texans, Southern Texans, and Coastal Texans, depending on the ingredients readily available in those areas. Thus the West Texans may eat more foods based on beef and wheat, while the coastal Texans' diet is rich in seafood and herbs.

So don't feel limited by ingredients called for that may or may not be available where you live. Substitute your own favorite foods! Since the cuisine is all about combining the best of many different cultures, don't be afraid to add your own twist.

Tex-Mex Ingredients

There are some special ingredients and food you will need in order to cook Tex-Mex, but the vast majority will be those with which you are already familiar. Once you master the new techniques and learn about the ingredients, you'll be able to create your own dishes using your family's favorite foods and flavors.

Specialty Foods

Over the years it has become much easier to purchase many of the special ingredients that make this food unique. Look for them in the ethnic, Hispanic, or Tex-Mex aisles of your grocery store.

- **Masa harina:** Processed corn flour used to make tortillas and tamales.
- **Hot sauce:** Ranges from mild to mind-blowing with hundreds of varieties.
- **Chile paste:** Chiles are picked and processed like tomatoes to make a paste.
- **Colored tortillas:** Tortillas that contain red chile powder or are made from blue or yellow corn.
- **Hominy:** Corn kernels processed in lime to remove the tough outer skin.
- **Corn husks:** Tough corncob leaves used to wrap tamales while they steam.
- **Cactus pads:** Thick leaves that can be bought precleaned and then scrubbed if necessary before use.
- **Tomatillos:** Can be purchased fresh or canned; should be husked and rinsed before use.
- **Chorizo:** Spicy hard sausage made of pork, garlic, salt, oregano, and chiles.
- **Adobo sauce:** Vinegar-based sauce; packed with chipotles or plain.

When you try a new ingredient, you will have to choose between several brands and varieties. Read labels closely to make sure you know what you are getting. You will also find favorites among different brands; when you do, write down the brand name next to the recipe it's used in.

Be sure to carefully follow preparation instructions for these foods. Tomatillos, for instance, must be rinsed to remove a sticky residue before chopping or cooking, and nopales, or cactus pads, sometimes need to be scrubbed with a plastic scrubbing utensil to remove tiny hairlike thorns, while corn husks are soaked in hot water before use.

Spices and Seasonings

Good quality spices and herbs are a critical part of the Tex-Mex cuisine. These ingredients add subtle or not-so-subtle flavors to most dishes. Many spices can be substituted for each other as long as you use approximately equal quantities.

- **Chili powder:** A blend of ground dried chiles, oregano, garlic, salt, and cumin.
- **Ground chile powder:** Dried chiles toasted and ground.
- **Cayenne pepper:** Cayenne chile, dried and ground into a red pepper.
- **Cumin:** A spice with a smoky flavor, used often in Tex-Mex cooking.
- **Cilantro:** A fresh herb with strong, citrusy, and almost astringent taste.
- **Epazote:** A very pungent herb used with cooked beans.
- **Mexican oregano:** More flavorful and intense than the Mediterranean variety.
- **Vanilla:** Used as a liquid extract and as the whole vanilla bean.

Other herbs such as basil, thyme, and marjoram also have their place in Tex-Mex cooking and can be used according to your tastes and mood. Remember when using herbs that 1 tablespoon of fresh herbs equals about 1 teaspoon of dried leaves or ⅛ teaspoon dried and ground.

Special Techniques

Many ingredients have special preparation methods. Each technique brings out the best characteristics of each food, whether to remove a tough skin, enhance flavors and aromas, or remove more undesirable parts of the ingredient.

Roasting Peppers

Many peppers are roasted and peeled before being added to dishes. Roasting adds a smoky flavor and removes the tough skins that may add an unpleasant texture to dishes. To roast peppers, broil them 4–6" from the heat source, turning frequently, until blackened all over. Or you can place them on the grill or hold them over a gas flame and char them.

Then place the peppers inside a paper bag and let them steam for about 10 minutes. The skin will come off easily; use your fingers or rub them with a paper towel or kitchen towel. Do NOT rinse the peppers off; you'll wash away a lot of flavor that developed during roasting.

Toasting Chiles, Seeds, Nuts, and Spices

Before many spices, nuts, and seeds are ground, they are toasted to remove excess moisture and to enhance the flavors and oils. To toast seeds, nuts, and spices, place them in a dry skillet and cook over medium heat until fragrant, shaking the pan frequently. Cool on kitchen towels. Dried chiles are often toasted to increase their flavor. When you buy them, dried chiles should still be pliable. Place them in a 325°F oven and bake for 3 to 8 minutes, depending on size, until the chiles are almost brittle.

FACT

Spices and chiles can be ground in a well-labeled spice grinder or a mortar and pestle, also called a molcajete. Traditionally, this implement was made of volcanic rock. Be sure that chiles, seeds, nuts, and spices are completely cool before grinding them.

Making Tortillas

Of course you can buy corn and flour tortillas, but making your own is easy and fun. Make the dough using masa harina for corn tortillas, or flour, water, and oil for flour tortillas, and form the dough into small balls.

A tortilla press looks like a waffle iron but is non-electric. Line the press with plastic wrap, or place the dough inside a plastic food bag, and then flatten the dough. Remove the plastic and cook the thin rounds on a comal or griddle until brown spots appear, turning once. Store them in an airtight container.

Preparing Tomatoes

Tomatoes may be peeled and seeded to remove tough skins and so sauces aren't diluted. To peel tomatoes, cut a small X in the end and plunge them into rapidly boiling water for about a minute. Remove and plunge into ice water. Let stand for 2–3 minutes, and then remove the peel with a knife. To seed tomatoes, cut them in half and squeeze out the seeds and clear liquid.

Using Lard

Lard is a common Tex-Mex ingredient that brings a unique flavor and texture to many foods, especially tamales. It actually isn't as bad for you as some think. It has half the cholesterol and one-third the saturated fat content of butter. Lard is easy to make yourself and better for you, too, since the processed types are usually hydrogenated.

ALERT!

Remember that melted lard is quite flammable and very hot; be careful when you are handling it. In a new crockpot, the lard may render in less time than in older crockpots, since the newer crockpots cook hotter. Start checking the crockpot after 6 hours.

Buy fatback pork (ask the butcher; you may be able to get it free) and cut it into small cubes. Place 2 pounds in a 4-quart crockpot and cook on low for 8–11 hours until the fat is rendered. Turn off the crockpot and let the lard cool for at least half an hour. The small pieces of fat and skin that do not dissolve may not get crisp enough in the crockpot to use them as cracklings; you can remove them from the fat and sauté in a heavy saucepan over medium heat until they become crisp and brown. Remove the brown bits, or cracklings, with a slotted spoon, drain them on a paper towel, and strain the fat from the crockpot and the saucepan into a container. Refrigerate or freeze the cracklings.

Cover the strained fat and refrigerate overnight. In the morning, scrape the light brown gelatin from the white solid fat; discard the gelatin and freeze the fat. Use cracklings to flavor Corn Bread (page 110) or tamales.

Making Tamales

Tamales are made of corn dough spread on corn husks that have been soaked in hot water, filled with meats or cheeses, then wrapped and steamed over boiling water. Making the dough is the tricky part. It is made by beating masa harina with fat and liquids until fluffy. The dough is ready when a spoonful of it, dropped into cold water, floats. Spread it evenly on the prepared corn husks to within 1" of edges, then top with fillings. Fold in the sides of the husks to meet in the middle and fold the top down and bottom up to cover the seam. Tie with string and steam until the corn husks pull away easily from the dough.

Cooking Methods

For your kitchen, you will need several good heavy skillets and saucepans, along with a selection of spoons, spatulas, and a good and sharp, well-balanced knife set. A sturdy charcoal or gas grill, a griddle, a crockpot, and a dual-contact indoor grill are also necessary tools.

Smoking Meats

Many meats are smoked in Mexican and Tex-Mex cooking. This adds a wonderful flavor to the meat and makes the meat portable, so it's readily available while traveling across the huge state. You can buy smokers that are specially designed to cook meat to perfection; use mesquite or other woods such as apple to add more flavor. The mesquite tree grows as scrub all through Texas and Mexico and is burned in grills and smokers to give a piquant flavor to foods. Mesquite and other flavored wood chunks should be soaked in water for about 30 minutes before being placed on hot coals.

Barbecue and Grilling

There's a difference between barbecue and grilling. To barbecue (or BBQ), meats are cooked for hours over low and slow coals, while grilled meats and vegetables are cooked quickly over a very hot flame. Both techniques use a charcoal or gas grill: choose one with a large surface area and a tight-fitting cover. Indoor grills are a good choice for cooking sandwiches and vegetables.

To truly barbecue, you need to be able to control the heat of the fire. Drip pans and water pans can be placed in the coals and used to create smoke, which drifts upward and flavors the meat. Sprinkle mesquite chips and other hardwoods such as apple or oak on the hot coals to add even more flavor.

The best meats for barbecue are cheaper cuts, which benefit from long slow cooking. For grilling, the meats must be more tender with a lower fat content: that means higher in quality and price.

Deep-Frying

Deep-frying is a common Tex-Mex cooking technique. Pour vegetable oil into a deep, heavy skillet or saucepan that is a bit larger than your burner, leaving at least 1" of space at the top of the pan to allow for expansion as cold and wet foods are added to the oil. Place pan over medium heat as directed in the recipes.

To judge temperature, use a deep-frying thermometer; also, at 350°F a 1" cube of bread will brown in about 1 minute; at 375°F the bread will brown in 30–40 seconds. When the oil is in this range, a few drops of water sprinkled into the oil will immediately sizzle and pop. You can reuse oil used for deep-frying up to five times—cool and strain it before storing—but for best results, use fresh oil each time you fry.

Cooking Beans

Beans are the backbone of Tex-Mex cooking; the cuisine uses pinto beans, pink beans, black-eyed peas, black beans, kidney beans, garbanzo beans, and pigeon peas. They are high in fiber and folic acid and other vitamins and minerals, and they taste delicious!

To cook dried beans, first carefully sort through them to remove any small stones or pieces of dirt. Then rinse the beans thoroughly and place them in a heavy saucepan. Cover with cold water to 1" over the beans, then bring to a boil; boil for 1 minute, then remove from the heat. Let beans stand for 1 hour. Then pour off the water and add fresh cold water or other liquid. Bring to a boil, reduce the heat, and simmer until the beans are tender. The cooking time can range from 30 minutes for tiny pink beans up to more than 70 minutes for black beans or garbanzo beans.

Of course, you can also use canned beans. Be sure to drain the beans and rinse well to remove the thick sweet liquid they are packed in.

The Name Game

Some names for Tex-Mex recipes and ingredients can be confusing. Many are named for their shape or appearance, and some recipes may even have more than one name.

For instance, chalupas are fried tortillas layered with ingredients. Tostadas are also fried tortillas layered with ingredients. Envueltos, or filled and folded tortillas, are so called because they look like envelopes. Flautas are tightly rolled, deep-fried filled tortillas that look like the flute they are named after; but the same dish is also called taquitos.

The names of chiles can also be confusing. Ancho chiles are sometimes called pasilla or Anaheim. But pasilla chiles are usually dried ancho chiles with a smoky flavor. It's best to ask when you shop for your recipes to make sure you're getting the pepper with the heat and flavor you want.

FACT

The outer crust on smoked and barbecued meat is called the bark, referring to the crisp dark brown layer that forms as the meat cooks. And bark is also a variety of cinnamon, as well as a recipe made with melted chocolate candy coating.

There are even different forms of tacos. A soft taco is filling folded inside a corn or flour tortilla. A puffy taco is made from a tortilla fried so the layers separate; it's a Tex-Mex pita bread, but very crisp, light, and crunchy. And a crispy taco is the traditional half moon shape you can buy packaged in any grocery store.

The point is to not be overly concerned with the names of foods, but be flexible and understand that, as with any fusion cuisine, there may be differences in food terms and ingredient definitions. Just relax and enjoy the process and the new discoveries!

Food Safety

It's important to follow basic food safety rules no matter which cuisine you're working with. Here are some of the basics.

- Refrigerate perishable foods after 2 hours at room temperature.
- Refrigerate perishable foods after 1 hour if the temperature is above 80°F.
- Separate cooked and raw foods at all times.
- Keep cold foods cold and hot foods hot—below 40°F or above 140°F.
- When working with chile peppers, wear gloves and NEVER touch your eyes.
- Wash your hands, cooking utensils, and work surfaces frequently.

- Use a meat thermometer to check doneness of meats.
- Do not serve raw or undercooked eggs, chicken, turkey, ground beef, or seafood.

Steaks can be cooked until medium rare or 145°F on a meat thermometer. Chicken should be cooked to 170°F; pork to 165°F; and all ground meats to 165°F.

When deep-frying, be especially careful. Keep the pot with the hot oil on a back burner and have a fire extinguisher and a tight-fitting lid nearby. Use oven mitts and tongs when putting cold or wet food into hot oil because spattering will occur. Don't leave the stove while you're frying, and carefully drain the food, first over the pot and then on paper or kitchen towels, before serving.

Remember to refrigerate and freeze foods promptly when you bring them home from the supermarket or farmer's market. Also, wipe off your countertops and cooking surfaces often with hot soapy water or antibacterial hand wipes. Just remember: cook, chill, clean, and separate, and your Tex-Mex kitchen will always produce safe and wholesome foods.

The Essential Cheese

Cheese is an important ingredient in the Tex-Mex cuisine. While the cuisine was evolving, yellow cheese was really the only cheese used: whether Cheddar, longhorn, or American, it was melted on top of many dishes. But fresh and cured Mexican and American cheeses such as queso fresco ("fresh cheese"), Monterey jack, Parmesan, and Muenster are now also used.

Look for these special cheeses in your grocer's dairy aisle, at the deli counter, or at a food co-op or farmer's market. Ask about the qualities of each cheese and also ask for a taste before you buy.

- **Queso fresco:** Mild crumbly fresh cheese; substitute fresh goat cheese.
- **Queso blanco:** Soft, mild white cheese that melts well; substitute Muenster.
- **Monterey jack:** Mild white cheese that melts well; farmer and provolone are substitutes.

- **American cheese:** Bright yellow or white mild cheese found in blocks or individually wrapped slices.
- **Colby cheese:** A very mild form of Cheddar, with a slightly softer texture.
- **Queso asadero:** Mexican string cheese, very mild; regular string cheese is a substitute.
- **Cotija:** Salty and sharp white cheese; feta and Parmesan are substitutes.
- **Aged Manchego:** Yellow sharp and salty cheese; Romano and aged Parmesan are substitutes.
- **Queso enchilada:** Hard grating cheese coated with red chile paste; substitute Romano.

If cheese becomes moldy while stored, cut off the mold along with 1" of the cheese next to it. The rest of the cheese can be safely used. Store cheese tightly wrapped in the refrigerator to prevent spoiling and to stop the transfer of flavors.

Very soft cheeses will be easier to work with if they are frozen for 15–20 minutes before use. Remember that most natural, or unprocessed, cheeses should not be cooked over high heat as they can separate and become tough. Most cheeses are sprinkled on foods a few minutes before cooking is finished and are allowed to melt, bubble, and begin to brown.

All about Chiles

Chile peppers are one of the most commonly used foods in Tex-Mex cuisine. They range from sweet bell peppers to incredibly hot habanero peppers, and are used in the fresh and dried form.

The ingredient in chiles that makes them taste hot and spicy is called capsaicin, a molecule most concentrated in the membranes and seeds. It's important that you know how hot each chile variety is so you can choose the correct heat level for the dishes you make. That's where knowledge of the Scoville Scale is useful.

The Scoville Scale

The Scoville Organoleptic Scale was developed by Wilbur Scoville in 1912 as a way to quantify a chile pepper's heat. Originally, tasters were asked to judge how many parts of sugar water added to one part of chile essence were needed to completely erase the chile's heat. Now a high-tech process called High Performance Liquid Chromatography (HPLC) measures capsaicin concentration in chiles in terms of parts per million.

It turns out that Wilbur Scoville knew what he was doing. The Scoville Scale is directly proportional to the HPLC tests, by a factor of a little less than sixteen. For example, a serrano pepper, with an HPLC number of 1,000, has a Scoville rating of 16,000.

The most common chiles used in Tex-Mex cooking are the Anaheim and poblano, which are roasted, peeled, and canned in 4-ounce containers. These chiles have a subtle spiciness acceptable to almost everyone. The jalapeño is also a very commonly used chile; choose this chile if you want heat but are new to Tex-Mex cooking. The rules change when you are dealing with Chile Heads, people who take pride in being able to eat the hottest peppers like popcorn; if they are among your guests, go ahead and use serrano and habanero peppers.

Fresh Chile Peppers

The following table of pepper types is arranged in order from mildest to hottest. You can substitute peppers for each other if the size is approximately the same. Remember, peppers of the same variety will vary in heat levels depending on where they were grown.

Fresh Chile Peppers

Name	Scoville Rating	Size	Use in Dishes
Sweet bell peppers	Zero	4" round	Stuffed, chopped
Cherry peppers	Zero to 500	1" round	Stuffed, garnish
Anaheim	500 to 2,500	1" wide 5" long	Roasted, chopped
Poblano	1,000 to 2,000	2" wide 6" long	Stuffed, roasted
Jalapeños	2,500 to 8,000	½" wide 2" long	Pickled, chopped
Serrano	8,000 to 22,000	¼" wide 2" long	Roasted, minced
Pequin	30,000 to 50,000	¼" round	Garnish, appetizer
Habanero	100,000 to 300,000	½" round	Roasted, chopped

Generally, the smaller the pepper the hotter the heat level; as an example, pequin and habanero chile peppers are very small, while bell peppers and Anaheim chiles are larger.

Since chile peppers always have a hotness range, it's sometimes difficult to predict heat level when used in a recipe. It's wise to start with a small amount of diced, minced, or ground chile; you can always add more.

ALERT!

Dried Chile Peppers

These peppers are also arranged in order from mildest to hottest. Reconstitute these peppers by soaking in boiling water for 15–20 minutes, or rinse and use them dried in recipes. You can also toast and grind them to make your own dried chile powder. When peppers are dried, their heat content usually increases.

Chipotle chiles, which are usually smoked and then dried, can be purchased plain and also canned in a vinegar-based sauce called *adobo*, which preserves the chiles and also can be used as an ingredient.

For a milder taste, remove the membranes and seeds from any fresh or dried chile pepper before adding it to recipes. Capsaicin is concentrated in those parts of the fruit.

Chile peppers provide not only heat, but other flavors and textures to Tex-Mex foods. The mild peppers have a slightly fruity taste and a citrus background. The roasted peppers have a hint of tobacco and prune, and may even add a coffee or chocolate essence to foods. Roasted and dried peppers also have a smoky, nutlike quality. Mild peppers are sweet and may taste slightly grassy.

Dried Chile Peppers

Name	Scoville Rating	Fresh Name	Size	Use
Ancho	1,000 to 2,000	Poblano	4" x 4"	Poached, mole and enchilada sauce
Pasilla	1,000 to 2,000	Chilaca	1" wide 4" long	Poached, chopped
Cascabel	2,000 to 2,500	None	1" round	Garnish
Chile Colorado	5,000	Anaheim	1" wide 3" long	Poached, ground
Chipotles	5,000 to 10,000	Red Jalapeños	½" wide 1½" long	Chopped
Dried Habanero	200,000	Habanero	½" round	Poached, chopped

Let's Cook!

Have fun experimenting with chiles and other Tex-Mex foods and ingredients and don't be afraid to substitute your own favorite foods for less familiar ones. But try the unusual foods at least once; they may become your favorites!

As we've seen, all in all Tex-Mex food is a robust combination of many flavors, along with a wonderful variety of textures. There's nothing better than a warm quesadilla made with queso fresco and Gulf shrimp, served with a cool and chunky tomatillo sauce.

Don't forget the "scorned" foods too; a platter of bean enchiladas topped with melted cheese can be delicious! Tex-Mex cooks know that Velveeta cheese and corn chips have their place in the cuisine as well. That's what is so fun about the cuisine: just about anything goes.

Now that you're an expert on chiles, cheeses, spices, and herbs, it's time to get started on your first Tex-Mex banquet.

Chapter Two

Appetizers

Guacamole

Yields about 2 cups

3 ripe Haas avocados
3 tablespoons lime juice
⅓ cup sour cream
2 tomatoes, seeded and
    chopped
½ cup minced sweet onion
2 tablespoons chopped
    cilantro
¼ teaspoon ground cumin
2 teaspoons chili powder
½ teaspoon salt
⅛ teaspoon pepper

*Guacamole is a basic recipe that is the essence of Tex-Mex cooking.
You can make it mild or spicy, creamy or chunky;
just be sure to use nicely ripened avocados.*

1. Cut avocados in half. Using a chef's knife, hit the pit sharply, then twist the knife to remove it; discard pit. Using a large spoon, scoop out the flesh and place in a bowl. As you work, sprinkle lime juice over avocados to stop oxidation. Sprinkle any remaining lime juice over avocados when you have finished.

2. Using a fork, coarsely mash the avocados, keeping some pieces intact for a chunky texture. Stir in remaining ingredients and mix well. You can serve this immediately, or cover by placing waxed paper directly on the guacamole's surface and refrigerating up to 24 hours.

3. Serve with tortilla chips and crudités such as jicama sticks, celery, carrot sticks, and bell pepper strips.

A Choice of Avocados

Haas avocados, with their dark pebbly skin, are the best choice for guacamole. There are other avocados available in the market; those with a thin green skin, called Fuerte, have a higher water content and aren't as creamy, so the guacamole made from them isn't as rich.

Texas Caviar

Black-eyed peas are the base for this delicious and colorful dip;
their round shape mimics the fish eggs in caviar.
Serve with blue corn tortilla chips for an exotic taste.

Ω

Serves 8

1 (15-ounce) can black-eyed
   peas, rinsed and drained
2 tomatoes, seeded and
   chopped
1 tablespoon seeded, minced
   jalapeño pepper
3 green onions, sliced
¼ cup chopped red onion
1 garlic clove, minced
2 tablespoons chopped
   cilantro
1 tablespoon olive oil
1 tablespoon apple cider
   vinegar
½ teaspoon salt
⅛ teaspoon cayenne pepper

1. Combine all ingredients in medium bowl and stir until well blended. Cover tightly and refrigerate for at least 2 hours to blend flavors.

2. Serve as a dip with blue corn and regular tortilla chips.

Fiery Pecans

This recipe can be made with just about any nut available. A combination of
pecans, cashews, and almonds makes an inauthentic but delicious snack mix.
Serve it with cold Mexican beer to start your party.

Ω

Yields 3 cups

3 cups whole pecan halves
½ cup butter
3 tablespoons chili powder
1 teaspoon salt
1 teaspoon cumin
¼ teaspoon cayenne pepper
¼ teaspoon white pepper
1 teaspoon cinnamon

1. Preheat oven to 300°F. Place pecan halves on a rimmed baking sheet, spreading evenly.

2. In small saucepan, melt butter and add remaining ingredients; stir until blended. Pour over pecans and toss to coat. Bake at 300°F for 30–35 minutes, stirring once during cooking, until pecans are crisp and toasted.

3. Cool on paper towels, then store in an airtight container.

Mini Tamales

Yields 24

8 corn husks
¾ cup solid shortening
¼ cup hot water
4 cups masa harina
1 egg, beaten
1 teaspoon baking powder
3 cups chicken broth
½ pound spicy bulk pork
    sausage
1 onion, chopped
2 chipotle chiles in adobo
    sauce, drained
1 tablespoon adobo sauce
2 tablespoons tomato paste

This easy version of traditional tamales is perfect for a buffet appetizer party. You can vary them any way you'd like: make the filling mild or spicy, and use any cooked meat or shredded cheese as a filling.

1. Soak corn husks in warm water for 2–3 hours, then drain well and cut into thirds. Preheat oven to 350°F. In medium bowl, combine shortening and hot water and beat with a fork until the shortening absorbs the water and becomes fluffy like whipped cream. Add the masa harina, beaten egg, baking powder, and enough chicken broth to make a fluffy spreading consistency. Set aside.

2. In heavy skillet, cook pork sausage and onion until pork is no longer pink, stirring frequently to break up meat. Drain well. Finely chop chipotle chiles and add to sausage mixture along with adobo sauce and tomato paste; mix well.

3. Place 1 corn husk piece in each 4" muffin cup and top with 2 tablespoons of the dough; spread to cover bottom. Place 1 tablespoon of the sausage filling on the dough, then top with 1 tablespoon of the dough, spreading to cover.

4. Bake at 350°F for 20–25 minutes or until tamales are set and light golden brown around edges. Let cool in muffin cups for 5 minutes, then remove and serve warm with guacamole, sour cream, and salsa.

Tamale-Eating Etiquette

Be sure to tell your guests they have to remove the corn husk before eating the tamale; it will peel away easily when the tamale is done. There is a famous picture of U.S. President Gerald Ford eating a tamale, corn husk and all; don't follow his example!

Jalapeño Poppers

These restaurant staples are so good when made from scratch that your guests will eat them like peanuts. Make sure you serve them with icy cold beer or soda pop as a cooling complement.

∩

1. Cut jalapeño peppers in half and gently remove seeds and membranes. In heavy skillet, over medium heat, brown chorizo sausage until thoroughly cooked; drain well and let cool for 10 minutes. Mix with cheese.

2. Stuff cheese filling into jalapeño halves. Combine eggs, salt, and pepper in shallow bowl. Combine cornmeal, flour, and crushed cereal in another shallow bowl. Dip each stuffed jalapeño in egg, then into cornmeal mixture to coat. Set on plate, cover, and chill for at least 1 hour.

3. When ready to serve, heat 1" of vegetable oil in deep heavy skillet over medium heat until temperature reaches 350°F. Fry stuffed jalapeños for 2–4 minutes until brown and crisp. Serve with warmed Nacho Cheese Sauce.

Stuffing Versatility

Use this sausage and cheese filling to stuff just about any fresh hot or mild pepper according to your tastes, or leave out the sausage and double the cheese in this recipe to make it vegetarian. Serve with a mixture of guacamole and sour cream for dipping.

Yields 24

12 small jalapeño peppers
¼ pound chorizo sausage
1½ cups shredded Cheddar cheese
2 eggs, beaten
¼ teaspoon salt
⅛ teaspoon pepper
¼ cup cornmeal
¼ cup flour
½ cup finely crushed corn flakes cereal
Vegetable oil
1 cup Nacho Cheese Sauce (page 99)

Tortilla Chips

Makes about 60

12 corn or flour tortilla chips
4 cups vegetable oil for frying
Salt to taste

You can bake or fry these delicious chips, according to your mood and waist-line. Use them as dippers for Guacamole (page 20), Nacho Cheese Sauce (page 99), Salsa Fresca (page 29), or Mexican Layered Dip (page 35).

1. Stack 4 tortillas and cut into 8 wedges. Separate pieces and repeat with remaining tortillas.

2. To fry, place enough oil in a deep, heavy saucepan to come within 1" of the top of the pan. Place over medium high heat until thermometer registers 375°F. Drop in chips and, stirring frequently, fry until chips are crisp and light golden brown.

3. Remove from oil using a stainless steel strainer and drain on paper towels. Sprinkle with salt.

Bake Your Chips

To bake tortilla chips, preheat oven to 400°F. Before cutting tortillas into wedges, brush each with vegetable oil. Spread in single layer on baking sheets and bake at 400°F for 10–12 minutes until chips are crisp and light golden brown; sprinkle with salt. Cool on paper towels. Store all tortilla chips in airtight containers.

Ruby Red Grapefruit Salsa

The deep red, super sweet Texas Ruby Red grapefruits are delicious in this fresh and clean-tasting salsa. If you can't get Ruby Reds, use any other grapefruit, but double the amount of honey in the recipe.

∩

Yields 2 cups

2 Ruby Red grapefruits
½ cup finely sliced sweet
   onion
1 avocado, peeled and diced
1 tablespoon grapefruit juice
2 tablespoons honey
2 teaspoons diced jalapeño
   pepper
½ teaspoon salt
⅛ teaspoon cayenne pepper

1. Peel grapefruits, removing all the white pith possible. Then cut between the membranes, freeing the grapefruit sections. Place in medium bowl with sliced onion. Prepare avocado and squeeze the grapefruit membranes over them. Add to grapefruit mixture along with honey and remaining ingredients.

2. Cover bowl tightly and refrigerate for at least 2 hours before serving. Serve with chips as a dip, or as a side with grilled chicken or steak.

What Are Sweet Onions?

Sweet onions, bred to be sweet and mild, must contain at least 6 percent sugar by weight to earn that label. Other varieties of sweet onions include the famous Vidalia from Georgia, the Maui from Hawaii, the Walla Walla from Washington, and the AmenSweet from Michigan.

Plain Nachos

Serves 8

3 cups plain tortilla chips
2 cups shredded Colby-jack
    cheese
1 onion, chopped
3 pickled jalapeños, sliced
Sour cream
Guacamole (page 20)
Picante Sauce (page 100)

Nachos are a true Tex-Mex appetizer. You could also substitute 1½ cups Nacho Cheese Sauce (page 99) for the cheese and onion topping.

1. Preheat oven to 400°F. Spread tortilla chips in an even layer on a large baking pan with sides. Sprinkle with shredded cheese, onion, and jalapeño slices.

2. Bake at 400°F for 5–8 minutes or until cheese is melted and beginning to brown and bubble around the edges. Remove from oven and serve with sour cream, Guacamole, and Picante Sauce.

More about Jalapeños

Pickled jalapeños are often used to garnish any cheesy appetizer or main dish. Be sure to thoroughly drain them and then slice thinly or chop fine, as their flavor is very sharp and spicy. For a tamer flavor, use ordinary canned jalapeños, well drained.

Tex-Mex Egg Rolls

Egg-roll wrappers are very thin crepes that become very crisp when filled, rolled, and deep-fried. Serve these spicy egg rolls with guacamole mixed with sour cream for a cooling dip.

Serves 10

1 onion, finely chopped
3 cloves garlic, minced
2 tablespoons olive oil
1 (15-ounce) can black beans,
    rinsed
2 cups chopped cooked
    chicken
1 jalapeño pepper, minced
½ teaspoon cumin
1 tablespoon chili powder
⅛ teaspoon cayenne pepper
1 cup shredded Muenster
    cheese
20 egg roll wrappers
3 cups vegetable oil

1. Preheat oven to 250°F. In heavy skillet, cook onion and garlic in olive oil until tender. Remove from heat and stir in drained black beans, chicken, jalapeño pepper, cumin, chili powder, cayenne pepper, and cheese until blended.

2. Place about 3 tablespoons mixture on 1 egg roll wrapper. Moisten edges of wrapper with water. Roll up wrapper, folding in ends, to form a roll. Repeat with remaining filling and wrappers.

3. In large saucepan, heat oil until a thermometer registers 375°F. Fry egg rolls, two at a time, for 5–8 minutes, turning once, until crisp and golden brown.

4. Remove and drain on paper towels. Keep warm in 250°F oven until all are done. Serve with sour cream, salsa, or ranch salad dressing for dipping.

Make-Ahead Tip

You can make these spicy little egg rolls ahead of time and keep them, tightly covered, in the refrigerator for up to 24 hours. Fry them up as your guests arrive, adding about 2–3 minutes of cooking time because the filling is chilled.

Serves 6–8

4 cups tortilla chips
1 (15-ounce) can refried
   beans
1 cup canned pinto beans
1 tablespoon chili powder
1 cup chunky salsa
1 tomato, seeded and
   chopped
1 serrano chile, seeded and
   chopped
2 cups shredded Cheddar
   cheese
1 cup shredded Muenster
   cheese
¼ cup chopped cilantro

Yields 4 cups

2 cups pitted, chopped
   cherries
1 cup seeded, chopped
   watermelon
2 kiwifruit, peeled and
   chopped
1 jalapeño pepper, minced
2 tablespoons lemon juice
2 tablespoons honey
½ teaspoon salt
⅛ teaspoon white pepper
2 teaspoons chili powder

Bean Nachos

The combination of smooth refried beans along with chunky whole beans is really nice in these nachos. They can be topped with just about anything you like; chopped cooked chicken or turkey works well.

1. Preheat oven to 400°F. Place tortilla chips on a large rimmed baking sheet and set aside. In medium saucepan, combine refried beans, pinto beans, chili powder, and salsa. Heat over medium heat until mixture just begins to bubble, stirring frequently.

2. Pour bean mixture evenly over chips. Sprinkle with tomato, chile, and cheeses. Bake at 400°F for 15–20 minutes until cheeses melt and begin to bubble.

3. Sprinkle with cilantro and serve with sour cream and guacamole.

Fruit Salsa

You can use your favorite fruits in this unusual sweet and spicy salsa. Choose fruits with similar textures for best results, and pick those that look best in the markets.

1. In medium bowl, combine cherries, watermelon, kiwi, and jalapeño pepper and toss gently. In small bowl, combine remaining ingredients and mix with wire whisk to blend. Pour over fruits and toss gently.

2. Cover salsa and chill for 2–4 hours to blend flavors.

Salsa Fresca

This classic sauce is an uncooked sauce. Make it using the best ripe tomatoes you can find in the market or in your garden.

Yields about 2 cups

2 pounds ripe tomatoes
1 sweet onion, chopped
1 serrano chile, minced
1 jalapeño chile, minced
3 tablespoons lime juice
1 teaspoon salt
¼ teaspoon cayenne pepper
1 tablespoon chili powder

1. Cut tomatoes in half and remove seeds. Coarsely chop pulp and place in medium bowl along with remaining ingredients. Cover and chill for 2–3 hours to blend flavors.

2. Serve as a dip or topping for grilled meats.

The Versatile Salsa

Salsa recipes are very versatile. Use different varieties of tomatoes, onions, spices, and chiles to make your own special recipe. When you hit upon a winner, be sure to write it down! It's very easy to forget exactly how you made a recipe, so record it for posterity.

Peanut Butter–Stuffed Jalapeños

Serrano or habanero peppers can also be stuffed with this creamy filling, depending on how hot you can stand them!

Serves 12

12 jalapeño peppers
⅓ cup peanut butter
1 tablespoon honey
¼ cup chopped honey roasted peanuts
Dash white pepper

1. Cut jalapeño peppers in half and carefully remove seeds and membranes. In small bowl, combine peanut butter, honey, peanuts, and white pepper and blend well.

2. Stuff into the prepared jalapeños, cover, and refrigerate for at least 1 hour before serving.

Queso con Chile

Serves 6–8

1 (8-ounce) package
    processed American
    cheese food
1 cup shredded pepper jack
    cheese
1 (14-ounce) can tomatoes
    with green chiles,
    undrained
½ cup sour cream

The only secret to this recipe is to use processed cheese food, simply because it melts perfectly and there's no danger that the recipe can be overcooked. Make sure you have tons of crisp tortilla chips on hand for dipping.

Cube cheese food and place in microwave-safe bowl along with pepper jack cheese and undrained tomatoes. Heat on high power for 2–3 minutes, stirring twice during cooking time, until mixture is melted and smooth. Stir in sour cream and serve.

Spicy Shrimp and Scallop Cocktail

Serves 6–8

½ cup minced onion
4 cloves garlic, minced
1 tablespoon butter
1 tablespoon oil
1½ pounds large shrimp,
    deveined and peeled
½ pound bay scallops
1 jalapeño pepper, minced
1 serrano pepper, minced
1 cup chunky salsa
1 tablespoon prepared
    horseradish
2 tablespoons lemon juice
1 red bell pepper, chopped
¼ cup chopped cilantro

If you prefer one over the other, use all shrimp or all scallops in this elegant cocktail recipe. Serve with warmed tortillas and crisp crackers or tortilla chips.

1. In heavy skillet, cook onion and garlic in butter and oil over medium heat until crisp-tender. Add shrimp and scallops; cook and stir until shrimp turn pink and scallops just turn opaque; remove skillet from heat.

2. Add minced peppers, salsa, horseradish, lemon juice, and bell pepper. Pour into serving bowl, cover, and chill for 3–4 hours to blend flavors. Sprinkle with cilantro and serve.

Ceviche

*For the safest Ceviche, the FDA recommends you freeze
raw fish for at least seven days to kill any bacteria.
Also, choose "sushi-grade" fish if you can find it, which is very fresh.*

∩

Serves 6

2 pounds ahi tuna or scallops
1 cup lime juice
1 cup grape tomatoes
1 sweet onion, chopped
1 clove garlic, minced
¼ cup chopped fresh cilantro
2 tablespoons olive oil
2 tablespoons orange juice
1 green bell pepper, chopped
1 jalapeño pepper, minced

1. Either freeze the seafood for seven days or cut tuna into cubes, rinse and dry scallops, and briefly sauté in butter. The scallops should be cooked just until opaque; the tuna can be seared and left raw in the center.

2. The frozen fish should be thawed and then marinated in the lime juice for 4 hours in the refrigerator. Cooked fish should be marinated for 1 hour in the refrigerator.

3. Drain fish and combine with remaining ingredients. Cover and chill for 3–4 hours, then serve with tortilla chips, flour tortillas, and crackers.

Food Safety Information

The lime juice in this recipe, which "cooks" the fish by denaturing the proteins and kills most bacteria, doesn't sufficiently kill parasites. To be perfectly safe, you could also briefly sauté the tuna and scallops in butter just until they turn opaque, then marinate in the lime juice mixture for 1 hour.

Tostaditas

Tostaditas is technically the name for tortilla chips.
These are topped with a mixture of shrimp, tomatoes, and chiles.

Serves 8

3 cups round tortilla chips
1 onion, chopped
2 tablespoons butter
1 pound medium shrimp,
    peeled and deveined
2 tomatoes, seeded and
    chopped
1 (3-ounce) package cream
    cheese, softened
½ cup sour cream
1 serrano pepper, minced
1 tablespoon chili powder
2 cups shredded Muenster
    cheese

1. Preheat oven to 400°F. Place tortilla chips on a large baking sheet and set aside. In heavy skillet over medium heat, cook onion in butter until crisp-tender. Add shrimp; cook and stir for 3–4 minutes until shrimp turn pink.

2. Add tomatoes and cream cheese; cook until cream cheese melts. Stir in sour cream, serrano pepper, and chili powder and remove from heat.

3. Pour shrimp mixture over tortillas and sprinkle with cheese. Bake at 400°F for 10–15 minutes or until cheese melts and starts to bubble.

Substitution Ideas

Substitute fresh or canned crab meat, scallops, or even cubes of red snapper, tuna, or swordfish for the shrimp in this or any recipe. The cooking time for the fresh seafood will be a little longer since these ingredients take more time to cook through than shrimp.

Corn Tartlets

These mini quiches can be filled with just about anything. Instead of the corn, use tiny shrimp, cooked chorizo sausage, or chopped cooked chicken.

∩

1. Preheat oven to 375°F. Let pie crust dough stand at room temperature for 20 minutes, then unroll onto work surface coated with cornmeal. Cut out 12 3" rounds from each crust and press, cornmeal side down, into bottom and sides of 1¾" muffin cups. Set aside.

2. In heavy skillet, cook onion in olive oil until tender. Remove from heat. In medium bowl, combine cream, eggs, and chili powder; beat well. Add onion, corn kernels, and jalapenos and mix well.

3. In bottom of each muffin cup, place 2 teaspoons of cheese. Pour egg mixture over cheese. Bake at 375°F for 18–22 minutes or until crusts are golden and filling is light golden brown and set. Serve warm.

Use a Homemade Crust

Instead of refrigerated pie dough, make a double pie crust using your favorite recipe, and chill the dough well before rolling out on a work surface finely dusted with cornmeal. Chill the lined cups in the refrigerator while preparing the filling for best results.

Yields 24

1 (9-ounce) package refrigerated pie crust dough
2 tablespoons yellow cornmeal
1 onion, minced
1 tablespoon olive oil
1 cup heavy cream
2 eggs
2 teaspoons chili powder
1 cup corn kernels
1 jalapeño pepper, minced
1 cup shredded pepper jack cheese

Queso Fundito

Serves 6

½ pound chorizo sausage
3 cloves garlic, minced
2 cups shredded Cheddar
  cheese
1 cup shredded pepper jack
  cheese
1 cup crumbled queso fresco
  or goat cheese
1 tomato, seeded and
  chopped
¼ cup chopped cilantro

*This combination of melted cheese, salsa, tomatoes,
and chorizo sausage is a classic; it's a variation of Swiss Raclette,
which consists of cheese melted with vegetables and served with dippers.*

1. Preheat oven to 325°F. In heavy skillet, sauté chorizo sausage with garlic until meat is browned and thoroughly cooked. Do not drain grease, but pour contents of skillet into an ovenproof serving dish.

2. Top chorizo with cheeses, distributing evenly around the dish. Top with tomato, then bake at 325°F for 10–15 minutes until cheese is melted and starts to bubble around the edges.

3. Remove from oven, sprinkle with cilantro, and serve with tortilla chips, warmed flour tortillas, and fresh vegetables for dipping.

More Cheese Combinations

Use any combination of your favorite cheeses in this easy fondue-like recipe. Muenster, Colby, mozzarella, provolone, Colby-jack, queso blanco, or cotija would all work well. Top the finished recipe with diced cold avocado and chopped fresh tomatoes for a nice flavor and texture contrast.

Mexican Layered Dip

*This hearty and beautiful layered dip is a real crowd pleaser.
You could add cooked ground beef, chorizo sausage,
or chopped cooked chicken or steak to the layers.*

∩

1. In medium bowl, place refried beans and stir to soften. Rinse and drain pinto beans and stir into refried beans along with taco sauce. Spread over a serving platter.

2. In another bowl, beat cream cheese until fluffy. Add sour cream, chili powder, cumin, salt, and cayenne pepper and beat until smooth. Spread over bean mixture on platter, leaving about 1" of bean mixture exposed around edges.

3. Top with Guacamole, then tomato, Colby cheese, serrano chile, green onions, and cilantro. Cover and chill for 1–2 hours to blend flavors. Serve with tortilla chips.

Serve a Crowd!

This dip, along with a hearty soup and lots of tortilla chips, crudités, and warmed flour tortillas, makes a great buffet offering that can easily replace a meal. You may want to make a double batch of this recipe, because it is very popular!

Serves 8

1 (16-ounce) can refried beans
1 (16-ounce) can pinto beans
½ cup taco sauce
1 (8-ounce) package cream cheese, softened
1 cup sour cream
3 tablespoons chili powder
½ teaspoon cumin
½ teaspoon salt
⅛ teaspoon cayenne pepper
2 cups Guacamole (page 20)
1½ cups tomato, chopped and seeded
1½ cups shredded Colby cheese
1 serrano chile, diced
3 green onions, sliced
¼ cup chopped cilantro

Deep-Fried Nopales

Serves 8–10

2 precleaned nopales pads
1 egg, beaten
½ cup milk
½ cup yellow cornmeal
½ cup flour
1 tablespoon chili powder
1 teaspoon salt
⅛ teaspoon cayenne pepper
Vegetable oil

Make sure to buy precleaned nopales, or cactus leaves, because it is very difficult to make sure that all of the tiny spines, or glochids, have been removed.

1. Rinse the nopales pads and scrub with a vegetable brush to make sure all spines are removed. Using a vegetable peeler, remove any nodules or discolored skin. Cut nopales into ¼" strips.

2. In shallow bowl, combine egg and milk and beat well. In another shallow bowl, combine cornmeal, flour, chili powder, salt, and cayenne pepper and mix well. Dip the nopales strips into egg mixture, then roll in cornmeal mixture to coat. Place on wire rack to dry for about 30 minutes.

3. Pour 1" of vegetable oil into a heavy saucepan and heat to 375°F. Fry coated nopales for 2–4 minutes until coating is brown and crisp. Drain on paper towels and serve.

Ingredient Substitutions

You can buy nopales already thoroughly cleaned, sliced, and canned in a water or vinegar solution, but they will be difficult to coat and fry. Other vegetables can be used in this recipe, including green beans, small mushrooms, pepper strips, and sliced yellow squash or zucchini.

Meatballs con Queso

*Meatballs are served in a creamy and rich cheese sauce
for a hearty appetizer. Serve this as part of a buffet at an open house
and your guests will not leave hungry!*

∩

Serves 8–10

1 tablespoon vegetable oil
1 onion, finely chopped
1 jalapeño chile, minced
½ cup crushed nacho cheese
    tortilla chips
2 eggs, beaten
½ teaspoon salt
⅛ teaspoon cayenne pepper
2 pounds ground beef
3 cups Nacho Cheese Sauce
    (page 99)

1. Preheat oven to 350°F. In heavy skillet, heat oil over medium heat and cook onion until tender. Remove from heat and place in large bowl. Add jalapeño, tortilla chips, eggs, salt, and cayenne pepper and mix well. Add ground beef and mix gently to combine. Form into 1" meatballs.

2. Place meatballs on baking sheets and bake at 350°F for 20–25 minutes or until no longer pink in the center. Meanwhile, prepare Nacho Cheese Sauce and pour into a 4-quart crockpot.

3. When meatballs are done, drain briefly on paper towels and gently stir into Nacho Cheese Sauce. Keep warm on low for 4 hours, stirring occasionally.

Label Containers!

Be sure to label containers and packages so you know what they contain. All chili and chile powders and spice blends tend to look the same, especially after they have been stored for a couple of weeks. Be sure to store them in a cool dry place, and discard after a year.

Chapter Three

Salads

Toasted Corn Bread Salad

Serves 6

1 (9-inch square) Corn Bread
(page 110)
1 (15-ounce) can black-eyed
peas, rinsed
1 (15-ounce) can pinto beans,
rinsed
1 green bell pepper, chopped
3 cups frozen corn, thawed
and drained
2 cups grape tomatoes
½ cup broken pecans
1 cup ranch salad dressing
½ cup salsa
½ cup plain yogurt
1 cup cubed pepper jack
cheese

Add anything you'd like to this versatile and delicious main-dish salad.
Leftover cooked chicken or turkey, diced ham, or even
leftover Oven Barbecued Beef Brisket (page 177) or Tex-Mex Smoked Brisket
(page 181) would make the salad even heartier.

∩

1. Preheat oven to 375°F. Cut corn bread into 1" cubes and place on baking sheet. Bake for 10–15 minutes or until cubes are light golden brown and toasted. Set aside.

2. Drain and rinse peas and beans and prepare vegetables. In medium bowl, combine salad dressing, salsa, and yogurt, and blend well. Combine with all ingredients in large serving bowl and toss gently. Serve immediately.

Give Your Salad Some Crunch

Most corn bread salads are made by layering crumbled corn bread with vegetables, cheese, meat, and dressing, chilling for a few hours, then tossing at the last minute. By toasting leftover corn bread cut into cubes and serving immediately, the salad retains crunch and texture.

Tex-Mex Slaw

This refreshing slaw has a dressing made of ranch dressing and salsa.
You can make the dressing as spicy or as mild as you like
by choosing a hot or mild salsa.

∩

1. In large bowl, combine cabbages, onion, corn, cheese, and pumpkin seeds, and toss gently. Dice chipotle chiles and add to mixture.

2. In small bowl, combine ranch salad dressing, salsa, yogurt, and chili powder; mix well. Pour over salad mixture and toss to coat. Cover and refrigerate at least 2 hours to blend flavors.

How to Toast Pumpkin Seeds

Wash and dry the seeds, then spread them on a baking sheet and drizzle with a bit of olive oil. Bake at 300°F for 30–40 minutes, stirring often, until seeds are crisp and light golden brown. You can toss them with seasonings and serve as a snack mix, too.

Serves 8-10

3 cups shredded purple cabbage

2 cups shredded green cabbage

⅓ cup thinly sliced sweet red onion

2 cups frozen corn, thawed and drained

1 cup diced pepper jack cheese

½ cup pumpkin seeds, toasted

2 chipotle chiles in adobo sauce, drained

½ cup ranch salad dressing

½ cup salsa

½ cup plain yogurt

2 teaspoons chili powder

Tex-Mex Potato Salad

Serves 8

4 pounds Yukon Gold
    potatoes
1 red onion, chopped
4 cloves garlic, chopped
3 tablespoons olive oil
2 tablespoons Taco
    Seasoning Mix (page 93)
1 cup plain yogurt
½ cup mayonnaise
½ cup salsa
2 cups frozen corn, thawed
    and drained
1 red bell pepper, chopped
1 green bell pepper, chopped
1 jalapeño chile, minced
½ cup queso blanco,
    crumbled

*This updated potato salad has a lot of colorful vegetables. You could make it a
main dish by adding some chopped ham, grilled chicken, or cooked shrimp.
Serve it with lettuce in a tostada shell for a nice presentation.*

1. Preheat oven to 400°F. Scrub potatoes and cut into cubes. Place in large
   baking pan along with red onion and garlic. Drizzle with olive oil; toss
   using hands, coating vegetables with oil. Bake at 400°F for 50–65 minutes, turning once with spatula, until potatoes are tender and crisp.

2. Meanwhile, in large bowl combine Taco Seasoning Mix, yogurt, mayonnaise, and salsa, and mix well. Add corn, bell peppers, and jalapeño
   and mix well. When potatoes are done, stir into mayonnaise mixture
   along with cheese, turning gently to coat.

3. Cover salad and refrigerate for at least 3 hours until chilled. Or you can
   serve the salad immediately.

Potato Substitutions

*Yukon Gold potatoes are a distinct variety of a buttery tasting potato
with a yellow tint. You can substitute russet potatoes for the Yukon Gold
potatoes in this recipe. Don't substitute red potatoes; they are waxy and
won't keep their shape after baking.*

Grapefruit Salad

*The combination of sweet and tart grapefruit along with other fruits
and the honey dressing is really delicious and refreshing.*

∩

1. Peel 2 grapefruits and remove the sections from the membranes; place sections in salad bowl. Cut third grapefruit in half; remove juice from one half and reserve juice. Peel and chop remaining grapefruit half and add to bowl. Cut strawberries in half and add to grapefruit along with grapes.

2. In small bowl, combine reserved grapefruit juice, oil, honey, salt, and pepper and mix well with whisk. Pour over fruit in bowl and top with raspberries; serve immediately.

All about Sweet Grapefruits

Ruby Red grapefruits are a special Texas variety with an incredible amount of sweetness. There are other varieties available too, including Rio Red, Flame, the white and sweet Oroblanco, and Indian River. If you can't find sweet grapefruit for this salad, use regular grapefruit and increase the honey amount to 4 tablespoons.

Serves 4–6

3 Ruby Red Grapefruit
1 pint strawberries
1 cup green grapes
¼ cup vegetable oil
2 tablespoons honey
½ teaspoon salt
⅛ teaspoon cayenne pepper
1 pint raspberries

Greens with Cilantro Dressing

Serves 4

2 cups butter lettuce
1 cup chicory
2 cups green leaf lettuce
1 avocado, peeled and
    chopped
2 tablespoons lemon juice
½ cup olive oil
2 tablespoons apple cider
    vinegar
2 tablespoons lime juice
1 avocado, peeled and sliced
¼ cup chopped cilantro
    leaves
½ teaspoon salt
⅛ teaspoon white pepper

Choose a variety of fresh greens for this refreshing salad.
Remember, the darker the green, the more vitamins and minerals it contains.

1. Prepare greens, dry, and tear into large serving bowl. Prepare 1 avocado, toss with lemon juice, and add to greens.

2. In blender container or food processor, place olive oil, vinegar, lime juice, and second avocado. Blend or process until mixture is smooth. Pour into small bowl and stir in cilantro leaves, salt, and pepper.

3. Drizzle half of the cilantro dressing over greens, toss gently, and serve with remaining dressing on the side.

Guacamole Salad

Serves 4–6

3 ripe Haas avocados
2 tablespoons lime juice
1 clove garlic
½ teaspoon salt
⅛ teaspoon white pepper
2 tablespoons olive oil
3 red tomatoes, seeded
1 yellow tomato, seeded
1 jalapeño pepper, minced
¼ cup chopped fresh cilantro

This rich salad can be served on a bed of mixed salad greens or
as a topping for grilled fish, chicken, or pork. It also makes a wonderful
appetizer served with a variety of tortilla chips.

1. Peel avocados and remove pit; scoop flesh from skin. Coarsely mash 2 of the avocados with the lime juice. Dice the third avocado and fold into the avocado and lime mixture.

2. In small bowl, mash garlic with salt, working together until a smooth paste forms. Add white pepper and olive oil; mix until blended. Fold into avocado mixture.

3. Chop tomatoes and add to avocado mixture along with jalapeño and cilantro. Cover with plastic wrap, pressing wrap onto surface of salad, and chill for 1–3 hours to blend flavors.

Roasted Corn and Tomatillo Salad

Roasting corn brings out its sweetness and concentrates the flavor. The kernels also become slightly chewy, giving this salad a nice texture contrast.

Serves 4

3 cups corn kerne
2 tablespoons oli
3 cloves garlic, ch
4 tomatoes
1 (10-ounce) can
   drained
1 tablespoon lin
½ cup plain yog
1 (4-ounce) can
   drained
½ cup chopped
⅓ cup chopped
9 cups mixed sa

1. Preheat oven to 400°F. Combine corn, olive oil, and garlic on baking pan and toss to coat. Roast at 400°F for 12–15 minutes until corn becomes light golden brown around edges. Remove and let cool. Chop tomatoes and place in bowl with corn mixture.

2. In blender container or food processor, place half of the drained tomatillos along with lime juice, yogurt, green chiles, and sweet onion. Cover and blend or process until mixture is smooth. Stir in fresh cilantro.

3. Chop remaining tomatillos and mix with roasted corn and tomatoes in bowl. Toss with salad greens and drizzle with half of tomatillo dressing. Serve with remaining dressing.

How to Remove Kernels from an Ear of Corn

Firmly hold cob upright on work surface. Using a sharp knife, carefully cut down the cob, removing the kernels but not cutting into the hard portion of the cob. Turn the cob a bit and repeat. After cutting the kernels, use the back of the knife to run down the cob, releasing juices.

Nopales Salad

*Nopales have the texture of blanched fresh green beans,
with a crisp citrusy bite. When combined with other ingredients,
they take on the flavors of those ingredients.*

∩

*s sliced fresh cleaned
opales
ion, quartered
ves garlic, cut in half
p minced sweet onion
bell pepper, chopped
-ounce) can black beans,
insed
s grape tomatoes
p olive oil
lespoons lime juice
lespoons mustard
aspoon salt
aspoon dried oregano
eaves
aspoon pepper
s butter lettuce*

1. Place nopales in large saucepan with quartered onion and garlic. Cover with cold water. Bring to a boil, reduce heat, and simmer for 30–40 minutes until nopales are no longer slimy. Remove nopales from water with slotted spoon; place in cold water to cool, then remove and drain on paper towels. Discard quartered onion and garlic.

2. In serving bowl, combine drained nopales with sweet onion, bell pepper, black beans, and grape tomatoes.

3. In small bowl, combine oil, lime juice, mustard, salt, oregano, and pepper and blend well with wire whisk. Drizzle half of this mixture over salad, toss gently, and serve on butter lettuce. Serve remaining dressing on the side.

All about Nopales

Nopales can have a slimy quality because they contain an ingredient called exopolysaccharides, a complex sugar, which is also found in okra. Boiling them in water with a quartered onion helps remove that texture because the onion absorbs the sugar.

Taco Salad

Find taco salad shells in the refrigerated dough section of your supermarket. You can use reheated leftover Classic Chili (page 67) in place of the ground beef mixture for a super-fast and hearty lunch or dinner.

∩

1. In heavy skillet, brown ground beef along with onion, garlic, and Anaheim chile. Drain if necessary. Stir in tomato sauce, salsa, chili powder, cumin, salt, and pepper. Bring to a boil, then reduce heat and simmer for 15–20 minutes until slightly thickened.

2. Meanwhile, heat refried beans in small pan over low heat, stirring frequently. Heat salad shells as directed on package until crisp.

3. To eat, spread heated refried beans on the bottom of each salad shell, then top with ground beef mixture. Top with lettuce, cheese, tomatoes, and avocados, and garnish with salsa and sour cream.

Make Your Own Taco Salad Shells

Place 3" of oil in a heavy deep saucepan over medium heat. Gently place an 8" flour tortilla on the hot oil, then using a ladle, press down to form a bowl shape. Fry tortilla, holding it down with the ladle, for 1–2 minutes until crisp. Carefully remove with tongs, tip over saucepan to remove oil, and drain on paper towels.

Serves 6

1½ pounds ground beef
1 onion, chopped
3 cloves garlic, minced
1 Anaheim chile, chopped
1 (8-ounce) can tomato sauce
1 cup salsa
2 tablespoons chili powder
1 teaspoon cumin
½ teaspoon salt
⅛ teaspoon pepper
1 (16-ounce) can refried beans
6 taco salad shells
3 cups shredded lettuce
2 cups shredded Cheddar cheese
2 tomatoes, seeded and chopped
2 avocados, peeled and chopped
1 cup chunky salsa
1 cup sour cream

1 recipe Chipotle Chile Corn
   Bread (page 108)
1 cup buttermilk
⅓ cup mayonnaise
1 tablespoon chili powder
½ teaspoon dried oregano
   leaves
½ teaspoon dried thyme
   leaves
¼ cup crumbled queso
   blanco cheese
½ teaspoon salt
⅛ teaspoon white pepper
1 green bell pepper, chopped
1 red bell pepper, chopped
1 (15-ounce) can black beans,
   rinsed
1 (15-ounce) can pinto beans,
   rinsed
2 cups frozen soybeans,
   thawed
1 cup crumbled queso fresco

Corn Bread Salad

*Typically, layered salads use cooked pasta or lettuce to separate the layers
of vegetables. Corn bread salad uses crumbled corn bread,
for wonderful flavor and texture. Soybeans, or edamame,
are nutty and tender and taste like lima beans.*

∩

1. Crumble corn bread and set aside. In medium bowl, combine butter-milk, mayonnaise, chili powder, oregano, thyme, queso blanco cheese, salt, and white pepper and mix well to blend.

2. Prepare remaining ingredients. In large glass serving bowl, place one-third of the crumbled corn bread. Drizzle with one-fourth of the dressing. Layer salad with one-third of the peppers, beans, and queso fresco cheese. Repeat layers, ending with cheese.

3. Cover and chill for 2–4 hours. Toss salad to mix just before serving.

Cheese with Something Extra

You may be able to find Mexican processed cheese food in the grocery store. It contains the usual blend of cheeses, emulsifiers, and seasonings, but also adds spicy ingredients such as chili powder, ground dried chiles, and onion powder, along with chopped fresh or dried chiles.

Three-Tomato Salad

The avocado dressing on this pretty salad is also excellent served over mixed salad greens, or drizzled on top of a hot chowder.

Ω

1. Cut red and yellow tomatoes into slices. Arrange on serving plate and sprinkle with grape tomatoes and green onions.

2. Peel avocado and remove pit. Place in blender or food processor along with lime juice, chili powder, buttermilk, salt, and pepper. Blend or process until smooth. Drizzle half of dressing over tomatoes and serve remainder on the side.

Serves 4

3 ripe red tomatoes
2 yellow tomatoes
1 pint grape tomatoes
4 green onions, chopped
1 ripe avocado
1 tablespoon lime juice
1 teaspoon chili powder
¼ cup buttermilk
½ teaspoon salt
⅛ teaspoon pepper

Margarita Fruit Salad

Frozen margarita mix can be found in the frozen drink aisle of your super-market. Thaw it by placing the desired amount in a microwave-safe bowl and microwaving on low for 30–45 seconds.

Ω

1. Using melon baller, remove flesh from cantaloupe and honeydew melon; place in serving bowl. Remove stems and slice strawberries and add to bowl. Top with blueberries and raspberries.

2. Thaw margarita mix. In small jar with screw-top lid, combine remaining ingredients and shake well to blend. Pour over fruit and serve.

Serves 6

1 cantaloupe
1 honeydew melon
1 pint strawberries
1 pint blueberries
½ pint raspberries
¾ cup frozen margarita mix
¼ cup orange juice
2 tablespoons vegetable oil
2 drops Tabasco sauce
½ teaspoon salt

Black-Eyed Pea Salad

*This refreshing salad can be served by itself,
or on a handful of mixed fresh salad greens. It's also delicious
as an appetizer dip served with tortilla chips or crackers.*

∩

Serves 4

2 (15-ounce) cans black-eyed
 peas
1 yellow bell pepper
1 red bell pepper
½ cup chopped sweet onion
1 serrano pepper
½ cup vegetable oil
¼ cup orange juice
2 tablespoons lime juice
½ teaspoon lime peel
½ teaspoon salt

1. Rinse and drain peas and place in serving bowl. Chop bell peppers and add to serving bowl. Sprinkle with onion.

2. Mince serrano pepper, and in small bowl, combine with remaining ingredients. Mix with wire whisk to blend. Pour over peas and vegetables in bowl and toss to coat.

In the Produce Department

Sometimes you can find fresh black-eyed peas in the supermarket in the produce section; when you can, snatch them up! They have a wonderful taste and texture, they are low in sodium, and they do not split when cooked so the presentation is beautiful.

Glorified Rice

This is a great way to use up leftover rice. It can be served as a salad or as a dessert, depending on your taste and mood.

1. Bring rice and water to a boil in a medium saucepan. Cover, reduce heat to low, and simmer for 15–20 minutes until rice is tender and water is absorbed. Remove from heat and let stand for 5 minutes, then fluff with fork. Let cool until warm.

2. In serving bowl, combine pudding mix and milk; stir with wire whisk until thickened. Fold in thawed whipped topping along with the lime juice, cooled rice, and remaining ingredients. Cover and chill for 3–4 hours to blend flavors.

Serves 6

1 cup Texmati rice
2 cups water
1 (3-ounce) package instant vanilla pudding mix
1 cup milk
1 cup frozen whipped topping, thawed
1 tablespoon lime juice
1 (15-ounce) can mandarin oranges, drained
1 (15-ounce) can crushed pineapple, drained
1 cup green grapes

Christmas Eve Salad

This beautiful salad is a meal in itself! Serve with warm corn bread or warmed flour or corn tortillas for an excellent light lunch. You can cook fresh beets or use canned ones.

1. In small bowl, combine oil, juices, honey, salt, and cayenne pepper; mix with wire whisk to blend and set aside.

2. Place salad greens in large serving bowl. Add pear, apple, pineapple chunks, and beets and toss gently. Drizzle with half of the salad dressing and sprinkle with peanuts. Serve remaining salad dressing on the side.

Serves 6

⅓ cup vegetable oil
3 tablespoons orange juice
1 tablespoon lime juice
3 tablespoons honey
½ teaspoon salt
⅛ teaspoon cayenne pepper
8 cups mixed salad greens
1 pear, peeled and chopped
1 apple, chopped
1 (8-ounce) can pineapple chunks, drained
½ cup diced cooked beets
⅓ cup honey roasted peanuts

Tex-Mex Pasta Salad

Serves 6–8

½ cup mayonnaise
1 cup plain yogurt
¼ cup milk
1 cup chunky salsa
2 teaspoons chile paste
1 green bell pepper, chopped
1 red bell pepper, chopped
1 jalapeño pepper, minced
1 (12-ounce) can chunk
　　chicken, drained
1 cup crumbled queso fresco
2 cups frozen corn
1 cup frozen baby peas
1 (16-ounce) package gemelli
　　pasta

Pasta salads are a great choice during the summer months. Make the salad in the morning or evening, then let it marinate until serving time.

1. In large bowl, combine mayonnaise, yogurt, milk, salsa, and chile paste and mix well. Stir in bell peppers, jalapeño pepper, chicken, and cheese and mix well. Place corn and peas on top of salad mixture.

2. Cook pasta according to package directions, drain, and stir into salad mixture while hot. Stir gently to coat all ingredients with dressing, cover, and refrigerate for 1–2 hours to blend flavors.

Tex-Mex Bean Salad

Serves 6–8

1 pound green beans
1 (15-ounce) can black-eyed
　　peas
1 (15-ounce) can pinto beans,
　　rinsed
½ cup minced sweet onion
4 green onions, chopped
2 cups chopped ham
½ cup olive oil
¼ cup lime juice
2 tablespoons lemon juice
3 tablespoons sugar
1 jalapeño chile, minced
½ teaspoon salt
⅛ teaspoon cayenne pepper
½ teaspoon cumin
6–8 romaine lettuce leaves

Three-bean salad typically has a sweet-and-sour dressing coating green beans and wax beans. This recipe adds ham, pinto beans, black-eyed peas, and the spice of minced jalapeño peppers. Serve it on a hot summer day with some cold beer or soda pop.

1. Trim green beans and steam over boiling water for 8–12 minutes until crisp-tender. Remove and place in serving bowl. Rinse and drain black-eyed peas and pinto beans and add to bowl along with sweet onion, green onions, and ham.

2. In small bowl, combine olive oil, lime and lemon juice, sugar, jalapeño chile, salt, cayenne pepper, and cumin and mix with wire whisk until blended. Pour over bean mixture, stir gently, cover, and refrigerate for at least 2 hours to blend flavors. Serve on lettuce leaves.

Pomegranate Green Salad

Pomegranates are in season from October to January. They are sold already ripe; choose fruits that are heavy for their size with no cracks or breaks in the skin.

Serves 4

4 cups torn romaine lettuce leaves
4 cups torn butter lettuce
1 large pomegranate
4 green onions, chopped
1 tablespoon chopped fresh chives
¼ cup toasted pumpkin seeds
½ cup oil
⅓ cup pomegranate juice
1 tablespoon lime juice
1 tablespoon mustard
½ teaspoon salt
⅛ teaspoon white pepper

1. In serving bowl, toss together lettuces. Remove seeds from pomegranate and sprinkle over lettuce. Squeeze the pomegranate shells over the salad to remove juice. Sprinkle with green onions, chives, and pumpkin seeds.

2. In small bowl, combine oil, pomegranate juice, lime juice, mustard, salt, and white pepper and beat with wire whisk to blend. Drizzle over salad, toss, and serve.

Seed a Pomegranate

To remove pomegranate seeds from the pomegranate, cut the large red fruit in half. Using the back of a knife or a large spoon, tap the rounded side of each half; the seeds will pop out from the cut edge. Squeeze the empty halves to remove the pomegranate juice and discard shell.

Corn and Rice Salad

Serves 6

1½ cups Texmati or Basmati
    rice
3 cups water
6 ears of corn
1 tablespoon olive oil
½ teaspoon salt
1 pint grape tomatoes
1 yellow squash, chopped
1 green bell pepper, chopped
1 cup ranch salad dressing
½ cup plain yogurt
½ cup green salsa
1 serrano chile, minced

*Tender roasted sweet corn along with fresh vegetables and
fragrant rice is a great combination in this easy salad.
Serve it with grilled steak and some warmed and buttered tortillas.*

1. Preheat oven to 400°F. In heavy saucepan, combine rice and water. Cover and bring to a boil over medium high heat. Reduce heat and simmer for 15–20 minutes until rice is tender and liquid is absorbed. Let stand for 5 minutes off the heat, then fluff with fork.

2. Cut kernels off the corn cobs and spread on baking pan. Drizzle with olive oil and sprinkle with salt; roast at 400°F for 12–15 minutes, stirring once during cooking time, until kernels are light golden brown around edges. Combine with rice, tomatoes, squash, and bell pepper in serving bowl.

3. In medium bowl, combine salad dressing, yogurt, green salsa, and minced chile and mix well. Pour over vegetables in serving bowl and toss gently. Serve immediately or cover and chill for 1–2 hours to blend flavors.

How to Ripen Tomatoes

Most tomatoes you buy at the store are not ripe. To ripen tomatoes, set them on a sunny windowsill until they give slightly when lightly pressed; try to buy tomatoes still on the vine. Do not store tomatoes in the refrigerator, as their texture will quickly become soft and mealy.

Four-Bean Salad

There are many different kinds of beans that can be used in this salad. Yellow wax beans, pink beans, pigeon peas, and green beans are all good choices.

Rinse and drain the canned beans and place in serving bowl. Microwave green beans according to package directions, drain well, and add to bowl. Combine salsa, yogurt, mayonnaise, buttermilk, and chili powder in small bowl and pour over beans, tossing to coat. Cover and chill for 2–4 hours to blend flavors. Serve over salad greens.

Serves 6

1 (15-ounce) can pinto beans
1 (15-ounce) can black beans
1 (16-ounce) can garbanzo
    beans
2 cups frozen green beans
1 cup chunky salsa
½ cup plain yogurt
¼ cup mayonnaise
¼ cup buttermilk
1 tablespoon chili powder

Greens with Jalapeño Dressing

This dressing also makes a wonderful marinade for chicken or turkey that you cook on the grill. Store it, covered, in the refrigerator up to 4 days.

1. Combine lettuces in serving bowl and set aside. In blender or food processor, combine peppers, sour cream, honey, lime juice, and salt. Blend or process until smooth.

2. Pour half of dressing over lettuce mixture and toss gently. Serve remaining dressing on the side.

Serves 4–6

4 cups butter lettuce
2 cups red lettuce
2 cups chicory
1 (4-ounce) can jalapeño
    peppers
½ cup sour cream
2 tablespoons honey
2 tablespoons lime juice
½ teaspoon salt

How to Prepare Greens

To prepare greens, fill a sink with cold water and add the greens. Swish the greens through the water and let stand for 2–3 minutes so any grit falls to the bottom of the sink. Remove the greens, separate if necessary, and lay on kitchen towels. Roll up towels and store in refrigerator for 1–2 hours.

Fruit and Avocado Salad

Serves 4–6

2 ripe avocados
2 tablespoons lime juice
1 pint strawberries, sliced
1 (15-ounce) can mandarin
    oranges, drained
1 cantaloupe
⅓ cup lime juice
3 tablespoons honey
⅓ cup olive oil
1 serrano chile, minced, if
    desired
½ teaspoon salt

Yes, avocado is a fruit! Its smooth, buttery texture and slightly nutty flavor is a great complement to sweet and tart fruits in this easy salad recipe.

1. Peel and chop avocados and sprinkle with lime juice. Place in serving bowl with strawberries and oranges. Make balls out of cantaloupe and add to fruits; toss gently to mix.

2. In small bowl, combine lime juice, honey, oil, chile, and salt and mix well to blend. Pour over fruits and serve immediately.

Keep Fruits Bright

If you use fruits that can turn dark after peeling and chopping, such as apples and pears, sprinkle lemon or lime juice over them before mixing with the other ingredients. These juices contain ascorbic acid, which helps prevents the enzymatic oxidation reaction that causes browning.

Chapter Four

Soups

Chilled Avocado Soup

Serves 4–6

3 ripe Haas avocados
3 tablespoons lemon juice
3 cups chicken broth
1 (3-ounce) package cream cheese, softened
½ cup plain yogurt
½ cup heavy cream
⅛ teaspoon cayenne pepper
½ teaspoon salt
1 chipotle pepper in adobo sauce
1 ripe Haas avocado
1 tablespoon lime juice
⅓ cup sour cream
½ teaspoon chili powder
½ cup chunky salsa

This rich and creamy soup can be a starter for a Tex-Mex party or part of a lunch menu served with a fruit salad and some warmed flour tortillas.

1. Slice 3 avocados and remove the pit. Scoop out the flesh and place in blender container or food processor. Sprinkle with 2 tablespoons lemon juice. Add ½ cup chicken broth and cream cheese; cover and blend or process until smooth.

2. Add remaining chicken broth, yogurt, cream, cayenne pepper, salt, and chipotle pepper and blend or process until smooth. Cover and chill in refrigerator for 1–2 hours.

3. When ready to serve, cut remaining avocado in half, remove pit, sprinkle with lime juice, then dice finely. Stir into chilled soup. In small bowl, combine sour cream and chili powder; use to garnish soup along with chunky salsa.

How to Ripen Avocados

Buy avocados that are firm and heavy for their size, with no breaks in the skin and no soft spots. Place them in a paper bag and fold down the top. Let stand at room temperature for 2–4 days, checking the avocados daily. They are ripe and ready to use when the flesh gives when lightly pressed.

Tortilla Soup

Two different chile peppers and three kinds of tomatoes build rich, long-simmered flavor in this easy 30-minute soup. Garnish it with sour cream, chopped avocado, chopped cilantro, and shredded cheese.

Serves 6

3 tablespoons vegetable oil
4 (10") flour tortillas
1 onion, chopped
3 cloves garlic, minced
1 green bell pepper, chopped
1 serrano chile, minced
2 tablespoons masa harina
1 (4-ounce) can diced green
   chiles, undrained
1 (14-ounce) can diced
   tomatoes, undrained
3 yellow tomatoes, chopped
1 (6-ounce) can tomato paste
3 (14-ounce) cans vegetable
   broth
2 teaspoons sugar
½ teaspoon pepper
⅛ teaspoon Tabasco sauce

1. In heavy saucepan, heat vegetable oil and fry the tortillas, one at a time, until crisp and golden; set aside to drain on paper towels. In same skillet in same oil, cook onions and garlic until crisp-tender; add bell pepper and serrano chile and cook 1–2 minutes longer.

2. Add masa harina to saucepan; cook and stir for 2 minutes. Add green chiles, diced tomatoes, yellow tomatoes, tomato paste, vegetable broth, sugar, and pepper. Bring to a boil, then reduce heat, partially cover, and simmer for 15 minutes until slightly thickened. Add Tabasco sauce and stir.

3. Crumble fried tortillas into soup bowls and top with soup; garnish as desired and serve.

Masa Harina Substitution

Masa harina helps to thicken soups and sauces and adds a nutty corn flavor. If you can't find it, you can thicken this soup with the same amount of flour; cook and stir it in the oil and vegetable mixture until the flour turns a very light golden brown.

A Bowl of Red

This is the classic Texas-Mexican chili, which has sustained many a traveler with its hearty ingredients and fiery taste. No beans or tomatoes are allowed in this chili: just beef, chiles, and onions.

Serves 8

2 pounds beef sirloin tips
¼ cup flour
1 teaspoon ground red chile powder
2 tablespoons lard or bacon grease
2 onions, chopped
4 cloves garlic, minced
3 dried ancho chiles
3 cups water
3 (14-ounce) cans beef broth
2 jalapeño chiles, minced
2 teaspoons chile paste
1 teaspoon cumin
3 tablespoons chili powder
½ teaspoon dried oregano
1½ teaspoons salt
½ teaspoon pepper

1. Cut beef into 1" pieces if necessary and toss with flour and red chile powder. Melt lard or bacon grease in large stockpot over medium heat. Sauté coated beef in batches until brown, about 4–5 minutes per batch. Remove each batch when cooked. Cook onions and garlic in drippings until crisp-tender, about 4–5 minutes.

2. Meanwhile, soak ancho chiles in ½ cup hot water for about 30 minutes. Drain and puree chiles and ¼ cup water in blender or food processor. Add to onions in pot along with beef and remaining ingredients. Bring to a boil, then cover pot, reduce heat to low, and simmer for 2½ hours, stirring occasionally.

Tex-Mex Gazpacho

Gazpacho is a Spanish recipe that adapts beautifully to Tex-Mex ingredients. Store the soup, covered, in the refrigerator up to 5 days. Garnish it with Guacamole (page 20) and salsa.

Serves 8

1 sweet onion, minced
2 cloves garlic, minced
1 (42-ounce) can tomato juice
¼ cup vegetable oil
2 tablespoons lime juice
3 tomatoes, chopped
1 cucumber, peeled and chopped
1 yellow squash, chopped
1 cup minced celery
1 pound cooked medium shrimp
2 jalapeño peppers, minced
1 tablespoon chili powder
1 teaspoon cumin
1 teaspoon salt
⅛ teaspoon cayenne pepper
⅛ teaspoon Tabasco sauce

1. In large bowl, stir together all ingredients and mix well. Cover and chill in refrigerator for at least 2 hours to blend flavors. Stir before serving. You can also place all ingredients except for shrimp and jalapeño peppers in a blender or food processor and blend or process until mixture is smooth; stir in shrimp and jalapeños and chill.

Beer Cheese Soup

Mince the onion, garlic, and carrots in a food processor so they are almost a pulp. The vegetables help thicken the soup and their flavor is maximized by being finely chopped.

1. Roast Anaheim chiles under broiler or over a gas flame until skin is blackened. Place in paper bag to steam for 10 minutes. Remove peel, seed peppers, and chop.

2. Meanwhile, in heavy saucepan, cook onion, garlic, and carrot in butter until tender, stirring constantly, about 4–6 minutes. Add red bell pepper, chipotle chile, and Anaheim chiles; cook and stir for 1 minute. Add flour; cook and stir until bubbly, about 5 minutes.

3. Add salt, pepper, evaporated milk, beer, chicken broth, and tequila. Cook and stir soup until slightly thickened, about 10–12 minutes. Add Colby and pepper jack cheeses and stir until cheese is melted and soup is thick. Top each serving with crumbled nacho chips.

About Beer

See if you can find a Mexican beer for this delicious and thick soup. If you can't, any dark ale would be wonderful. Nonalcoholic beer can be substituted. Since even nonalcoholic beer does contain some alcohol, you can substitute the same amount of chicken broth for the beer if you'd like.

Serves 6

2 Anaheim chiles
1 onion, minced
3 cloves garlic, minced
1 cup minced carrots
½ cup butter
1 red bell pepper, chopped
1 chipotle chile in adobo
    sauce, minced
½ cup flour
1 teaspoon salt
⅛ teaspoon cayenne pepper
1 (12-ounce) can evaporated
    milk
1 (12-ounce) bottle beer
2 (14-ounce) cans ready-to-
    serve chicken broth
2 tablespoons tequila, if
    desired
2 cups grated Colby cheese
1 cup grated pepper jack
    cheese
2 cups crumbled nacho chips

Mexicali Tomato Bisque

A bisque is a combination of vegetables or seafood and milk.
This delicious and beautiful soup can be served with warmed tortillas
or some crisp Bolillos (page 122).

Serves 4

4 red tomatoes
2 yellow tomatoes
2 tablespoons butter
½ cup chopped onion
1 chipotle chile in adobo
    sauce
½ teaspoon dried oregano
1 cup chicken stock
1½ cups half-and-half
½ teaspoon salt
⅛ teaspoon cayenne pepper

1. Peel and seed tomatoes and chop. Melt butter in heavy saucepan and cook tomatoes and onion for 3–4 minutes. Chop chipotle chile and add to saucepan with oregano and chicken stock. Simmer for 10 minutes, stirring frequently.

2. Mash tomatoes using a potato masher. Stir in half-and-half, salt, and cayenne pepper and heat soup, stirring, until almost simmering.

Triple Corn Chowder

Chowders are thicker than stews and usually have cheese
or another dairy product in the recipe. Serve this hearty chowder with
some breadsticks and a fruit salad.

Serves 4–6

1 onion, chopped
2 tablespoons butter
2 cups frozen corn
1 (15-ounce) can creamed
    corn
2 cups chicken broth
2 tablespoons masa harina
1 cup heavy cream
1 red bell pepper, chopped
1 (4-ounce) can diced chiles
½ teaspoon cumin

1. In heavy saucepan, cook onion in butter until crisp-tender, about 4 minutes. Stir in frozen corn, creamed corn, and half of chicken broth; bring to a boil. Meanwhile, in small saucepan combine remaining chicken broth with masa harina; bring to a boil, stirring constantly.

2. Stir chicken broth and masa harina mixture into onion mixture along with cream, bell pepper, chiles, and cumin; simmer for 5–8 minutes, stirring frequently, until blended.

Black Bean Soup

Black beans, also called turtle beans, make the most wonderful soup.
Their meaty flavor and creamy texture enhance the vegetables in this easy recipe.

∩

1. Sort and rinse black beans and cover with cold water. Let stand overnight. In the morning, drain beans, discard soaking water, and combine in a 4- to 5-quart crockpot with remaining ingredients except masa harina and $\frac{1}{3}$ cup water. Cover and cook on low for 8–10 hours until beans are soft.

2. Remove ham bone and take meat off the bone; chop and return to soup. Turn crockpot to high. In small bowl, mix masa harina with water and blend well. Stir into soup, mixing well. Cook on high for 30 minutes, stirring once during cooking, until soup is thickened.

Ham Bones

You can usually buy ham bones right in your supermarket's meat aisle.
You may have to ask the butcher for the bones. A ham bone adds a rich
flavor to soups, especially when simmered long as in crockpot recipes.
If you can't find one, substitute 1 cup of chopped cooked ham.

Serves 6

1 pound dried black beans
1 onion, chopped
3 cloves garlic, minced
2 stalks celery, minced
2 jalapeño peppers, minced
½ teaspoon minced epazote, if desired
2 tablespoons chili powder
1 teaspoon cumin
¼ teaspoon cayenne pepper
1 ham bone
4 cups water
6 cups chicken stock
2 tablespoons masa harina
⅓ cup water

Pumpkin Soup

Serves 6

1 pasilla chile
2 tablespoons butter
1 tablespoon vegetable oil
1 onion, minced
3 cloves garlic, minced
1 jalapeño pepper, minced
Dash nutmeg
3 (10-ounce) cans chicken
  broth
1 (15-ounce) can solid-pack
  pumpkin
1 (12-ounce) can evaporated
  milk
½ cup sour cream
1 avocado, peeled and diced

*Think about serving this soup at Thanksgiving dinner as a first course.
It can be made ahead of time; store in the refrigerator up to 2 days
and reheat in a double boiler until steaming.*

1. Place pasilla chile in small bowl and cover with boiling water. Let stand for 1 hour, then puree chile with ¼ cup soaking water in food processor. Set aside.

2. In heavy stockpot, heat butter and oil over medium heat and cook onion, garlic, and jalapeño pepper until crisp-tender, about 4 minutes. Stir in remaining ingredients including chile puree, except for evaporated milk, sour cream, and avocado; stir well. Bring to a simmer, then stir in evaporated milk and cook for 1–2 minutes longer.

3. Remove from heat and garnish with sour cream and avocado.

Serving Suggestions

Serve this delicious soup topped with Tomatillo Salsa (page 104), alongside hot Corn Bread (page 110) and Grapefruit Salad (page 43). For dessert, Pineapple Cake (page 269) is a refreshing and elegant choice. Or serve the soup as a starter for an elegant meal, including Tex-Mex Smoked Brisket (page 181), Tex-Mex Crockpot Rice (page 80) and Fruit and Avocado Salad (page 56).

Puchero

*This rich Mexican meat and vegetable stew is like
the pot-au-feu of France with many classic Tex-Mex ingredients.
Serve it with warmed flour tortillas and fresh fruit.*

∩

Serves 6

2 pounds beef soup bones
2 onions, chopped
4 cloves garlic, minced
3 quarts water
1 tablespoon salt
1 russet potato
1 sweet potato
2 boneless, skinless chicken
    thighs
1 (15-ounce) can garbanzo
    beans, drained
3 carrots, cut into 1" chunks
1 serrano chile, minced
2 chipotle chiles in adobo
    sauce, minced
2 cups frozen corn
1 plantain, peeled and sliced
½ head cabbage, cut into
    chunks
1 cup frozen green beans

1. Preheat oven to 400°F. Place soup bones on a baking sheet and bake at 400°F for 45–55 minutes or until bones are browned. Place in large stockpot along with onion, garlic, water, and salt. Bring to a boil, then cover, reduce heat, and simmer for 1 hour.

2. Peel and dice potatoes and add to soup. Remove beef bones and cut meat off the bones. Return meat to soup along with chicken thighs, garbanzo beans, and carrots. Simmer for 1 hour longer, then shred chicken with 2 forks. Add chiles, frozen corn, plantain, cabbage, and green beans and simmer for 20–30 minutes longer or until all ingredients are tender.

3. Serve with Guacamole (page 20), Pico de Gallo (page 91), more chopped chiles, and fresh cilantro.

How to Warm Tortillas

Serve any dish that has a lot of sauce with a bunch of warmed flour or corn tortillas. To warm tortillas, wrap them in foil and place them in a 350°F oven for about 10 minutes. Or wrap in microwave-safe paper towels and microwave on high for 20–30 seconds. Place them in a tortilla warmer and serve.

Crockpot Pozole

Serves 6

3 Anaheim chiles
1-pound boneless pork loin
    roast
1 onion, chopped
4 cloves garlic, minced
2 (15-ounce) cans hominy,
    drained
4 cups water
1 (4-ounce) can diced green
    chiles, undrained
2 tablespoons chili powder
1 teaspoon cumin
1 teaspoon salt
½ teaspoon dried oregano
Pequin chiles

*Chiles, pork, and hominy combine in your slow cooker to make
a rich hearty soup perfect for a cold day. Serve it with a crisp green salad
and some hot corn bread.*

1. Roast Anaheim chiles under a broiler or over a gas flame until skin is charred. Place in paper bag and let steam for 10 minutes. Peel off skin, cut chiles open and discard seeds and membranes; coarsely chop.

2. Cut pork into 1" cubes and place in a 4- to 5-quart crockpot with all remaining ingredients; stir well. Cover and cook on low for 6–8 hours until pork is very tender. Garnish with sour cream, tortilla chips, chopped avocado, and pequin chiles.

Crockpot Hints

Make sure that your crockpot is filled ½ to ⅔ full for best results. Don't lift the lid to stir the food or check on progress, especially when cooking on low, because you lose 20 minutes of cooking time each time it's lifted. Place vegetables on the bottom and chop or slice food so it's all the same size.

White Chicken Chili

This rich chili is best garnished with Salsa Verde (page 92) or Cilantro Pesto (page 90), to keep the cool green color constant.

∩

1. Cut chicken into pieces and coat with flour and garlic salt. Heat vegetable oil in large saucepan and cook chicken until lightly browned.

2. Add onion; cook and stir until crisp-tender. Add chicken broth and drained beans and simmer for 15 minutes. Add bell pepper and chiles and simmer for 10 minutes. Add cheese; stir until melted and serve.

Serves 6

3 boneless, skinless chicken breasts
3 tablespoons flour
½ teaspoon garlic salt
2 tablespoons vegetable oil
1 onion, chopped
3 (14-ounce) cans chicken broth
2 (15-ounce) cans pinto beans
1 green bell pepper, chopped
1 (4-ounce) can diced green chiles
2 cups shredded pepper jack cheese

Classic Chili with Beans

"Classic" chili doesn't have beans, but this recipe does. Beans help stretch the meat, add lots of fiber, and taste wonderful. So use them without shame.

∩

1. In large saucepan, brown ground beef with onion and garlic until beef is cooked, stirring frequently. Drain if necessary.

2. Add remaining ingredients along with 1 cup of water and stir gently. Simmer for 20–30 minutes until flavors are blended.

Serves 4–6

1 pound ground beef
1 onion, chopped
3 cloves garlic, minced
1 (14-ounce) can diced tomatoes
1 (8-ounce) can tomato sauce
1 (6-ounce) can tomato paste
2 tablespoons chili powder
2 (15-ounce) cans kidney beans
1 (4-ounce) can diced green chiles

Chili Condiments

There are so many things you can serve with your chili. Sour cream is an obvious choice, as is shredded Cheddar cheese. A fresh salsa, made with tomatoes or tomatillos, adds a nice kick of flavor. Crumbled taco chips, especially the nacho- or guacamole-flavored varieties, add some nice crunch.

Chili Colorado

Serves 6

1 tablespoon vegetable oil
1 onion, chopped
1 pound boneless pork chops
1 (14-ounce) can diced
    tomatoes with garlic,
    undrained
½ teaspoon dried oregano
    leaves
½ teaspoon salt
⅛ teaspoon crushed red
    pepper flakes
1½ cups water
3 cups Colorado Sauce (page
    101)

*This quick soup uses Colorado Sauce as its base. You can substitute canned
enchilada sauce for the fresh sauce if you'd like.*

1. Heat vegetable oil in large stockpot over medium heat and cook onion
    until crisp-tender. Meanwhile, cut pork chops into 1" pieces, discard-
    ing excess fat. Add to pot; cook and stir until pork is browned, about
    7–8 minutes.

2. Add remaining ingredients and bring to a boil. Cover, reduce heat, and
    simmer for 20–25 minutes until pork is thoroughly cooked and mixture
    is slightly thickened. Garnish with fresh cilantro, tortilla chips, and sour
    cream.

10-Minute Chicken Soup

Serves 4–6

3 (14-ounce) cans ready-to-
    serve chicken broth
1 (9-ounce) package frozen
    cooked southwest
    seasoned chicken breast
    strips
1 chipotle chile in adobo
    sauce, minced
2 cups frozen onion and
    pepper stir-fry mix
1 cup refrigerated hash
    brown potatoes
1 tablespoon chili powder
¼ teaspoon garlic salt
1 cup diced pasteurized
    processed cheese

*Convenience foods can be real lifesavers. In this recipe, combining already cooked
frozen ingredients means the soup will be on the table in ten minutes. Olé!*

1. In heavy saucepan, combine all ingredients except cheese and bring to
    a boil. Reduce heat and simmer for 3 minutes.

2. Add cheese, lower heat, and cook and stir until cheese melts and soup
    is thickened.

Cowboy Soup

This thick soup, more like a stew, is an excellent choice for lunch on a cold winter day. Serve with warmed flour tortillas, sour cream, and Guacamole (page 20).

∩

1. In heavy stockpot, cook beef, onion, chiles, and garlic over medium heat, stirring to break up beef, until browned, about 7–8 minutes. Add flour; cook and stir for 3–4 minutes until bubbly. Add soup, chili powder, cumin, and beef stock; bring to a boil, then cover and simmer for 5 minutes.

2. Stir in frozen corn and bring back to a simmer. Stir in the rice, cover, and simmer for 15–20 minutes until rice is tender. Stir in cheese until melted, and serve.

Convenience Foods

Every once in a while, take some time and stroll through your supermarket looking for new foods. In the United States, 20,000 new food products are introduced each year. You never know what you'll find that may become a new favorite you can add to your weekly grocery list.

Serves 4–6

1 pound lean ground beef
1 onion, chopped
2 jalapeño chiles, minced
4 cloves garlic, minced
2 tablespoons flour
1 (10-ounce) can condensed tomato soup
1 tablespoon chili powder
1 teaspoon cumin
5 cups beef stock
2 cups frozen corn
½ cup Texmati rice
1 cup cubed processed American cheese

Green Gazpacho

*Top this delicious cold soup with some sour cream, guacamole,
and tiny cooked shrimp or fresh lump crabmeat.*

Serves 4–6

2 tablespoons vegetable oil
1 onion, chopped
3 cloves garlic, minced
1 (10-ounce) can tomatillos,
    drained
2 jalapeños, minced
1 cucumber, peeled
1 avocado, peeled
2 tablespoons lime juice
1 green bell pepper, chopped
2 cups chicken broth
1 teaspoon salt
⅛ teaspoon white pepper
½ cup chopped cilantro

1. Heat vegetable oil in heavy skillet over medium heat and cook onion and garlic until crisp-tender. Remove from heat and place in blender container or food processor; let cool for 30 minutes.

2. Add drained tomatillos, jalapeños, cucumber, avocado, lime juice, and bell pepper to blender or food processor; blend or process until mixture is still slightly chunky.

3. Remove to serving bowl or glass pitcher and stir in chicken broth, salt, pepper, and cilantro. Cover and chill for at least 4 hours before serving.

Proportion

Ingredient proportions for soups and many main dish recipes can be changed according to your own personal tastes. For example, in the Green Gazpacho recipe, add another cucumber or avocado, and cut the tomatillos in half. Or omit the onion and garlic and increase the bell peppers. The point? Have fun with your recipes.

Crab and Tomatillo Chowder

If you don't care for tomatillos, you can just leave them out and increase the fish stock to 3 cups. This rich soup is hearty enough to serve as a main course with a simple salad and some corn bread.

∩

1. In heavy saucepan over medium heat, cook bacon until crisp. Drain bacon on paper towels, crumble, and place in refrigerator. Add butter to drippings in skillet and cook onion, garlic, jalapeño pepper, and potato until potatoes start to turn golden, about 6–8 minutes, stirring frequently. Add flour; cook and stir for 2–3 minutes until bubbly.

2. Add corn to potato mixture. Using kitchen scissors, cut up tomatillos in the can and add to saucepan along with fish stock, salt, pepper, and milk. Bring to a boil, reduce heat, and simmer for about 8 minutes until potatoes are tender.

3. Stir in heavy cream, crabmeat, and reserved bacon; bring to a simmer, then add cheese, stir, sprinkle with cilantro, and serve.

Using Dairy Products in Soups

When a soup recipe calls for milk or cream, be sure that you don't let the mixture boil after the dairy products are added. The casein protein in the milk can denature and cause curdling, which is undesirable. Just let the soup simmer briefly to heat through and be sure to stir the soup constantly.

Serves 6–8

2 slices bacon
1 tablespoon butter
1 onion, chopped
2 cloves garlic, minced
1 jalapeño pepper, minced
1 potato, peeled and diced
2 tablespoons flour
2 cups frozen corn
1 (10-ounce) can tomatillos, drained
2 cups fish stock
1 teaspoon salt
⅛ teaspoon white pepper
1½ cups milk
1 cup heavy cream
2 (6-ounce) cans crabmeat, drained
1 cup shredded Muenster cheese
⅓ cup chopped cilantro

Spicy Shrimp Chowder

Serves 6

3 tablespoons butter
1 tablespoon vegetable oil
1 onion, chopped
3 cloves garlic, minced
1 jalapeño pepper, minced
3 carrots, sliced
2 tablespoons flour
1 teaspoon salt
1 chipotle chile in adobo
    sauce, minced
1½ cups milk
2 cups frozen corn
1 cup frozen hash brown
    potatoes
1 pound raw shrimp
1 (8-ounce) package cream
    cheese
1½ cups shredded Muenster
    cheese

Two kinds of chiles add a rich depth of flavor to this delicious and hearty chowder. Garnish it with some fresh tomato salsa and avocado slices.

1. In large saucepan, melt butter and oil over medium heat. Cook onion, garlic, jalapeño pepper, and carrots until crisp-tender, about 4–5 minutes. Add flour and salt; cook and stir until bubbly.

2. Stir in chipotle chile and milk and bring just to a simmer. Add corn and potatoes and bring back to a simmer. Add shrimp and bring to a simmer; cook for 4–5 minutes until shrimp just begin to curl and turn pink.

3. Cut cream cheese into cubes and add to chowder; cook and stir for a few minutes until cheese melts. Add Muenster cheese, stir, and serve.

Frozen Vegetables

Don't be afraid to use frozen vegetables. Since the vegetables are picked, processed, and frozen within hours, the quality is very high. Frozen peas, especially, are almost always better than fresh, unless you have your own garden. Stock up on frozen vegetables and you can whip up a chowder or soup in minutes.

Bacon and Black-Eyed Pea Soup

This rich soup simmers all day in your crockpot. Serve it with Chipotle Chile Corn Bread (page 108) for a fabulous lunch or dinner.

∩

1. In heavy skillet, cook bacon over medium heat until crisp; remove bacon, drain on paper towels, crumble, and set aside in refrigerator.

2. In drippings remaining in skillet, cook onion, garlic, and serrano chile until vegetables are crisp-tender, about 4–5 minutes. Place in a 4- to 5-quart crockpot. Add remaining ingredients to crockpot, cover, and cook on low for 8–9 hours until vegetables are tender.

3. Add reserved bacon to soup, stir, and cook on high for 20–30 minutes. Top with cheese and serve.

Food Lore

Black-eyed peas are considered a good luck food in the South. Every Southerner eats this legume in one form or another on New Year's Eve and New Year's Day to guarantee good luck for the rest of the year. Serve this soup at your New Year's party and join the tradition.

Serves 6

4 slices bacon
1 onion, chopped
4 cloves garlic, minced
1 serrano chile, minced
2 tablespoons Taco Seasoning Mix (page 93)
3 (14-ounce) cans chicken broth
1 (14-ounce) can diced tomatoes with chiles
2 (15-ounce) cans black-eyed peas, drained
1 (9-ounce) bag baby carrots
2 cups grated Muenster cheese

Chapter Five

Side Dishes

Asparagus with Avocado

Serves 4

1 pound asparagus spears
2 tablespoons butter
½ teaspoon salt
Dash pepper
1 avocado, peeled and diced
1 tablespoon lemon juice

This simple side dish combines tender, slightly sour hot asparagus spears with cold sweet avocado cubes for a wonderful taste sensation.

1. In large pan, place asparagus spears in water to cover and bring to a boil. Boil for 2–5 minutes until asparagus is crisp-tender. Drain asparagus thoroughly, return to pan and add butter. Place pan over low heat to melt butter, and sprinkle with salt and pepper, tossing gently to coat.

2. Dice avocado and sprinkle with lemon juice. Place asparagus on serving platter and sprinkle with avocado.

Grilled Corn on the Cob

Serves 6

6 ears sweet corn
6 tablespoons butter
¼ teaspoon fresh nutmeg
1 tablespoon chili powder
Salt and pepper to taste

There's an old saying about fresh sweet corn: Stroll down to the garden to pick it, but run back to the kitchen to cook it. Corn begins to convert its sugars into starches the second it is picked; for the sweetest corn, freshest is best.

1. Pull back corn husks but leave attached at bottom. Remove silk. Spread each cob with 1 tablespoon butter.

2. In small bowl, combine nutmeg and chili powder and mix well. Sprinkle evenly over each buttered cob; pull husks back over corn kernels. Tie closed, then cook on medium grill 4–6" from heat for 20–30 minutes until corn is tender.

3. Serve with salt and pepper to taste.

Frijoles Refritas

This recipe can be expanded depending on how many people you want to feed. You can use just about any flavoring you like to season this rich and creamy side dish.

∩

1. In large saucepan, melt lard or bacon drippings and cook onion until tender.

2. Add beans, salt, pepper, and chili powder and cook, mashing beans with a potato masher or fork, until beans absorb the fat and mixture is as smooth or chunky as you like.

Menu Suggestions

Any cooked beans can be "refried" or recooked using this method. Be sure the beans are soft and very well drained. Serve these beans with Spanish Rice (page 79) and Cheese Quesadillas (page 204) for a great traditional Tex-Mex meal.

Serves 6

3 cups cooked Pinto Beans (page 83)
3 tablespoons lard or bacon drippings
1 onion, finely chopped
½ teaspoon salt
⅛ teaspoon cayenne pepper
1 tablespoon chili powder

Green Rice

Green rice is full of flavor, is a beautiful color,
and is a wonderful side dish to serve with simple grilled meats.

½ cup diced onion
1 clove garlic, minced
2 tablespoons butter
1 cup long-grain rice
1½ cups chicken broth
1 cup water
1 cup baby spinach leaves
¼ cup cilantro leaves
1 serrano pepper, seeded
2 tablespoons olive oil
½ teaspoon salt
Dash pepper

1. In heavy skillet, cook onion and garlic in butter over medium heat until transparent. Stir in rice and cook for 2–3 minutes until rice is opaque. Add broth and water, bring to a boil, then cover, reduce heat, and simmer for 15–20 minutes until rice is tender.

2. Meanwhile, combine spinach, cilantro, pepper, olive oil, salt, and pepper in mortar and pestle or in food processor. Pound or process until mixture is smooth.

3. When rice is cooked, fluff with fork, then stir in spinach mixture. Cook over low heat, stirring constantly, until mixture is hot, about 2–3 minutes.

Food Safety Update

Food scientists have found that cilantro has an antibacterial effect, especially against the Salmonella bacteria. Eating lots of cilantro will help protect you from food poisoning, but it is NOT a substitute for safe food-handling techniques.

Spanish Rice

Rice cooked with onions, garlic, peppers, and tomatoes is a fabulous
side dish—you can serve it with everything from grilled steaks to chicken soup.

∩

Serves 6

2 tablespoons vegetable oil
1 onion, chopped
3 cloves garlic, minced
1 jalapeño pepper, minced
1½ cups Texmati rice
2½ cups water
1 (14-ounce) can diced
    tomatoes, undrained
1 tablespoon chili powder
½ teaspoon cumin
½ teaspoon salt
Dash pepper

1. In large saucepan, heat vegetable oil over medium heat and cook onion, garlic, and pepper until crisp-tender. Add rice; cook and stir for 5–8 minutes until rice becomes opaque.

2. Stir in remaining ingredients and bring to a boil. Cover, reduce heat, and simmer for 20–30 minutes or until rice is tender. Let stand off heat for 5 minutes. Fluff with fork and serve.

Crockpot Red Beans

Serve this hearty and rich dish with some cooked Texmati rice and some
chilled Sweet Tea (page 241) for a perfect light lunch.

∩

Serves 6

3 slices bacon
1 onion, chopped
3 cloves garlic, minced
2 jalapeño peppers, minced
8 ounces dried red beans
8 cups water
2 tomatoes, seeded and diced
1 tablespoon chili powder
1 teaspoon salt
⅛ teaspoon pepper
½ teaspoon dried oregano
½ teaspoon cumin

1. In heavy skillet, cook bacon until crisp. Drain bacon on paper towels, crumble, cover, and refrigerate. In drippings remaining in pan, cook onion, garlic, and jalapeños until crisp-tender, 4–5 minutes, stirring frequently.

2. Meanwhile, sort over dried beans, then rinse them thoroughly. Place in 4-quart crockpot along with onion mixture and water. Cover and cook on high for 4 hours.

3. Stir beans and add remaining ingredients, including reserved bacon. Cover and cook on low for 4–6 hours or until beans are very tender.

Cheesy Corn and Tomatoes

Serve this rich and cheesy side dish with a grilled steak or Beer-Can Chicken (page 152), with a plain, crisp green salad on the side.

Serves 6

2 tablespoons butter
1 onion, chopped
2 cloves garlic, minced
1 serrano pepper, minced
1 tablespoon flour
1 cup cubed pasteurized processed cheese
2 tomatoes, seeded and chopped
2 cups frozen corn, thawed
½ teaspoon salt
Dash pepper

1. Melt butter in large skillet over medium heat and cook onion, garlic, and serrano pepper until crisp-tender. Add flour; cook and stir for 2 minutes.

2. Add remaining ingredients; cook and stir until cheese is melted and corn is hot. Season with salt and pepper and serve.

Tex-Mex Crockpot Rice

Serve this hearty side dish with a simple grilled steak or grilled chicken breasts, with some corn on the cob on the side.

Serves 6

1 (15-ounce) can black beans, rinsed
1 cup brown rice
1½ cups boiling water
1 cup frozen corn
½ cup chunky salsa
1 serrano chile, minced
4 cloves garlic, minced
½ teaspoon salt
⅛ teaspoon white pepper
2 tablespoons lime juice
¼ cup chopped cilantro

1. In a 3- to 4-quart crockpot, combine beans, rice, water, corn, salsa, chile, garlic, salt, and pepper. Stir well, then cover and cook on low for 2½ to 3 hours, until rice is tender.

2. Stir in lime juice and cilantro, mix well, and serve.

Rice in the Crockpot

When cooked in the crockpot, brown rice becomes moist and tender—more tender than when cooked on the stovetop. Do not substitute regular or instant rice for the brown rice; it will overcook. Even Texmati and Basmati rice do not work well in this appliance.

Squash con Queso

*Two different kinds of squash, yellow squash and zucchini,
are cooked with onion and then topped with two different kinds of cheese
for a wonderfully flavored side dish.*

∩

Serves 6

1 tablespoon vegetable oil
1 tablespoon butter
1 onion, chopped
3 cloves garlic, minced
3 yellow squash, sliced
2 zucchini, sliced
½ teaspoon salt
Dash pepper
1 cup cubed processed
    American cheese
1 cup shredded Monterey jack
    cheese

1. Heat oil and butter in heavy skillet over medium heat. Cook onion and garlic until crisp-tender, about 4–5 minutes.

2. Add squash and zucchini, sprinkle with salt and pepper, and stir-fry for 4–6 minutes until tender. Sprinkle with the two cheeses, cover pan, and remove from heat.

3. Let stand for 3–4 minutes until cheese melts. Stir gently and serve.

Ingredient Substitution

You can substitute other forms of squash in this recipe, but the squash must be partially cooked first. Use a butternut or acorn squash, cut it in half, scoop out seeds, brush with butter, and bake in a 350°F oven for 20–45 minutes until almost tender. Then scoop out the flesh, chop it, and use it in the recipe.

Scalloped Corn

Serves 8

¼ cup butter
3 tablespoons vegetable oil
1 onion, chopped
1 green bell pepper, chopped
2 cups frozen corn
1 (16-ounce) can creamed
   corn
1 jalapeño pepper, minced
1 (8-ounce) package corn
   muffin mix
2 eggs, beaten
1 cup sour cream
⅓ cup milk
1 cup shredded pepper jack
   cheese
½ cup shredded Colby cheese
¼ cup grated cotija or
   Parmesan cheese

This hearty side dish is a great choice to serve with barbecued or smoked meats, along with a green salad and some fresh fruit.

1. Preheat oven to 350°F. Grease a 2½-quart baking dish and set aside. In heavy skillet, melt butter with oil and sauté onion and green bell pepper until crisp-tender, about 4 minutes. Stir in frozen corn; cook and stir until corn is thawed, 3–4 minutes longer.

2. Stir in remaining ingredients except cotija or Parmesan cheese and mix well until blended. Pour into prepared pan. Sprinkle with cotija or Parmesan cheese and bake at 350°F for 40–50 minutes or until casserole is set and golden brown. Serve immediately.

Jalapeño Roasted Squash

Serves 4

2 tablespoons vegetable oil
1 butternut squash
⅛ teaspoon nutmeg
½ teaspoon salt
Dash pepper
2 jalapeño peppers

Sweet squash combined with spicy and hot jalapeño peppers makes a wonderful side dish perfect with any grilled or barbecued meat.

1. Preheat oven to 350°F. Drizzle a baking pan with the vegetable oil and set aside. Peel squash, discard membranes and seeds, and cut into 1" cubes. Place in baking pan and toss with your hands to coat the squash with the oil.

2. Sprinkle squash with the nutmeg, salt, and pepper. Roast in 350°F oven for 20–25 minutes or until squash is almost tender. Cut jalapeño peppers into slices and sprinkle over the squash. Roast for another 10–15 minutes or until squash is tender; stir, and serve.

Roasted Corn

You can expand this recipe to serve more people;
just add ½ cup corn and a bit of oil for each additional person.

Serves 4

2 cups frozen corn kernels
2 tablespoons vegetable oil
4 cloves garlic, minced
1 teaspoon salt
⅛ teaspoon cayenne pepper
⅓ cup heavy cream

1. Preheat oven to 400°F. Combine all ingredients except cream on baking sheet and stir to mix well. Roast at 400°F for 15 minutes. Stir mixture, and roast for another 10–15 minutes or until corn is golden brown around the edges.

2. Transfer corn mixture from baking sheet to saucepan and place over medium heat. Stir in cream and bring to a simmer. Cover pan, remove from heat, and let stand for 5 minutes, then serve.

Pinto Beans

You can omit the onion for plain beans. This basic recipe is a staple in Tex-Mex
and Mexican cooking; beans are good for you, cheap, tasty, and filling.

Serves 6

2 cups dried pinto beans
1 onion, chopped
8 cups water

Sort over pinto beans and discard any shriveled beans or small stones. Rinse well and drain. Place in 4-quart crockpot with onion and water; stir well. Cover and cook on low for 8–10 hours or until beans are very tender.

Cook Dried Legumes

Cook any dried legume using this easy method—black beans (add a bit of epazote), kidney or red beans, black-eyed peas, and garbanzo beans all work well. You can flavor this dish any way you'd like; adding chile peppers, garlic, chili powder, or dried herbs will boost the flavor.

Corn and Squash Sauté

Serves 4

4 ears fresh corn
2 tablespoons butter
2 yellow squash, sliced
3 green onions, chopped
½ teaspoon cumin
½ teaspoon garlic salt
Dash pepper
¼ cup sour cream

Not every Tex-Mex recipe has to include chile peppers. This simple and mild side dish is a good accompaniment to spicy main dishes such as Rib-Eye Steak (page 176) or BBQ Ribs (page 192).

∩

1. Cut the kernels off the corn cobs. In heavy skillet over medium heat, melt butter and add corn. Cook and stir for 4–5 minutes or until corn just begins to turn golden around the edges.

2. Add squash and green onions; cook and stir for 3–4 minutes longer or until vegetables are crisp-tender. Sprinkle with cumin, garlic salt, and pepper and add sour cream. Cook and stir for a few minutes longer until blended; serve.

Serving Suggestion

This flavorful recipe can be served in warm tortillas with some shredded cheese for a great vegetarian main dish. Or top a simple omelet, vegetable soup, or a frittata with this mixture. Think about serving dishes in different ways and you'll automatically expand your repertoire.

Roasted Sweet Potatoes

*You can cook just about any hard skin, or winter, squash using this method.
It's a great side dish for grilled meats or fish.*

1. Preheat oven to 375°F. Peel sweet potatoes and cut into ½" cubes. Place in roasting pan and set aside. In medium skillet, melt butter and cook onion and garlic until tender. Add sugar, salt, and pepper and cook until onions just begin to become golden at the edges.

2. Pour onion mixture over sweet potatoes, toss gently, and roast at 375°F for 35–45 minutes, stirring twice during cooking time, until potatoes are tender and crisp around the edges. Sprinkle with parsley and serve.

Serves 4–6

3 sweet potatoes
¼ cup butter
1 onion, chopped
2 cloves garlic, minced
1 tablespoon brown sugar
1 teaspoon salt
⅛ teaspoon pepper
¼ cup chopped parsley

Black Beans and Corn

*This simple side dish is excellent served with Beer-Can Chicken (page 152)
and Grapefruit Salad (page 43).*

1. In heavy skillet, melt butter and cook onion over medium heat until crisp-tender, about 4 minutes.

2. Rinse and drain black beans and add to skillet along with drained corn, undrained creamed corn, salt, and pepper. Cover and bring to a simmer; simmer for 4–5 minutes until thoroughly heated.

3. Stir in epazote, cilantro, and parsley and serve.

Serves 6

2 tablespoons butter or
   bacon grease
1 onion, chopped
1 (15-ounce) can black beans,
   rinsed
1 (15-ounce) can corn,
   drained
1 (15-ounce) can creamed
   corn
½ teaspoon salt
Dash cayenne pepper
1 teaspoon chopped epazote,
   if desired
2 tablespoons chopped
   cilantro
2 tablespoons chopped
   parsley

Chipotle Potatoes

Serves 6

2 pounds small red potatoes
3 tablespoons vegetable oil
3 cloves garlic, minced
1 teaspoon hot salt
⅛ teaspoon pepper
½ teaspoon cumin
3 chipotle chiles in adobo
    sauce
3 tablespoons adobo sauce

*This easy side-dish recipe is really delicious served with
a simple grilled steak or turkey tenderloin.*

1. Preheat oven to 400°F. Cut each potato into quarters and toss with vegetable oil in roasting pan. Sprinkle with garlic, hot salt, pepper, and cumin, and toss again. Bake at 400°F for 30 minutes.

2. Meanwhile, chop chipotle chiles. Remove pan from oven and sprinkle chiles over potatoes. Return to oven and bake 10 minutes longer. Remove pan from oven and drizzle with adobo sauce.

3. Return to oven and bake 10–15 minutes longer until potatoes are golden and crisp, but tender when tested with fork.

Drunken Beans

Serves 8

1½ pounds dried pinto beans
3 strips bacon
1 onion, chopped
3 cloves garlic, minced
1 (12-ounce) bottle beer
4 cups water
1 (4-ounce) can diced green
    chiles
2 cups chunky salsa
1 teaspoon salt
⅛ teaspoon pepper
½ cup chopped cilantro

*These beans are made easier by cooking in the crockpot, so you don't have to keep
an eye on them. They taste even better the next day; reheat them by pouring into a
saucepan and cooking over low heat, stirring frequently, until beans simmer.*

1. Sort through beans and rinse thoroughly. Cover with water and let soak overnight.

2. When ready to cook, fry bacon in a heavy skillet until crisp; drain on paper towels, crumble, and refrigerate. Cook onion and garlic in bacon drippings until crisp-tender. Drain beans and add to a 4- to 5-quart crockpot along with onion mixture, beer, and water. Cover and cook on low for 6–7 hours until beans are tender.

3. Stir beans and add chiles, salsa, salt, and pepper. Cover and cook for 1–2 hours longer until beans are very tender. Sprinkle with cilantro and reserved bacon pieces, stir, and serve.

Roasted Tomatoes

Use these smoky and flavorful tomatoes in Ranchero Sauce (page 97) or Picante Sauce (page 100) or in your own favorite salsa recipe.

1. Preheat oven to 400°F. Cut plum tomatoes in half and place, cut side up, on baking pan. Drizzle with olive oil and sprinkle with salt and pepper. Bake tomatoes at 400°F for 15 minutes.

2. Meanwhile, cut grape tomatoes in half. Remove pan from oven and add grape tomatoes and minced garlic to plum tomatoes; toss gently. Return to oven and bake for another 10–15 minutes or until all tomatoes are brown around the edges. Serve immediately or cover and refrigerate up to 3 days.

About Roasting

When you roast vegetables or meats, the food cooks in dry heat and the moisture in the food evaporates. This concentrates the flavors in the food. When roasted food turns brown, the sugars in the food have caramelized, forming many compounds that provide smoky, rich, intense flavors and aromas.

Serves 6–8

2 pounds plum tomatoes
2 tablespoons olive oil
1 teaspoon salt
⅛ teaspoon pepper
1 pint grape tomatoes
4 cloves garlic, minced

Rice with Avocado

Serves 4–6

¼ cup butter

1 onion, minced

½ cup finely chopped
    mushrooms

1 cup Texmati rice

1 tablespoon tequila

2½ cups chicken stock

½ teaspoon dried oregano

½ teaspoon salt

Dash pepper

1 avocado

1 tablespoon lime juice

¼ cup crumbled queso
    blanco

The flavors and textures of this side dish are outstanding. Serve with a simple grilled steak, steamed baby carrots, and a spinach salad.

∩

1. In heavy saucepan, melt butter until foamy. Add onion and mushrooms; cook and stir for 4 minutes. Add rice; cook and stir until rice is opaque, about 4–5 minutes longer. Add tequila, chicken stock, oregano, salt, and pepper and bring to a boil.

2. Cover pan, reduce heat, and simmer for 15–18 minutes until rice is tender and liquid is absorbed. Peel avocado and dice; toss with lime juice and fold into rice along with cheese. Cover and let stand for a few minutes, then serve.

About Avocados

Avocados can become bitter when they are heated, which is why you almost never see a recipe for cooked avocados. But you can freeze avocados! Puree the flesh with lime or lemon juice, pack into a freezer container, and freeze for up to three months. You can use this mixture in Guacamole (page 20) or Chilled Avocado Soup (page 58).

Chapter Six

Sauces

Cilantro Pesto

Yields about 1 cup

2 cups packed fresh cilantro
    leaves
½ cup toasted pine nuts
¼ cup lime juice
2 cloves garlic
¼ cup minced onion
1 tablespoon minced
    jalapeño peppers
½ cup olive oil
⅓ cup crumbled queso fresco
    or feta cheese

This flavorful sauce can be served in many ways. Use it as an appetizer dip with tortilla chips and fresh vegetables; top grilled chicken breasts with a spoonful or two; or garnish a creamy corn chowder.

1. In blender or food processor, combine all ingredients except olive oil and cheese; blend or process until mixture is finely chopped. With motor running, gradually add olive oil through feed tube, then add enough water to form a smooth sauce if necessary. Stir in cheese by hand.

2. Cover with plastic wrap, pressing wrap to the surface of the sauce, and chill for 2–3 hours before serving.

How to Freeze Pesto

It's easy to freeze cilantro pesto for later use. Place a tablespoon of the pesto into each ice cube tray section and freeze until solid, then remove from trays and store in a labeled freezer bag for up to three months. To use, let thaw in refrigerator, then add to recipes or stir, add more cheese, and serve as is.

Pico de Gallo

Pico de gallo means "beak of the rooster." This may refer to the sound the knife makes chopping up the vegetables or the fact that the peppers "peck" at your tongue. At any rate, this fresh sauce is a delicious Tex-Mex staple.

∩

1. Cut tomatoes in half, seed them, then cut into small pieces. Dice onion and combine with tomatoes in a medium bowl. Sprinkle with lemon and orange juice.

2. Seed and dice jalapeño pepper. Add to tomato mixture along with parsley. Sprinkle with salt and cayenne pepper and toss to coat. Cover and chill for 1–2 hours to blend flavors, or serve immediately. Store leftovers, covered, in refrigerator.

Yields about 2 cups

3 ripe red tomatoes
2 ripe golden tomatoes
½ sweet onion
2 tablespoons lemon juice
1 tablespoon orange juice
1 jalapeño pepper
¼ cup chopped fresh parsley
1 teaspoon salt
⅛ teaspoon cayenne pepper

Tomatillo Chutney

Chutney is a sweet-and-sour cooked sauce that can be used as a condiment for any grilled meats, as a dip for tortilla chips mixed with some yogurt or mayonnaise, or as part of a salad dressing.

∩

1. Roast Anaheim chile under broiler or over gas flame until skin is blackened. Place in paper bag and let steam for 10 minutes. Peel, seed, and coarsely chop.

2. In medium saucepan, combine prepared chile, tomatillos, raisins, onion, garlic, vinegar, lime juice, jalapeño, sugar, salt, pepper, and cumin and bring to a boil. Reduce heat and simmer for 45–50 minutes or until mixture begins to thicken, stirring occasionally.

3. Store chutney, covered, in refrigerator for 2 weeks or freeze up to 3 months.

Yields 2 cups

1 Anaheim chile
1½ cups chopped tomatillos
1 cup golden raisins
½ cup chopped sweet onion
2 cloves garlic, minced
½ cup apple cider vinegar
2 tablespoons lime juice
1 jalapeño pepper, minced
¼ cup sugar
1 teaspoon salt
½ teaspoon pepper
½ teaspoon cumin

Salsa Verde

Yields 2 cups

1 poblano chile
1 green bell pepper, chopped
12 tomatillos
1 green tomato
½ cup chopped sweet onion
1 serrano chile, minced
1 clove garlic, minced
2 tablespoons lime juice
1 teaspoon salt

Green salsa is an excellent sauce for chicken and fish. Keep this fresh sauce refrigerated, well covered, for up to a week.

1. Place poblano chile and green bell pepper on broiler pan. Broil 4–5" from heat source, turning frequently, until vegetable skins are blackened. Place in paper bag and let steam for 10 minutes. Peel vegetables, remove seeds, and chop.

2. Remove husks from tomatillos, rinse, and chop. Seed and chop green tomato. Combine all ingredients in medium bowl and mix thoroughly. Store salsa in an airtight container in the refrigerator up to 1 week.

Ingredient Substitutions

Green tomatoes can be difficult to find. If you aren't able to locate any, add three more tomatillos to the recipe and another tablespoon of lime juice. This salsa can also be frozen in ice cube trays, and stored up to 3 months in the freezer.

Taco Seasoning Mix

You can purchase envelopes of taco seasoning mix in the grocery store, but this recipe is more flavorful and lets you control the sodium and spice levels. 2 tablespoons is equal to a 1¼-ounce package.

∩

1. Place dried onion and garlic powder in a spice grinder. Grind until a powder forms. Combine with all remaining ingredients and store in an airtight container.

2. Use 2 tablespoons as substitute for store-bought taco seasoning mix.

Yields 12 tablespoons

4 tablespoons dried onion
1 teaspoon garlic powder
4 tablespoons chili powder
1 tablespoon ground red chile powder
2½ teaspoons salt
1 teaspoon black pepper
½ teaspoon cayenne pepper
2 teaspoons ground coriander
3 tablespoons cornstarch
1 teaspoon cumin

Three-Chile Rub

Use this recipe as a substitute for any ground chile powder, and use it as a dry rub for grilled, barbecued, and smoked meats.

∩

1. In small heavy skillet, toast chipotle peppers until fragrant, stirring frequently; remove to a kitchen towel to let cool.

2. Toast the ancho peppers in same skillet until fragrant and let cool on kitchen towel. Remove stems and grind the cooled chiles in a spice grinder. Combine with remaining ingredients and mix well. Store in an airtight container.

Yields ½ cup

2 dried chipotle peppers
2 dried ancho chile peppers
1 teaspoon cayenne pepper
2 tablespoons brown sugar
1 teaspoon salt
½ teaspoon garlic pepper

Enchilada Sauce

Yields 3 cups

1 Anaheim chile
2 dried ancho chiles
1 tablespoon butter
2 tablespoons vegetable oil
1 onion, finely chopped
3 cloves garlic, minced
3 tablespoons flour
1 teaspoon salt
¼ teaspoon pepper
2 tablespoons chili powder
1 teaspoon cumin
1 (6-ounce) can tomato paste
1 (8-ounce) can tomato sauce
2 cups water or chicken broth

This sauce differs from Chili Gravy in that it adds tomatoes and tomato paste. Use it for enchiladas, tamales, and Mixed-Bean Lasagna (page 225) and as a dip for cheese quesadillas.

∩

1. Roast Anaheim chile under a broiler or over a gas flame, turning frequently, until charred. Place in paper bag to steam for 10 minutes. Meanwhile, toast the dried ancho chiles under a broiler or in a dry saucepan for 4–5 minutes, watching carefully, until fragrant. Let cool. Peel the Anaheim chile, remove seeds, and chop. Grind the ancho chiles in a spice grinder or molcajete.

2. In large saucepan, melt butter with oil over medium heat and sauté onion and garlic until transparent. Stir in flour, salt, and pepper; cook and stir until flour just begins to turn light golden. Add chili powder, cumin, tomato paste, sauce, water or broth, chopped Anaheim chile, and ancho chile powder. Bring to a boil, then reduce heat, cover, and simmer for 30–40 minutes until slightly thickened.

Spice It Up

Add more Anaheim and ancho chiles to make this sauce spicier, or use different colors of plain bell papers for a milder mixture. You could also add a couple of minced jalapeño or serrano peppers along with the roasted chopped chiles to really heat things up.

Mole Sauce

Using both cocoa powder and unsweetened chocolate, along with raisins, adds a nice depth of flavor to this classic sauce. Use it in Grilled Chicken in Mole Sauce (page 152), or with barbecued and smoked beef.

∩

Yields 2–3 cups

1 poblano chile
2 tablespoons vegetable oil
1 onion, chopped
3 garlic cloves, minced
2 tomatoes, seeded and
    chopped
1 (8-ounce) can tomato sauce
1½ cups chicken broth
½ cup water
1 tablespoon chili powder
1 tablespoon cocoa powder
1 (1-ounce) square
    unsweetened chocolate
¼ cup raisins
¼ teaspoon cayenne pepper
½ teaspoon cinnamon
½ teaspoon salt
¼ teaspoon pepper

1. Roast poblano chile under broiler or over gas flame until skin is blackened; place in paper bag to steam. Then peel, remove seeds, and chop.

2. Heat vegetable oil in large skillet. Add onion and garlic cloves; sauté until tender. Add tomatoes, tomato sauce, chicken broth, water, and remaining ingredients including chopped poblano chile.

3. Cover and simmer for 15 minutes to blend flavors. Using one-third of the sauce at a time, puree in blender or food processor until sauce is smooth. Use to baste meats as they grill, in recipes calling for the sauce, or cover and store in refrigerator up to 1 week.

What Are Heirloom Tomatoes?

Heirloom tomatoes are those passed down through the generations without genetic alteration, and they are making a comeback. If you have a garden or just some pots on a balcony, plant red or yellow Brandywines, Moonglow, Amish Red, or Peppermint tomatoes, which are striped like peppermint candies, to use in your salsas.

Jalapeño Pesto

Yields 2 cups

½ cup pumpkin seeds
1 tablespoon vegetable oil
½ cup chopped onion
2 cloves garlic, minced
5 jalapeño peppers
1 cup cilantro leaves
1 cup flat leaf parsley
2 tablespoons lime juice
½ teaspoon salt
¼ teaspoon pepper
½ cup olive oil
⅓ cup grated Manchego or
 Romano cheese

*This pesto can be tossed with some hot cooked pasta for an instant lunch,
or mixed with sour cream for an easy appetizer. It too freezes well,
in ice cube trays, and keeps for about 3 months.*

∩

1. In small skillet, toast pumpkin seeds over medium heat until light brown and fragrant. Remove to kitchen towel to cool. In same skillet, heat vegetable oil and sauté onion and garlic until tender. Remove to blender or food processor bowl.

2. Add cooled seeds, jalapeños, cilantro, parsley, lime juice, salt, and pepper and blend or process until finely chopped. With motor running, add olive oil in a thin stream until a paste forms. Remove to bowl and stir in cheese.

3. Press plastic wrap onto surface and refrigerate up to 2 days, or freeze up to 3 months.

Ingredient Substitutions

Other nuts can be substituted for pumpkin seeds. Peanuts, pine nuts, and slivered almonds have about the same texture and similar flavor. For a richer flavor, use pecans or cashews. Remember to let all nuts cool thoroughly after roasting and before chopping or processing, or they will be soggy.

Tomato Salsa

*This simple salsa is served with many Tex-Mex foods—
from an appetizer dip to the garnish for a grilled steak.
Keep this fresh sauce refrigerated, well covered, for up to a week.*

∩

1. Place poblano chile on broiler pan. Broil 4–5" from heat source, turning frequently, until skin is charred. Place in paper bag and let steam for 10 minutes. Peel chile, remove seeds, and chop.

2. Combine bell pepper, poblano chile, and chopped tomatoes in medium bowl. Cut cherry tomatoes in half and add to bowl along with remaining ingredients; mix thoroughly. Store salsa in an airtight container in the refrigerator up to 1 week.

Yields 2 cups

1 poblano chile
1 green bell pepper, chopped
4 tomatoes, seeded and
    chopped
1 pint cherry tomatoes
½ cup chopped sweet onion
1 serrano chile, minced
1 clove garlic, minced
2 tablespoons lime juice
1 teaspoon salt

Ranchero Sauce

*This is the sauce to use when you want to make anything "Ranchero"—
that is, Huevos Rancheros (page 221), Grilled Ranchero Swordfish (page 132),
and Potatoes Rancheros (page 229).*

∩

1. Heat oil in heavy skillet over medium heat. Cook onion and garlic in oil for 4–5 minutes, stirring frequently, until crisp-tender. Add bell pepper, jalapeños, chopped tomatoes with their liquid, tomato paste, chili powder, salt, and pepper.

2. Bring to a boil, then cover pan, reduce heat, and simmer for 15–20 minutes until sauce thickens.

3. Cool the sauce and store, covered, in the refrigerator up to 3 days, or freeze for longer storage. Reheat before use.

Yields about 2 cups

1 tablespoon vegetable oil
1 onion, chopped
2 cloves garlic, minced
1 green bell pepper, chopped
2 jalapeño peppers, minced
1 (14-ounce) can fire-roasted
    chopped tomatoes
3 tablespoons tomato paste
1 tablespoon chili powder
1 teaspoon salt
¼ teaspoon pepper

Chili Gravy

2 ancho chiles
½ cup warm chicken stock
¼ cup shortening or lard
1 onion, minced
4 cloves garlic, minced
¼ cup flour
1 teaspoon salt
⅛ teaspoon pepper
1 teaspoon cumin
½ teaspoon dried oregano
  leaves
1 tablespoon chili powder
1½ cups beef stock

*This versatile sauce can be used to top just about any Tex-Mex entrée.
It's good served over enchiladas, with tamales for dipping,
and as a table sauce with grilled and barbecued meats.*

1. Break ancho chiles into pieces and discard stems. Place in food processor or blender with chicken stock; let stand for 10 minutes, then blend until smooth. Set aside.

2. In heavy saucepan, melt shortening and add onion and garlic. Cook and stir over medium heat until onions are transparent. Add flour; cook and stir over medium heat for 5–8 minutes or until flour turns a light golden brown.

3. Add salt, pepper, cumin, oregano, chili powder, and the ancho chile puree along with beef stock. Stir well with wire whisk to combine. Lower heat and simmer for 20–30 minutes until sauce is thickened.

What's a Roux?

Gravies and sauces are started with a roux, which is flour cooked in meat drippings, butter, oil, or shortening. When the flour is browned in the fat, lots of good flavor compounds are created. Watch the roux carefully as it cooks, for if the roux burns you'll have to start all over.

Tamale Sauce

This sauce is very quick to make, and you can vary it as you like with different spices, herbs, and seasonings. Serve it as a dipping sauce with freshly steamed tamales or pour over enchiladas.

1. In heavy saucepan, combine all ingredients and stir well to mix. Bring to a boil over medium heat, then cover, reduce heat to low, and simmer for 20–30 minutes to blend flavors.

2. Use immediately or cover and refrigerate; use within three days.

Nacho Cheese Sauce

This sauce can be served warm with tortilla chips for an appetizer, or can be used as a topping for enchiladas and tacos. It reheats very well in the microwave.

1. In microwave-safe bowl, combine all ingredients. Microwave on medium for 1 minute, then remove and stir. Repeat microwaving at 1 minute intervals, stirring after each minute, until sauce is smooth and blended, about 3-6 minutes.

2. Use or cover and refrigerate up to 2 days; reheat before using.

About Spices

Powdered vegetables and spices lose their intensity over time. When you bring them home from the grocery store, mark the date of purchase right on the bottle. Store them in a dark, cool, and dry place, and be sure to discard spices that are more than a year old.

Rib Mopping Sauce

Yields 2 cups

1 (12-ounce) can beer
¼ cup butter
1 onion, finely chopped
4 cloves garlic, minced
1 (6-ounce) can tomato paste
2 tablespoons mustard
1 teaspoon Tabasco sauce
2 jalapeño peppers, minced
½ cup water
¼ cup sugar
1 teaspoon salt
¼ teaspoon pepper

Beer adds great flavor to this rich sauce used to "mop" ribs or other meats on the grill. Use a pastry brush, a barbecue mop, or a bunch of fresh herbs tied together to apply this sauce to the food toward the end of cooking time.

1. Open beer and let stand while preparing other ingredients. In heavy saucepan, melt butter and cook onion and garlic until very soft. Add beer and other ingredients; mix well.

2. Bring to a boil over medium heat, then cover, lower heat, and cook for about 40–50 minutes or until flavors are blended and sauce is slightly thickened. Rub sauce over meat several times while it cooks, toward the end of cooking time.

Picante Sauce

Yields 2 cups

4 red tomatoes, seeded and
    chopped
1 yellow tomato, seeded and
    chopped
1 orange bell pepper,
    chopped
½ cup diced sweet onion
2 garlic cloves, minced
2 tablespoons lime juice
1 serrano chile, minced
2 teaspoons chili powder
1 teaspoon sugar
1 teaspoon salt
⅛ teaspoon cayenne pepper

This fresh sauce is a must served with warm and crisp tortilla chips as an appetizer. Use a sweet onion if you can find it.

1. Combine all ingredients in large bowl and toss to mix. You can also put everything into a blender or food processor and blend or process until mixture is almost smooth.

2. Cover and refrigerate up to 4 days. Serve as a condiment with tamales and tacos, or as an appetizer dip.

Colorado Sauce

Colorado chiles are dried Anaheim peppers.
This is an excellent sauce to use to top enchiladas or to serve with tamales.

∩

1. Rinse chiles and place in large bowl. Bring broth to a boil and pour over chiles; let stand for 30–40 minutes until softened. Meanwhile, cook onion and garlic in lard until soft.

2. Place in blender or food processor with softened chiles and remaining ingredients. Blend or process until smooth, adding chicken broth as needed. Strain mixture through strainer, pressing with back of spoon. Store covered in refrigerator up to 1 week.

Yields 3 cups

4 dried Colorado chiles
2½ cups chicken broth
1 onion, chopped
3 cloves garlic, chopped
2 tablespoons lard or vegetable oil
½ teaspoon coriander seeds
2 tablespoons red chile powder
½ teaspoon salt
⅛ teaspoon pepper

Taco Sauce

Serve this smooth and spicy sauce as part of a taco buffet,
or add to tomato sauce and pour over enchiladas.

∩

1. Combine all ingredients in heavy saucepan and bring to a boil over medium heat. Reduce heat, cover, and simmer for 10–15 minutes or until sauce is slightly thickened.

2. Store sauce, covered, in refrigerator for up to 1 week.

Yields about 3 cups

1 (6-ounce) can tomato paste
2 cups water or chicken broth
¼ cup grated onion
1 chipotle pepper in adobo sauce, minced
1 tablespoon adobo sauce
1 tablespoon corn syrup
1 jalapeño pepper, minced
½ teaspoon cayenne pepper
½ teaspoon salt
1 tablespoon apple cider vinegar

How to Make Chicken Broth

To make chicken broth, place 2 pounds chicken parts in 8 cups of water along with an onion, garlic cloves, carrot slices, and celery. Bring to a boil, cover, and simmer for 1½ hours. Strain broth, cool, and store in refrigerator up to 4 days or freeze up to 3 months.

Crockpot BBQ Sauce

Let this sauce slowly simmer and blend in your crockpot
while you start the ribs on the grill. During the last half-hour of cooking,
slather this sauce all over the ribs.

Yields 5 cups

2 (8-ounce) cans tomato
    sauce
2 cups ketchup
4 chipotle chiles in adobo
    sauce, minced
1 tablespoon red chile
    powder
4 tablespoons Worcestershire
    sauce
1 teaspoon chile paste
4 tablespoons mustard
1 teaspoon cumin
¼ teaspoon cayenne pepper
½ cup grated onion
1 teaspoon garlic pepper
    (or ½ teaspoon garlic
    powder and ½ teaspoon
    black pepper)
4 tablespoons molasses
4 tablespoons apple cider
    vinegar

Combine all ingredients in 3-quart crockpot and cook on low for 2–3 hours, stirring twice during cooking time, until blended and slightly thickened. Do not use a larger crockpot, as the sauce may burn.

How to Freeze Sauce

Freeze any remaining barbecue sauce in ice cube trays, then package the cubes into well-labeled freezer storage bags and freeze for up to 3 months. Thaw the cubes in the microwave oven or in a saucepan over very low heat, then use as directed.

Brisket Mopping Sauce

Coffee is the secret ingredient in this rich sauce. You can substitute 2 table-spoons of red chile powder for the roasted pasilla chile if you'd like.

∩

1. Place pasilla chile on baking sheet and roast at 400°F for 5–6 minutes until fragrant. Place on kitchen towel to cool. Break into chunks and place in blender or food processor with coffee. Blend or process until smooth.

2. Combine with remaining ingredients in heavy saucepan and bring to a boil. Reduce heat and simmer for 15–25 minutes or until slightly thickened.

The Secret Ingredient

Coffee is also the main ingredient in Red Eye Gravy, a Southern specialty usually served with ham. It adds a nice deep flavor, a bit of smokiness, and wonderful color to any sauce. Brew your own favorite blend, or make instant coffee double-strength for best results.

Yields 4 cups

1 pasilla chile
1 cup strong coffee
1 (8-ounce) can tomato sauce
¼ cup apple cider vinegar
2 cups beef broth
1 serrano or habanero chile, minced
½ teaspoon salt
⅛ teaspoon pepper
2 tablespoons chili powder
½ teaspoon Tabasco sauce

Tomatillo Salsa

Yields 2 cups

1 pint fresh tomatillos
1 tablespoon vegetable oil
1 onion, chopped
2 cloves garlic, minced
1 minced serrano chile
½ cup chopped cilantro
1 teaspoon salt
⅛ teaspoon pepper
⅛ teaspoon cayenne pepper

This salsa is excellent served as an appetizer with different-colored tortilla chips. Or use it in Mexican Layered Dip (page 35) in place of the tomatoes.

1. Remove husks from tomatillos and rinse. Dry well and coarsely chop. Heat vegetable oil in heavy saucepan and sauté onion and garlic until crisp-tender. Add chopped tomatillos and cook for 2–3 minutes until tomatillos begin to soften.

2. Remove from heat and add remaining ingredients. Cool to room temperature, then place in container, cover, and refrigerate up to 4 days or freeze up to 3 months.

Red Chile Sauce

Yields about 3 cups

1 dried ancho chile
½ cup hot water
1 Anaheim chile
⅓ cup lard or vegetable oil
⅓ cup flour
1 teaspoon salt
¼ teaspoon pepper
1 teaspoon cumin
2 tablespoons chili powder
3 cups beef broth

The beef broth, ancho chile, browned roux, and chili powder all combine to make this sauce a deep rich brownish red color. Use it as a sauce when you're making enchiladas, or serve it on the side with any kind of tamale.

1. Cover ancho chile with hot water and let stand for 30 minutes. Meanwhile, place Anaheim chile under broiler or hold over a gas flame until skin is blackened. Place in paper bag for 10 minutes to steam, then peel. Remove seeds and coarsely chop. Stem and coarsely chop the ancho chile.

2. In heavy skillet, melt lard and stir in flour. Cook and stir over low heat for 5–8 minutes until mixture turns light brown. Add salt, pepper, cumin, chili powder, chopped chiles, and beef broth. Cook, stirring frequently, over low heat for 20–25 minutes or until sauce thickens.

Chile Puree

*Make this sauce in many different ways using different chiles.
It freezes very well; place in ice cube trays and freeze solid, then remove
cubes from trays and package them in freezer-storage plastic bags.
When needed, drop the cubes into any red sauce (while cooking) or heat
and use for enchiladas or a table sauce.*

Yields 2 cups

*3 dried ancho chiles
2 Anaheim chiles
4 garlic cloves, peeled
1 jalapeño chile
1½ cups chicken broth
1 tablespoon honey
½ teaspoon salt*

1. Place ancho chiles in saucepan and cover with boiling water. Let stand for about 1 hour. Meanwhile, roast the Anaheim chiles under the broiler or over a gas flame until blackened. Place in paper bag for 10 minutes to steam, then peel and remove seeds. Place garlic in small saucepan and toast over low heat for 3–6 minutes until fragrant.

2. Place soaked ancho chiles, seeded Anaheim chiles, toasted garlic, jalapeño chile, and ½ cup chicken broth in a blender or food processor. Blend or process until smooth. Strain mixture into a heavy saucepan.

3. Add remaining chicken broth, honey, and salt; bring to a boil. Reduce heat and simmer for 5–10 minutes until mixture is blended. Use or cover and refrigerate up to 1 week, or freeze up to 3 months.

Sweet or Spicy?

For a sweeter flavor in this puree, use dried pasilla chiles instead of the dried ancho chiles, and increase the amount of honey to 2 tablespoons. For a spicier sauce, use smoked chipotle chiles instead of the ancho chiles, and add another jalapeño chile.

Chapter Seven

Bread and Tortillas

Chipotle Chile Corn Bread

Hot and smoky chipotle chiles add a wonderful depth of flavor to this simple corn bread recipe. Serve it with any chili for a fabulous lunch.

∩

Serves 8

2 chipotle peppers in adobo
    sauce, drained
1½ cups flour
1 cup yellow cornmeal
1 tablespoon baking powder
½ teaspoon salt
¼ cup sugar
2 eggs
½ cup milk
½ cup plain yogurt
⅓ cup vegetable oil
1 cup crumbled queso blanco

1. Preheat oven to 400°F. Grease a 9" square pan with solid shortening or nonstick baking spray and set aside. Finely chop chipotle peppers and set aside.

2. In large bowl, combine flour, cornmeal, baking powder, salt, and sugar and blend well. In small bowl, combine eggs, milk, yogurt, and oil and mix until blended. Add to dry ingredients along with chipotle peppers and cheese and stir just until blended.

3. Pour into prepared pan; bake at 400°F for 25–30 minutes or until bread is firm to the touch and light golden brown. Serve warm.

Colored Cornmeal

Corn bread can be made with yellow cornmeal, red cornmeal, white cornmeal, or even blue cornmeal. All of it tastes about the same; the difference will be in the appearance of the finished product, although red cornmeal may have ground chiles added. If not, red cornmeal is made from a special variety of red corn that is sweeter than white or yellow.

Texts Toast

Texas Toast is usually served alongside a nicely grilled steak. It can be used to make the steak seem larger; place the toast under the meat and it will soak up all the wonderful juices.

Serves 8

1 loaf white bread, unsliced
½ cup butter
4 cloves garlic, smashed
2 tablespoons chili powder
½ teaspoon salt
⅛ teaspoon cayenne pepper

∩

1. Cut the bread into 1" thick slices. In small saucepan, melt butter and add garlic cloves. Simmer over medium low heat for 3–4 minutes to flavor butter. Discard garlic.

2. Add chili powder, salt, and cayenne pepper to butter. Briefly dip each slice of bread into the butter mixture, turning to coat both sides. Place on broiler pan or hot grill; broil or grill 4–6" from heat source, turning once, until bread is golden brown, about 4–5 minutes total.

Make It Your Own

As with everything in Texas, their toast is larger than usual. You can use any spices, herbs, and peppers that you'd like in this simple recipe; just be sure to watch carefully when the toast is under the broiler or on the grill because it burns very easily.

Corn Bread

Serves 8–10

1½ cups yellow cornmeal
1 cup buttermilk
½ cup milk
1 cup canned cream-style
    corn
1¾ cups flour
⅓ cup sugar
1 cup corn kernels
2 teaspoons baking powder
1 teaspoon baking soda
2 eggs, beaten
½ cup oil

*Three different kinds of corn make this corn bread moist and delicious,
with a superb flavor. Serve it hot with butter;
remember to save some to make Toasted Corn Bread Salad (page 40).*

∩

1. Preheat oven to 400°F. Grease a 9" x 13" pan with solid shortening and
    set aside. In medium bowl, combine cornmeal, buttermilk, milk, and
    cream-style corn and mix well; set aside.

2. In large bowl, combine flour, sugar, corn kernels, baking powder, bak-
    ing soda, eggs, and oil until well mixed. Add cornmeal mixture and
    mix just until combined. Pour into prepared pan.

3. Bake corn bread at 400°F for 30–35 minutes or until corn bread is light
    golden brown and pulling away from sides of pan. Serve hot with butter.

Hush Puppies

Makes 24

1 cup yellow cornmeal
1 cup flour
1 teaspoon baking powder
½ teaspoon baking soda
½ teaspoon smoked paprika
⅓ cup buttermilk
2 eggs
½ cup chopped sweet onion
4 cups vegetable oil

*Hush puppies were first made in the Deep South
when fishermen would fry extra batter in little round balls
and throw them to their hunting dogs, saying "Hush, puppies!"*

∩

1. In large bowl, combine cornmeal, flour, baking powder, baking soda,
    and paprika and mix well. In medium bowl, combine buttermilk, eggs,
    and sweet onion and beat well. Mix dry and wet ingredients together
    just until blended.

2. Heat oil in large heavy saucepan to 375°F. Drop batter by spoonfuls into
    hot oil, about five or six at a time, and fry until golden brown. Remove
    and drain on paper towels. Serve hot.

Hot-Water Hoecakes

Yes, these little cakes were originally cooked on a (clean) hoe over a campfire. They must be served hot, preferably with butter and salsa or honey.

∩

1. Heat a griddle to 375°F. In medium bowl, combine cornmeal, salt, and chili powder. Add water and stir to combine. Let stand for 5 minutes.

2. Add butter to hot griddle and drop cornmeal batter in tablespoon amounts onto hot butter. Cook 2–3 minutes until golden; turn and cook 2–3 minutes on the other side. Serve hot with cold butter.

Serves 6

1 cup white cornmeal
½ teaspoon salt
½ teaspoon chili powder
2 cups boiling water
3 tablespoons butter

Tex-Mex Beer Bread

Serve this super-easy bread hot out of the oven with butter seasoned with chili powder, oregano, and cumin to taste. It's excellent served with any soup or chili.

∩

1. Preheat oven to 375°F. In large bowl, combine all ingredients and mix just until blended.

2. Spray 9" x 5" loaf pan with nonstick baking spray; pour batter into prepared pan. Bake at 375°F for 50–55 minutes or until bread is firm and light golden brown and pulls away from edge of pan. Serve warm.

Serves 8

2½ cups self-rising flour
⅓ cup yellow cornmeal
1 teaspoon chili powder
1 (12-ounce) can beer
2 tablespoons butter, melted

Funnel Cakes

Yields 12–14

¼ cup sugar
2 cups flour
1 teaspoon baking powder
½ teaspoon cinnamon
2 eggs, beaten
1½ cups half-and-half
1 teaspoon vanilla
3 cups vegetable oil
½ cup powdered sugar
1 teaspoon cinnamon

Funnel cakes really are made using a funnel. The soft batter is poured into a funnel and drips through the opening into hot oil, forming a tangled shape that becomes brown and crisp.

1. Combine sugar, flour, baking powder, and cinnamon in a large bowl and mix well. In medium bowl, combine eggs, half-and-half, and vanilla and beat well. Add to dry ingredients and mix just until combined. You may need to add more flour or half-and-half to reach the desired consistency.

2. Heat the oil to 375°F in a large and deep heavy saucepan, making sure there is at least 1" of space between the oil and the top of the pan. Hold your finger over the opening of a funnel or pastry bag and ladle in ½ cup of the batter. Holding the funnel over hot oil, remove your finger and release the batter, making spirals and criss-crossed circles in the oil. Fry until golden brown, turn, and fry second side until golden brown. Drain on paper towels.

3. In small bowl, combine powdered sugar and cinnamon and mix well. Using a strainer, sift this mixture over the hot funnel cakes.

Tool Options

If you don't want to use a funnel, you could use a pastry bag to get the batter into the hot oil. Or use a clean plastic squeeze bottle. Most bottles have a smaller opening than funnels or pastry bags, so the funnel cakes will be finer and will cook more quickly.

Pan Dulce Rolls

Pan dulce, which means "sweet bread" in Spanish, is a classic breakfast dish served on special occasions. The slightly sweet and soft dough is topped with a mixture of sugar, butter, and egg yolks that browns to a crisp crunch.

∩

Makes 16

2 tablespoons warm water
1 (0.25-ounce) package active dry yeast
1 teaspoon sugar
1 (12-ounce) can evaporated milk
¼ cup butter
⅓ cup sugar
½ teaspoon salt
3 eggs
4 to 5 cups flour
½ cup butter, softened
½ cup powdered sugar
½ cup brown sugar
2 egg yolks
1 teaspoon lemon peel
½ cup flour

1. In small bowl, combine warm water with yeast and 1 teaspoon sugar and mix well. Let sit until foamy, about 5 minutes. Meanwhile, combine the evaporated milk, ¼ cup butter, ⅓ cup sugar, and salt in a medium saucepan. Heat until butter melts. Pour mixture into a mixing bowl and let stand until lukewarm.

2. Add eggs to milk mixture, beating well after each addition. Then add yeast mixture. Gradually stir in enough flour until a soft dough forms. Knead the dough on a flour-dusted surface until smooth and satiny. Place in a greased bowl, turning to grease top, cover, and let rise until double, about 1 hour.

3. Divide dough into 16 balls and form into oval shapes. Flatten with palm of hand and place on greased baking sheets. Cover with a kitchen towel and let rise until double, about 45 minutes.

4. Preheat oven to 350°F. In medium bowl, combine ½ cup butter, powdered sugar, brown sugar, and egg yolks and beat until smooth. Stir in lemon peel and flour. Spread this mixture over each of the rolls, covering completely. Bake at 350°F for 15–25 minutes, until rolls are browned and topping is crisp. Serve warm.

Ingredient Substitutions

The topping for these sweet rolls can be flavored any number of ways. Use orange peel instead of the lemon peel, add a few tablespoons of cocoa powder, or use a couple of teaspoons of cinnamon. You can also add raisins or currants to the dough, or form each roll around a piece of dark chocolate.

Corn Fritters

You can make these fritters spicy or sweet—or both!
Add a minced serrano or jalapeño pepper and a few tablespoons grated
cheese for spicy, or increase the sugar to ⅓ cup and serve with warm honey.

Ω

1 ear fresh corn
½ cup buttermilk
2 eggs, beaten
¼ cup sugar
3 tablespoons melted butter
1¼ cups flour
½ teaspoon baking soda
½ teaspoon salt
3 cups vegetable oil

1. Cut the kernels from the cob, then using the back of a knife scrape the cob to remove juices. Place corn and juices in medium bowl along with buttermilk, eggs, sugar, and butter; beat well.

2. Stir in flour, baking soda, and salt until a stiff batter forms. You may need to add more flour to reach desired consistency.

3. Place vegetable oil in a large heavy skillet leaving 1" of headspace, and heat to 375°F. Drop fritters by tablespoons into the hot oil, a few at a time, and fry until golden. Turn over and fry on second side until golden, then drain on paper towels. Serve hot.

Ingredient Substitutions

To substitute for 1 ear of fresh corn, use a 10-ounce can of corn kernels, well drained, or 1 cup frozen corn, thawed and drained. Don't cook the canned or frozen corn before using it in recipes or it will be too soft and add too much moisture to the recipe.

Corn Tortillas

You can make your own blue corn or red corn tortillas by using blue corn masa harina, or by adding about a tablespoon of chili powder to the dough for red.

∩

Yields 16 4" tortillas

2 cups masa harina
½ teaspoon salt
1 ⅓ cups warm water

1. In medium bowl, combine the masa harina and the salt and mix well. Add enough warm water to form a firm but moist dough. Run a kitchen towel under warm water and wring out; place over dough while you work with each tortilla.

2. Heat a griddle or comal over medium heat. Pinch off about 2 tablespoons of the dough and press in a tortilla press between 2 sheets of plastic wrap. If the dough sticks to the plastic wrap, it's too wet; stir in more masa harina. If the dough crumbles in the press, it's too dry; add some more water. Don't be afraid of overworking the dough; that's not possible.

3. Peel off 1 sheet of plastic wrap and transfer the tortilla to your hand. Peel off the second sheet and drop onto the heated griddle. Cook for about 1 minute on each side, turning tortilla only once, until small brown spots appear on the surface.

4. Serve immediately, or reheat by wrapping a stack of cooled tortillas in heavy-duty foil and baking at 350°F for 8–10 minutes until hot and tender.

Don't Handle with Care

Because there is no gluten (wheat protein) in corn flour, the corn tortilla dough can be manipulated a lot without fear of ending up with tough tortillas. Add flour or water as necessary to make a firm but moist dough.

Pumpkin Corn Bread

Serves 9

1 cup flour
1 cup cornmeal
½ cup brown sugar
2 teaspoons baking powder
1 teaspoon baking soda
½ teaspoon salt
½ teaspoon cinnamon
2 eggs, beaten
¼ cup vegetable oil
¾ cup solid-pack pumpkin
⅔ cup buttermilk

Pumpkin adds smoothness to this easy corn bread, along with a great color and some added vitamin A. Serve this bread hot with butter and honey.

1. Preheat oven to 350°F. Grease and flour a 9" x 9" square pan and set aside. In large bowl, combine flour, cornmeal, brown sugar, baking powder, baking soda, salt, and cinnamon and mix well with wire whisk to blend.

2. In medium bowl, combine eggs, oil, pumpkin, and buttermilk and beat well to combine. Add all at once to dry ingredients and stir just until dry ingredients are moistened. Pour into prepared pan and bake at 350°F for 20–30 minutes or until bread is golden brown and edges pull away from sides of pan. Serve hot.

Jalapeño Cheese Crackers

Yields 50 crackers

½ cup butter, softened
1½ cups shredded Cheddar
    cheese
½ cup grated cotija cheese
1 jalapeño pepper, minced
2 tablespoons cornmeal
½ teaspoon ground red chile
    powder
1¼ cups flour
½ cup finely chopped pecans

Store these crisp little crackers tightly covered in a cool dry place. You can reheat them before serving, if you'd like, in a toaster oven.

1. Preheat oven to 350°F. In large bowl, combine butter, Cheddar and cotija cheeses, and jalapeño pepper; mix together until blended. Add cornmeal, chile powder, and flour; mix until a dough forms; work pecans into the dough.

2. Form dough into 1" balls and place on cookie sheet. Flatten with 2 forks or the bottom of a glass to ¼" thickness. Bake at 350°F for 10–15 minutes until crackers are golden brown around the edges. Cool on wire rack.

Tex-Mex Spoon Bread

Spoon bread is a softer version of corn bread, more like a soufflé. Cooking the cornmeal before baking the bread ensures a smoother texture in this easy side-dish recipe.

∩

Serves 6–8

1 (16-ounce) can creamed corn
1½ cups milk
1 cup yellow or white cornmeal
1 tablespoon sugar
½ teaspoon salt
⅛ teaspoon cayenne pepper
⅓ cup butter
3 eggs, separated
1 cup grated Colby cheese

1. In heavy saucepan, combine creamed corn, milk, cornmeal, sugar, salt, and pepper. Bring to a boil, then reduce heat and simmer, stirring frequently, for 5 minutes or until thickened. Remove from heat and stir in butter until melted; cool completely.

2. Preheat oven to 400°F. Stir egg yolks into the cornmeal mixture. In medium bowl, beat egg whites until stiff peaks form. Place egg whites on top of cornmeal mixture and sprinkle with cheese. Gently fold into cornmeal mixture just until blended. Pour into a greased 9" square pan and bake at 400°F for 40–50 minutes or until golden brown and puffed. Serve immediately.

Fleeting Spoon Bread

Spoon bread, like a soufflé, will deflate as soon as it comes out of the oven because the dough doesn't have gluten (wheat protein) to strengthen the structure. Don't worry about it—the bread will still taste wonderful. Unfortunately, spoon bread doesn't store and reheat well, so eat it all when you make it.

Pumpkin Bread

½ cup butter, softened
½ cup sugar
⅓ cup brown sugar
1 egg, beaten
3 tablespoons buttermilk
1 cup solid-pack pumpkin
½ teaspoon cinnamon
¼ teaspoon allspice
½ teaspoon salt
2¼ cups flour
1½ teaspoons baking powder
1 teaspoon baking soda
3 tablespoons sugar
½ teaspoon cinnamon

This excellent quick bread has a wonderful silky texture. For a nice twist, substitute 1 cup of whole wheat flour for 1 cup of the all-purpose flour, and add a tiny pinch of cayenne pepper to bring out the spices.

∩

1. Preheat oven to 350°F. Spray a 9" x 5" loaf pan with nonstick baking spray and set aside. In large bowl, combine butter with sugars and beat until light and fluffy. Beat in egg, buttermilk, and pumpkin.

2. In medium bowl, combine cinnamon, allspice, salt, flour, baking powder, and baking soda, and stir with wire whisk to blend. Add to pumpkin mixture and mix just until combined.

3. Spoon batter into prepared pan. In small bowl, combine 3 tablespoons sugar and ½ teaspoon cinnamon, mix well, and sprinkle over batter. Bake at 350°F for 40–50 minutes until loaf is dark golden brown and toothpick inserted in center comes out clean. Remove from pan and cool on wire rack.

Self-Rising Flour

Self-rising flour is sold primarily in the Southern United States. It combines flour with salt and baking powder, in proportions of ½ teaspoon salt and 1½ teaspoons baking powder per cup of flour. If you want to substitute it in a recipe that calls for plain flour and baking powder, make sure the proportions of baking powder to flour in the recipe are approximately the same.

Plain Tamales

Plain tamales are a nice addition to any Tex-Mex feast. Serve them with Enchilada Sauce (page 94) or Pico de Gallo (page 91) for dipping.

∩

Yields 16

16 corn husks
½ cup lard
¼ cup sour cream
¼ cup water
2 cups masa harina
½ teaspoon salt
⅛ teaspoon cayenne pepper
1¼ cups chicken broth

1. Cover corn husks with hot water and set aside to let soak. In large bowl, combine lard, sour cream, and water and beat on medium speed until light and fluffy.

2. Add masa harina, salt, and cayenne pepper and beat well. Add chicken broth as necessary to make the mixture spongy and fluffy (dough dropped into cold water should float).

3. Drain husks and spread tamale dough on husks to within 1" of edges. Fold sides of husks to the middle so edges meet, then fold up bottom and fold down top to enclose filling. Tie with kitchen string. Place in single layer in steaming basket, and steam over simmering water for 1 hour.

Substitution for Corn Husks

You can substitute parchment paper for the corn husks when you're making tamales, especially these plain ones. Cut the paper to 4" x 8" rectangles and spread the dough to within 1" of the edges. Fold the sides in toward the middle so they touch, fold the top down and the bottom up, tie with string, and steam until the paper comes away from the dough.

Chorizo Pepper Bread

¼ pound chorizo sausage
½ cup chopped red bell
   pepper
3 green onions, chopped
1¾ cups flour
1 tablespoon sugar
2 teaspoons baking powder
½ teaspoon baking soda
½ teaspoon salt
⅛ teaspoon cayenne pepper
1 egg
¾ cup buttermilk
1 tablespoon honey
¼ cup vegetable oil
1 cup shredded Cheddar
   cheese

*Serve this rich and hearty bread with grilled steak and fruit salad for
a great entertaining menu. Leftover slices can be buttered
and toasted for a quick snack.*

1. Preheat oven to 400°F. Spray 9" x 5" loaf pan with nonstick baking spray and set aside. In heavy skillet, cook chorizo sausage with red bell pepper until sausage is thoroughly cooked, stirring to break up sausage. Drain well, remove from heat, stir in green onions, and cool.

2. In large bowl, combine flour, sugar, baking powder and soda, salt, and cayenne pepper and stir to combine. In small bowl, combine egg, buttermilk, honey, and vegetable oil and beat until combined. Add to dry ingredients and stir just until combined. Add cheese along with chorizo mixture and stir gently.

3. Pour batter into prepared pan and bake at 400°F for 30–40 minutes until bread is deep golden brown and bread pulls away from edges of pan. Remove from pan and cool slightly on wire rack. Cut into thick slices and serve warm.

How to Make Quick Bread

For the best quick breads, be sure to mix the dry and wet ingredients separately, and when you combine them, stir just until the dry ingredients disappear. Overmixing will result in a tough loaf. And don't worry about the crack that develops in the center – that's the way quick breads are supposed to look!

Tex-Mex Corn Muffins

These tender little muffins make a great quick breakfast on the run along with a juice box or two. You can omit the serrano chile and use Monterey jack cheese instead of pepper jack for a totally mild muffin.

Yields 12

⅓ cup butter, softened
⅓ cup sugar
3 eggs, beaten
⅔ cup buttermilk
1 serrano chile, minced
¾ cup yellow cornmeal
1 cup flour
1 teaspoon baking powder
½ teaspoon baking soda
½ teaspoon salt
1 cup frozen corn, thawed
1½ cups shredded pepper
   jack cheese

1. Preheat oven to 375°F. Line 12 muffin cups with paper liners and set aside. In large bowl, combine butter with sugar and beat until fluffy. Add eggs, buttermilk, and serrano chile and beat until combined.

2. In medium bowl, combine cornmeal, flour, baking powder, baking soda, and salt, and mix well. Add to butter mixture and stir just until combined. Fold in corn and pepper jack cheese.

3. Spoon batter into prepared muffin cups. Bake at 375°F for 20–30 minutes until golden brown. Remove from pans immediately; serve warm.

Gorditas

These little pockets are like Mexican pita breads. You can flavor them any way you'd like: add ground chile powder, fresh or dried herbs, or a bit of grated cheese.

Yields 8

1½ cups masa harina
½ cup flour
1 teaspoon salt
1 teaspoon baking powder
1 teaspoon chili powder
2 tablespoons lard
1 cup hot water
2 cups vegetable oil

1. In large bowl, combine masa harina, flour, salt, baking powder, and chili powder and mix well. Cut in lard with 2 knives until well blended. Stir in enough hot water to make a firm yet pliable dough.

2. Divide dough into 8 pieces. On floured surface, press or roll dough to make ovals ¼" thick. Heat vegetable oil in heavy skillet to 375°F. Fry each gordita until puffed and dotted with brown spots, carefully turning once during cooking. Remove to paper towels to drain.

3. When cool enough to handle, slit the tops and pull open to fill.

Bolillos

Yields 24

1 package active dry yeast
¼ cup warm water
1 teaspoon sugar
½ cup milk
1 tablespoon butter
1 cup water
2 tablespoons sugar
½ teaspoon salt
¼ teaspoon cinnamon
6 cups bread flour
1 egg white

Bolillos, or Mexican hard rolls, really take a back seat to tortillas in the Tex-Mex kitchen, but they are delicious. The touch of cinnamon gives them a wonderful fragrance. Serve them with a fruit salad for a wonderful lunch, or use for sandwiches.

∩

1. In small bowl, combine yeast, ¼ cup warm water, and 1 teaspoon sugar. Let stand until bubbly. Meanwhile, combine milk, butter, 1 cup water, sugar, and salt in heavy saucepan over medium heat until butter melts. Remove and let cool to lukewarm.

2. In large mixing bowl, combine cooled milk mixture, yeast mixture, cinnamon, and 2 cups flour; beat at medium speed for 1 minute. Gradually add remaining flour until dough is too stiff to beat. Remove to a flour-dusted work surface and knead in enough of the remaining flour to make smooth and elastic dough.

3. Place dough in a greased bowl, turning to grease top. Cover and let rise in warm place until doubled in size, about 1 hour. Punch down dough and turn onto floured work surface; cover with bowl and let sit for 10 minutes.

4. Divide dough into 24 pieces and form into football shapes. Place on greased baking sheets, cover, and let rise until doubled, 30–40 minutes. Preheat oven to 375°F. In small bowl, beat egg white until frothy; gently brush over rolls. Bake at 375°F for 20–30 minutes or until rolls are light golden brown and sound hollow when tapped on bottom. Cool completely on wire racks.

How to Freeze Rolls

These rolls—and all yeast breads—freeze very well. Make sure they are completely cooled, then package into freezer bags, label well, seal, and freeze up to 3 months. To thaw, let stand, uncovered, at room temperature for about 1½ hours. You can reheat the rolls in the microwave oven.

Tex-Mex Gougere

Gougere is a classic French quick bread made from pâte à choux pastry, also used to make cream puffs. Tex-Mex vegetables and seasonings add a nice twist to this cheesy, crisp, and tender bread that's a tribute to the French love of the cuisine.

∩

1. Preheat oven to 375°F. Melt butter in large saucepan over medium heat and cook onion and garlic until tender, 4–5 minutes. Add pimentos and chiles; cook and stir for 1–2 minutes.

2. Add milk, salt, and pepper and bring to a rolling boil. All at once, add the flour and chili powder and cook and stir over medium heat until the mixture forms a ball and cleans the sides of the pan.

3. Remove from heat and add eggs, one at a time, beating well after each addition. Fold in Muenster and Manchego cheeses. Line a cookie or baking sheet with Silpat or Exopat silicon liner. Scoop out dough in spoonfuls the size of an egg and arrange into an 8" ring on the liner, edges just touching, leaving the center open. Spoon a smaller ring of dough spoonfuls on top of the first. Brush bread with cream and sprinkle with cotija cheese.

4. Bake the bread at 375°F for about 35–45 minutes, or until the bread is puffy, deep golden brown, and firm. Serve immediately.

Making Choux Pastry

It's not difficult to make choux pastry; it just takes some time and a little bit of muscle. Make sure that the butter and milk mixture comes to a rolling boil; stir constantly while the flour is cooking, and be sure to beat in each egg one at a time. Baking these breads on a nonstick Silpat or Exopat liner is a must.

Yields 1 ring loaf

¼ cup butter
¼ cup minced onion
1 clove garlic, minced
2 tablespoons chopped drained pimentos
2 tablespoons diced green chiles, drained
1 cup milk
½ teaspoon salt
⅛ teaspoon white pepper
1¼ cups flour
2 teaspoons chili powder
4 eggs
½ cup diced Muenster cheese
⅓ cup crumbled Manchego cheese
1 tablespoon heavy cream
2 tablespoons finely grated cotija cheese

Puffy Tacos

2 cups masa harina
½ teaspoon salt
1 ⅓ cups warm water
2 cups vegetable oil

Puffy tacos are basically corn tortillas that are briefly cooked on a dry griddle, then deep-fried so they become puffy and crisp. Once you've tried these, it's hard to go back to commercial crisp taco shells.

∩

1. In medium bowl, combine masa harina and salt and mix well. Add enough water to make a firm but moist dough. Divide dough into 12 pieces; cover remaining dough with damp cloth while working with each piece.

2. Using plastic wrap and a tortilla press, press out each ball of dough. Now start an assembly line: heat a comal or griddle over medium heat and heat vegetable oil in a heavy skillet over medium heat to 350°F. Cook the dough on the griddle for 30 seconds on each side. Remove and immediately slip into the hot oil. Fry the tortilla until it puffs, carefully spooning hot oil over the top. When it puffs, gently press down on the center of the tortilla to form an indentation.

3. Remove from hot oil when crisp and drain on paper towels. Repeat until all the dough is used.

Tortilla Choices

If you use corn tortillas for quesadillas, you'll need to use less cheese and other fillings because corn tortillas are smaller than the flour variety. Or use flavored flour tortillas: green are made with spinach leaves, while red are made with a special variety of corn or with added chile powder.

Flour Tortillas

Homemade flour tortillas, served warm from the griddle, are a wonderful treat. You can also roll the dough out between 2 sheets of plastic wrap instead of using a tortilla press. Make them as thick or thin as you like.

∩

Yields 9

3 cups flour
½ teaspoon salt
⅓ cup lard or vegetable shortening
1 cup warm water

1. Combine flour and salt in large bowl. Cut in lard or vegetable shortening using 2 knives until mixture is crumbly. Add enough warm water to make a firm but moist dough. Cover and let stand for 10 minutes.

2. Divide dough into 9 balls and press on tortilla press or between sheets of plastic wrap. Heat a griddle or comal over medium heat, peel off plastic wrap, and cook tortillas, 1–2 minutes per side, until speckled with gold and light brown spots. Serve warm.

Color Your World

What about colored tortillas? To make green tortillas, drain liquid from frozen spinach and use instead of the water in the recipe. For red tortillas, add 1 tablespoon of red chile powder. And for yellow tortillas, dissolve 1 teaspoon turmeric in the water.

Churros

Yields 24

¾ cup water
¼ cup milk
½ cup butter
¼ teaspoon salt
¼ teaspoon cinnamon
¾ cup flour
¼ cup masa harina
2 eggs
2 cups vegetable oil
½ cup sugar
1 teaspoon cinnamon

This dough is also known as choux pastry, a French recipe used to make cream puffs. (See sidebar "Making Choux Pastry" (page 123).) For churros, the dough is squeezed through a pastry bag into hot oil and fried until crisp and golden, then rolled in cinnamon sugar.

1. In heavy saucepan, combine water, milk, and butter; bring to a boil over medium heat. In small bowl, combine salt, cinnamon, flour, and masa harina and mix well. Add all at once to butter mixture, beating with a wooden spoon. Cook mixture over medium heat until dough leaves the sides of the pan.

2. Remove from heat and, one at a time, stir in eggs, beating until dough is smooth and shiny. Set aside to let cool for a few minutes. Meanwhile, heat vegetable oil in a heavy skillet until it reaches 350°F.

3. Using a pastry bag or a churros maker, attach the star tip and spoon one-fourth of the dough into the bag. Press the dough into 4" strips directly into the oil, using a knife to cut off the dough and release it. Fry three or four churros at a time in the hot oil, turning once, until golden brown, about 1–2 minutes on each side. Remove to paper towels to drain.

4. While still warm, sprinkle with mixture of ½ cup sugar and 1 teaspoon cinnamon. Serve warm.

Pan Dulce Loaves

*These beautiful loaves of bread are marvelous lightly toasted for breakfast.
Or use them to make Caramel Bread Pudding (page 250).*

∩

1. In small bowl, dissolve yeast in warm water with 1 teaspoon sugar; let stand for 10 minutes. Meanwhile, combine half-and-half, butter, ¾ cup sugar, salt, and orange peel in heavy saucepan; cook and stir over medium heat until butter melts. Let stand until lukewarm.

2. Stir vanilla and eggs into lukewarm butter mixture along with the dissolved yeast mixture. Gradually add flour, mixing until a soft dough forms.

3. On floured surface, knead dough until smooth and elastic (about 8 minutes), then mix in raisins and almonds. Put dough in greased bowl, turning to grease top. Cover and let rise until double, about 1 hour.

4. Punch down dough and shape into 2 rounds. Place into 2 greased 9" round pans and set on baking sheet. Cover with towel and let rise until double, about 45 minutes. Preheat oven to 325°F. Bake loaves for 35–45 minutes or until golden brown and cooked through. Remove to wire rack. In small bowl, combine orange juice and powdered sugar and brush over loaves. Let stand until cool.

Cinnamon Honey Butter

Make Cinnamon Honey Butter to serve with this bread or any toasted bread. In small bowl, combine ¼ cup softened butter with ⅓ cup honey and ½ teaspoon cinnamon; mix well. Store butter, covered, for up to 1 week (if there's any left!).

Yields 2 round loaves

2 packages active dry yeast
½ cup warm water
1 teaspoon sugar
1 cup half-and-half
½ cup butter
¾ cup sugar
1 teaspoon salt
1 teaspoon grated orange peel
1 teaspoon vanilla
4 eggs, beaten
6½ to 7½ cups flour
2 cups raisins
1 cup chopped slivered almonds
2 tablespoons orange juice
¼ cup powdered sugar

Chapter Eight

Seafood

Fish Tacos

Serves 4–6

1 pound red snapper fillets
3 tablespoons cornmeal
1 tablespoon flour
½ teaspoon salt
2 teaspoons chili powder
¼ teaspoon cumin
¼ teaspoon pepper
1 egg, beaten
3 tablespoons heavy cream
1 cup Cilantro Pesto (page 90)
⅓ cup sour cream
¼ cup olive oil
1 avocado
1 tablespoon lime juice
1 (15-ounce) can cannelloni
   beans, rinsed
2 cups shredded lettuce
1 cup shredded Monterey jack
   cheese
8 crisp taco shells, heated

This is a more upscale recipe, typically served near Texas's Gulf Coast. You can certainly substitute breaded fish sticks for the fresh fish, but try it this way once. The combination of textures and flavors is really wonderful.

1. Cut fish fillets into 1" pieces and set aside. In shallow bowl, combine cornmeal, flour, salt, chili powder, cumin, and pepper and mix well. In another shallow bowl, combine egg and cream and beat until combined. Dip fish pieces into egg mixture, then roll in cornmeal mixture to coat; set on wire rack.

2. In small bowl, combine pesto and sour cream; blend well, cover, and place in refrigerator. Heat olive oil in heavy skillet over medium heat. Cook coated fish pieces in oil for 3–4 minutes, turning once, until golden brown. Peel and dice avocado and sprinkle with lime juice.

3. Make tacos by filling heated taco shells with fish, beans, avocado, cilantro sauce, lettuce, and cheese.

For a Special Feast

If you're entertaining some very special people, make Puffy Tacos (page 124) and use them in the recipe for Fish Tacos instead of purchased taco shells. The Puffy Tacos are a bit more work, but their ultra crispiness elevates any taco to a feast.

Tex-Mex Shrimp Tart

There's some French influence in this elegant recipe; tarts are traditionally made in a pan with a removable bottom to make them easier to serve.

Ω

1. In large skillet, heat oil over medium heat. Add onion and garlic; cook and stir for 1 minute. Add red bell pepper and serrano chile and cook 1 minute more. Stir in chile powder, cumin, shrimp, sour cream, cream, flour, and salt and mix well. Remove from heat and let cool for 10 minutes.

2. Preheat oven to 400°F. Beat eggs in small bowl and add to shrimp mixture in skillet; stir until combined.

3. Sprinkle almonds over bottom of tart shell and top with shrimp filling. Bake at 400°F for 20–35 minutes until filling is puffed and golden brown. Serve immediately.

Menu Ideas

Garnish this beautiful tart with some fresh chopped cilantro and pass bowls of sour cream and Pico de Gallo (page 91). It's perfect for a summer lunch served with some wedges of honeydew melon and cantaloupe; for dessert, serve Pineapple Cake (page 269).

Serves 6

2 tablespoons vegetable oil
½ cup chopped onion
2 cloves garlic, minced
1 chopped red bell pepper
1 serrano chile, minced
½ teaspoon ground red chile powder
½ teaspoon cumin
2½ cups small cooked shrimp
½ cup sour cream
½ cup light cream
2 tablespoons flour
½ teaspoon salt
2 eggs
3 tablespoons chopped almonds
1 (10") tart shell

Grilled Ranchero Swordfish

Serves 4

1½ cups Ranchero Sauce
    (page 97)
4 swordfish steaks
1 tablespoon vegetable oil
1 tablespoon chili powder
½ teaspoon dried oregano
1 teaspoon salt
¼ teaspoon pepper

Make this delicious recipe with salmon steaks or tuna steaks if you'd like. Serve it with some warmed flour tortillas and Corn and Rice Salad (page 54).

1. Place Ranchero Sauce in a saucepan and bring to a simmer over medium heat while preparing fish. Brush steaks with oil and sprinkle with seasonings. Prepare and preheat grill.

2. Cook fish on the grill, covered, for about 5 minutes. Turn and brush with Ranchero Sauce. Cook, covered, until fish flakes when tested with fork, 5–6 minutes longer; keep sauce simmering.

3. Place on serving platter, dollop each steak with more sauce, and serve remaining sauce on the side.

Grilled Prawns with Fruit Salsa

Serves 4

2 pounds cleaned prawns
1 teaspoon salt
⅛ teaspoon cayenne pepper
1 teaspoon red chile powder
2 tablespoons lemon juice
1 cup Fruit Salsa (page 28)

Prawns and shrimp are actually two different but closely related species of shellfish, though many people use the terms interchangeably. For this recipe, prawns are simply large shrimp.

1. Prepare and heat grill. Shell and devein prawns but do not remove tail. Place in large bowl. In small bowl, combine salt, pepper, and chile powder. Sprinkle lemon juice over prawns and sprinkle with salt mixture; toss gently.

2. Grill prawns over medium coals for 4–5 minutes or until they curl and turn pink. Serve with Fruit Salsa.

Tex-Mex Salmon Quiche

You can substitute canned chicken or canned deviled ham for the salmon in this beautiful and easy quiche recipe.
Serve it with a fruit salad for a heavenly brunch.

∩

1. Preheat oven to 400°F. In heavy skillet over medium heat, cook onion and garlic in butter until crisp-tender. Add chipotle chile and stir. Sprinkle flour, chili powder, salt, and pepper over onion mixture; cook and stir for 3–4 minutes. Stir in evaporated milk and sour cream; cook and stir for 2–3 minutes until thick. Remove from heat and cool for 10 minutes.

2. Meanwhile, drain salmon and remove and discard skin and bones. Drain beans, rinse, and drain again.

3. In medium bowl, beat eggs until foamy; add oregano. Stir egg mixture into onion mixture and blend well.

4. Sprinkle half of the pepper jack cheese into bottom of pie crust. Break salmon into chunks and scatter over cheese; sprinkle with black beans. Pour onion/egg mixture over salmon and top with remaining pepper jack cheese. Sprinkle with cotija or Parmesan cheese. Bake at 400°F for 30–35 minutes until golden brown and set.

Read Labels for Health

You can find low-fat or even fat-free versions of sweetened condensed milk, evaporated milk, and half-and-half to add to your coffee and use in your recipes. These healthier ingredients can be used in place of full-fat versions in most cooking and baking recipes.

Serves 6

1 (9") unbaked pie crust
1 onion, chopped
3 cloves garlic, minced
¼ cup butter
1 chipotle chile in adobo sauce, minced
¼ cup flour
1 tablespoon chili powder
½ teaspoon salt
⅛ teaspoon cayenne pepper
1 (12-ounce) can evaporated milk
¼ cup sour cream
1 (14-ounce) can red salmon
1 (15-ounce) can black beans, rinsed
3 eggs, beaten
½ teaspoon dried oregano
1½ cups shredded pepper jack cheese
¼ cup grated cotija or Parmesan cheese

Shrimp and Corn Pot Pie

Serves 8–10

1 sheet puff pastry, thawed
1 tablespoon cornmeal
½ teaspoon chili powder
¼ cup butter
1 onion, chopped
3 cloves garlic, minced
1 serrano pepper, minced
¼ cup flour
½ teaspoon salt
⅛ teaspoon pepper
2 cups half-and-half
1 egg, beaten
1½ cups shredded pepper
    jack cheese
2 cups frozen corn, thawed
1 cup refrigerated hash
    brown potatoes
1 (10-ounce) package frozen
    cooked shrimp, thawed
1 egg, beaten

Puff pastry is the French accent in this delicious pie. You can substitute canned crabmeat or frozen surimi for the shrimp if you'd like.

1. Place thawed puff pastry on surface dusted with cornmeal and cut out a 10" round. Cut out small decorative shapes from center of pastry (for venting) and from scraps (for decorating) and dust with chili powder. Cover and refrigerate while preparing filling.

2. In heavy saucepan, sauté onion and garlic in butter until crisp-tender; stir in serrano pepper. Sprinkle flour, salt, and pepper over onions; cook and stir until bubbly. Stir in half-and-half; cook and stir until slightly thickened. Remove from heat and stir in 1 egg and cheese until blended. Drain corn, potatoes, and shrimp very well and stir into pan.

3. Preheat oven to 375°F. Pour mixture into a 2-quart baking dish and top with puff pastry round; flute edges. Beat 1 egg in small bowl and brush over pastry. Use a bit of egg to attach cutouts to decorate pie.

4. Bake pie at 375°F for 20–30 minutes or until pastry is puffed and golden brown and the filling bubbles. Let stand for 10 minutes before serving.

About Puff Pastry

You can find puff pastry in the frozen foods aisle of your local supermarket. Follow the directions for thawing carefully for best results. The pastry has dozens of layers of dough and butter so it puffs up and becomes very crisp and flaky when baked.

Tex-Mex Shrimp

Serve this great stir-fry over some cooked Green Rice (page 78),
with Grapefruit Salad (page 43) on the side for a cooling contrast.

∩

1. Thaw shrimp as directed on package. In heavy skillet, heat butter over medium heat and sauté onion and garlic until almost crisp-tender. Add bell peppers and chipotle peppers; cook and stir 2 minutes longer. Add undrained tomatoes, tomato paste, adobo sauce, water, cayenne pepper, and Tabasco sauce; simmer 10 minutes, stirring frequently.

2. Stir in thawed and drained shrimp; bring to a simmer and cook for 4–8 minutes until shrimp is curled, pink, and cooked through. Serve over rice.

Thawing Frozen Shrimp

Most frozen shrimp, whether raw or cooked, is thawed by placing it in a colander and running cold water over it for a few minutes, tossing and turning shrimp a few times. Do not thaw shrimp by letting it stand at room temperature, for food safety reasons.

Serves 6–8

2 pounds frozen raw medium shrimp
2 tablespoons butter
1 onion, chopped
5 cloves garlic, minced
2 red bell peppers, chopped
2 chipotle peppers in adobo sauce, minced
2 (14-ounce) cans diced tomatoes with green chiles
1 (6-ounce) can tomato paste
3 tablespoons adobo sauce
¼ cup water
⅛ teaspoon cayenne pepper
¼ teaspoon Tabasco sauce

Red Snapper Veracruz

6 (6-ounce) red snapper fillets
2 tablespoons lime juice
1 tablespoon chili powder
1 teaspoon salt
2 tablespoons butter
1 tablespoon oil
1 onion, sliced
4 cloves garlic, minced
1 serrano chile, minced
4 tomatoes, seeded and diced
2 tablespoons tomato paste
½ teaspoon dried oregano
2 tablespoons tequila
⅓ cup sliced green olives
1 tablespoon capers
Salt and pepper to taste
¼ cup chopped cilantro
1 avocado, sliced

This very classic dish is delicious served over Spanish Rice (page 79) or over plain long-grain rice, along with a fruit salad and a spinach salad.

1. Preheat oven to 350°F. Place red snapper in glass baking dish in single layer; sprinkle with lime juice, chili powder, and salt; set aside.

2. In heavy skillet, melt butter and oil over medium heat and cook onion, garlic, and serrano chile until crisp-tender, about 4–5 minutes. Add tomatoes, tomato paste, oregano, and tequila; simmer for 5–10 minutes over medium heat. Stir in olives, capers, and salt and pepper to taste; pour over red snapper in baking dish.

3. Bake at 350°F for 12–18 minutes or until fish flakes when tested with fork. Sprinkle fish with cilantro and garnish with avocado; serve immediately.

Shrimp Quesadillas

1 pound raw medium shrimp
1 tablespoon chili powder
½ teaspoon salt
⅛ teaspoon cayenne pepper
2 tablespoons butter
1 red bell pepper, cut into strips
2 cloves garlic, minced
2 tablespoons lemon juice
1 cup crumbled queso fresco
10 (10″) flour tortillas

Serve these fresh-tasting quesadillas with sour cream, your favorite guacamole recipe, or Tomatillo Salsa (page 104).

1. Preheat oven to 350°F. In medium bowl, toss shrimp with chili powder, salt, and cayenne pepper. In heavy skillet over medium heat, melt butter and cook shrimp until they curl and just turn pink; remove from skillet. Add bell pepper and garlic; cook and stir for 2–3 minutes until crisp-tender.

2. Return shrimp to pan along with lemon juice. Warm tortillas, then place on work surface and, using a slotted spoon, divide shrimp mixture among them. Top with queso fresco, fold over, and press gently; place on baking sheet. Bake quesadillas at 350°F for 10–15 minutes until cheese is melted and tortillas are light golden brown. Serve immediately.

Spicy Crabmeat Spread

You could substitute cooked chopped shrimp or surimi for the fresh crabmeat in this delicious recipe. And as always, make it as spicy or mild as you like with your choice of peppers.

∩

1. Pick over crabmeat, removing any pieces of shell or cartilage; set aside. In large bowl, beat cream cheese until soft and fluffy; stir in sour cream, cocktail sauce, salt, and pepper. Add green onions, lime juice, and jalapeño peppers and mix well. Stir in crabmeat and the two cheeses; mix gently.

2. Cover and refrigerate for 2–4 hours to blend flavors. Use within 3 days.

Serves 8

1 pound lump crabmeat
1 (3-ounce) package cream cheese, softened
1 cup sour cream
½ cup cocktail sauce
½ teaspoon salt
⅛ teaspoon cayenne pepper
4 green onions, chopped
2 tablespoons lime juice
1–2 jalapeño peppers, minced
1 cup shredded Muenster cheese
1 cup crumbled queso fresco

Shrimp Tamales

It's best to keep the filling for tamales simple yet very flavorful, since you don't use a lot of it. And always serve something to dip the tamales in; Tamale Sauce (page 99) or Taco Sauce (page 101) are good choices.

∩

1. Soak corn husks in hot water for 1 hour. Prepare Plain Tamale dough. In small bowl, combine remaining ingredients and mix well.

2. Drain husks and spread tamale dough on husks to within 1" of edges. Place 1 tablespoon shrimp filling in center of dough. Fold sides of husks to the middle so edges meet, then fold up bottom and fold down top to enclose filling; tie with kitchen string. Place in colander and steam for about 1 hour until corn husks peel away from tamales.

Yields 16

16 corn husks
1 batch dough from Plain Tamales (page 119)
⅔ cup chopped cooked shrimp
3 tablespoons sour cream
2 tablespoons adobo sauce
2 green onions, chopped
1 tablespoon chili powder

Red Snapper Flautas

Serves 4–6

1 (6-ounce) red snapper fillet
1 tablespoon chili powder
1 tablespoon vegetable oil
½ cup minced onion
4 tomatillos, chopped
¼ cup Salsa Verde (page 92)
2 cups vegetable oil
12 (10") flour tortillas
1 cup shredded pepper jack
   cheese

This versatile recipe can be made with canned tuna, chopped shrimp,
or even canned chicken if you'd like. Or substitute 1 tomato for the tomatillos
and use red salsa instead of the Salsa Verde.

1. Sprinkle red snapper with chili powder and let stand for 15 minutes. Heat 1 tablespoon oil in heavy skillet over medium heat and cook snapper for 4–5 minutes, turning once, until fish flakes easily. Remove from skillet.

2. Sauté onion and tomatillos in same skillet until crisp-tender; transfer to medium bowl. Flake fish and add to onion mixture along with Salsa Verde; mix gently. Rinse out skillet and dry; add 2 cups vegetable oil and heat to 375°F.

3. Warm flour tortillas and place on work surface. Top with a spoonful of fish mixture, then a bit of cheese; roll up tightly. Fry in oil for 2–3 minutes until crisp and golden brown. Remove from oil and tip from side to side to drain; let rest for a few minutes on paper or kitchen towels. Serve with salsa and guacamole.

Cooking Shrimp

It's very easy to overcook shrimp, so whether you're cooking them in a saucepan or on the grill, watch them carefully. Fresh shrimp is gray in color and only slightly curled. When properly cooked, shrimp will turn pink and curl up tightly: it just takes a few minutes.

Grilled Tilapia with Avocado Pesto

Use this pesto and glaze for just about any fillet of white fish; red snapper, grouper, cod, or orange roughy would all work well.

∩

1. Peel avocado and cut into chunks. Place in blender or food processor with lemon juice, cilantro, queso fresco, and pine nuts. Blend or process until mixture is smooth. Meanwhile, prepare and preheat grill.

2. Combine mayonnaise and adobo sauce in small bowl. Place fish fillets on grill and brush with mayonnaise mixture. Cover and cook for 2–3 minutes, then turn fish, brush with remaining mayonnaise mixture, cover grill, and cook for about 3 minutes until fish flakes easily. Serve with avocado pesto.

Serves 4

1 avocado
2 tablespoons lemon juice
¼ cup chopped cilantro
¼ cup crumbled queso fresco
2 tablespoons pine nuts
2 tablespoons mayonnaise
2 tablespoons adobo sauce
4 tilapia fillets

Grill Baskets

There are many accessories for your gas or charcoal grill. Grill baskets are a great way to cook smaller pieces of vegetables or meat, and to cook fragile foods such as fish fillets and shrimp. Brush the basket lightly with oil and add the food, then cook on the grill, using an oven mitt to handle the basket.

Fish Stick Fajitas

Serves 4

8 breaded fish sticks
1 tablespoon chili powder
½ teaspoon cumin
1 tablespoon vegetable oil
1 onion, sliced
1 yellow squash, sliced
1 serrano chile, minced
2 tomatoes, seeded and
　　chopped
½ cup sour cream
1 tablespoon lime juice
1 avocado
1 cup shredded Monterey jack
　　cheese
4 (10″) flour tortillas

Breaded fish sticks are a great convenience food that adds an American twist to fajitas. Serve these with lots of cold beer, guacamole, and tortilla chips.

1. Place fish sticks on baking sheet and sprinkle with chili powder and cumin. Bake according to package directions. Meanwhile, heat oil in heavy skillet and add onion, yellow squash, and serrano chile. Cook and stir over medium heat for 3–4 minutes until crisp-tender.

2. In small bowl, combine tomatoes, sour cream, and lime juice. Peel and dice avocado and add to sour cream mixture along with cheese. Wrap tortillas in foil and warm in oven for 5 minutes.

3. Make each fajita using 2 hot fish sticks, a spoonful of the onion mixture, and a dollop of sour cream mixture.

For Kids

To make this recipe more kid-friendly, leave out the yellow squash and serrano chile and think about omitting the spice coating on the fish sticks. Put a mild salsa on the table along with the onion mixture and avocado mixture and let the kids fix their own fajitas.

Crab Chile Rellenos

This delicate filling can be made with any cooked and flaked fish; try using salmon or swordfish. Serve with white wine, a mild salsa, and a fruit salad.

Serves 6

6 poblano chiles
1½ cups lump crabmeat
2 tablespoons butter
½ cup chopped onion
½ cup chopped yellow squash
1 clove garlic, minced
1 tomato, seeded and
    chopped
2 tablespoons lemon juice
1½ cups shredded pepper
    jack cheese
2 tablespoons flour
4 eggs, separated
¼ cup flour
1 teaspoon salt
2 cups vegetable oil

1. Roast poblano chiles under a broiler or over a gas flame until skin is charred. Place in paper bag and let steam for 10 minutes. Peel peppers, cut a slit in the side, and remove membranes and seeds.

2. Pick over crabmeat, getting rid of cartilage and shell. In heavy skillet, melt butter over medium heat and cook onion until crisp-tender. Add squash, garlic, tomato, and lemon juice; cook and stir for 3–4 minutes. Stir in crabmeat, then remove pan from heat and let it cool for 30 minutes.

3. Stuff peppers with crab mixture and 2 tablespoons pepper jack cheese. Sprinkle with 2 tablespoons flour and shake off excess. In medium bowl, beat egg whites until stiff. In another medium bowl, beat egg yolks with ¼ cup flour, and salt; fold into egg whites.

4. Heat vegetable oil to 350°F in deep heavy skillet. Dip stuffed chiles, one at a time, into egg batter and gently lower into oil. Fry for 2–4 minutes on each side until golden brown. Drain on kitchen or paper towels and serve with salsa.

About Crabmeat

Bulk crabmeat purchased frozen has been processed and frozen within hours of the catch. Lump crabmeat is the most expensive, since it comes from the body of the crab. Backfin and flake consist of smaller pieces that come from the leg and other body parts. Crab should smell fresh and be white, colored with a bit of brown or red.

Crab Cakes with Tomatillo Salsa

Serves 6

1 pound lump crabmeat
2 tablespoons oil
½ cup minced onion
3 cloves garlic, minced
1 jalapeño pepper, minced
3 green onions, minced
1½ cups corn bread crumbs
2 eggs
⅓ cup mayonnaise
1 tablespoon lime juice
3 tablespoons chopped
   cilantro
1 teaspoon salt
¼ teaspoon white pepper
2 tablespoons flour
½ cup vegetable oil
⅓ cup mayonnaise
½ cup Tomatillo Salsa
   (page 104)

*You can substitute three 6-ounce cans of crabmeat
for the lump crabmeat if you like; be sure to drain it well.*

1. Pick over crabmeat, removing any cartilage or shells; set aside. In heavy skillet, heat 1 tablespoon oil over medium heat. Add onion, garlic, and jalapeño pepper; cook and stir for 4–5 minutes until crisp-tender. Remove from heat and stir in green onions and corn bread crumbs; mix gently.

2. In large bowl, combine eggs with ⅓ cup mayonnaise, lime juice, cilantro, salt, and pepper. Add onion mixture and stir well. Add crabmeat and fold together gently. Cover and chill mixture for 1–2 hours until firm.

3. When ready to cook, form crab mixture into 6 patties. Sprinkle with flour and place on waxed paper. Heat ½ cup oil in heavy skillet over medium heat. Cook patties for 3–5 minutes on each side, turning once, or until golden brown. Drain on paper or kitchen towels. Combine ⅓ cup mayonnaise and Tomatillo Salsa in small bowl; serve with hot crab cakes.

Serving Suggestion

Since these crab cakes are such a wonderful, decadent treat, serve them as a first course rather than an appetizer. Cook the crab cakes and serve them at the table on a bed of spinach or arugula for color contrast. Place the tomatillo mixture in a small cut-glass bowl and enjoy the cakes with a knife and fork.

Grilled Snapper with Cilantro Pesto

*Cooking these well-seasoned fish fillets in foil packets means
you won't have any problem with them sticking to the grill,
and all of the flavors infuse the flesh as it cooks.*

∩

1. Place fillets in a glass baking dish; sprinkle with Taco Seasoning Mix and lime juice. Cover and place in refrigerator for 30 minutes. Meanwhile, prepare grill for indirect grilling.

2. In heavy skillet, heat butter over medium heat and sauté onion, garlic, and bell pepper until crisp-tender, about 4–5 minutes. Tear off 6
18" x 12" pieces of heavy-duty aluminum foil and place on work surface. Place 1 fish fillet in the center of each piece of foil; top with onion mixture. Place 1 lemon slice on top of each fillet and fold together edges of foil, sealing with double folds, leaving some room for expansion.

3. Place foil packets on grill; cover grill, and cook for 15–25 minutes or until fish flakes easily when tested with fork. Let your guests open the packets, warning them to be careful of the hot steam. Serve with Cilantro Pesto.

Marinating Fish

Fish fillets should only be marinated for a short time because they are so delicate. If you marinate them longer than an hour, the flesh will be mushy because the acid in the marinade will break the protein bonds in the fish. Marinate fish in the refrigerator for about 30 minutes while you prepare the coals, then grill immediately.

6 (6-ounce) red snapper fillets
1 tablespoon Taco Seasoning
    Mix (page 93)
2 tablespoons lime juice
1 tablespoon butter
½ cup chopped sweet onion
3 cloves garlic, minced
1 red bell pepper, chopped
6 lemon slices
1 cup Cilantro Pesto (page 90)

Tex-Mex Shrimp Tacos

You can certainly use frozen guacamole and jarred salsa verde in these easy tacos if you'd like. But be sure the shrimp are fresh!

Serves 6

2 cups Tex-Mex Shrimp (page 135)
2 tomatoes, seeded and chopped
1 jalapeño chile, minced
1 cup frozen corn, thawed
6 (10") flour tortillas
1 cup shredded Muenster cheese
2 cups shredded lettuce
1 cup Guacamole (page 20)
1 cup Salsa Verde (page 92)

1. Prepare all ingredients. Combine tomatoes with chile and corn in small bowl. Warm tortillas by wrapping in microwave-safe paper towels and heating at 50% power for 2–3 minutes.

2. Make tacos with shrimp, lettuce, tomato mixture, cheese, Guacamole, and Salsa Verde.

Baja Shrimp and Scallop Skewers

Serve these colorful kabobs with Green Rice (page 78) and a variety of fresh salsas, along with Margarita Fruit Salad (page 49).

Serves 6

2 garlic cloves, crushed
¼ cup Taco Sauce (page 101)
1 tablespoon lime juice
1 pound large shrimp
1 pound sea scallops
12 small plum tomatoes
12 large button mushrooms
12 (1") pieces yellow squash

1. In small bowl, combine garlic, Taco Sauce, and lime juice; mix well. Shell and devein shrimp, leaving tail section on. Thread shrimp, scallops, tomatoes, mushrooms, and squash onto metal skewers.

2. Prepare and preheat grill. Cook kabobs over medium coals for 6–8 minutes, turning twice during cooking and brushing with garlic mixture. Kabobs are done when shrimp curl and turn pink and scallops are opaque.

Spicy Salmon Steaks

Serve these wonderful spicy steaks with Asparagus with Avocado (page 76) and Grilled Corn on the Cob (page 76).

∩

1. Place salmon steaks in a glass baking dish. In small bowl, combine Three-Chile Rub, mayonnaise, and lime juice and mix well. Spread over salmon, turn steaks to coat both sides, cover, and refrigerate for 1–2 hours.

2. Place steaks on a broiler pan 4–6" from heat source. Cook for 5 minutes, then turn fish and cook for 5–7 minutes longer until desired doneness. Meanwhile, combine tomatoes, sour cream, salt, and pepper in small bowl. Serve with steaks along with Guacamole.

Salmon Steaks

Salmon steaks are cut from the center part of the fish; they are shaped like a thick horseshoe. They have a wonderful meaty texture and rich flavor; don't overcook them. When serving, tell your guests to remove the skin and to avoid the bones around the center of the steak.

Serves 6

6 (8-ounce) salmon steaks
2 tablespoons Three-Chile Rub (page 93)
¼ cup mayonnaise
1 tablespoon lime juice
2 tomatoes, seeded and chopped
½ cup sour cream
½ teaspoon salt
⅛ teaspoon pepper
1 cup Guacamole (page 20)

Seafood Enchiladas

Serves 6

2 tablespoons butter

½ cup chopped onion

2 cloves garlic, minced

1 red snapper fillet

½ pound cleaned raw shrimp

½ pound lump crabmeat

1 cup frozen baby peas

1 cup sour cream

¼ cup Enchilada Sauce
(page 94)

12 (6") corn tortillas

1½ cups shredded Muenster
cheese

1 cup Enchilada Sauce
(page 94)

⅔ cup heavy cream

½ cup crumbled queso
blanco

Enchilada sauce is combined with some cream to lighten it so it doesn't overwhelm the flavors in these mild enchiladas. Serve them for a special occasion.

1. Preheat oven to 350°F. In heavy skillet, melt butter over medium heat and cook onion and garlic until crisp-tender, about 4–5 minutes. Add snapper fillet; cover skillet, and cook for 7–9 minutes until fish flakes when tested with fork. Remove fillet from pan and set aside.

2. Add shrimp to skillet; cook and stir until shrimp turn pink. Place contents of skillet in a large bowl. Flake snapper fillet and add to bowl along with crabmeat and baby peas. Stir in sour cream and ¼ cup Enchilada Sauce; mix gently.

3. Heat corn tortillas in microwave or oven. Spread each tortilla with a small amount of Enchilada Sauce. Divide filling among tortillas and top with Muenster cheese; roll up and place in 9" x 13" glass baking dish. In medium bowl, combine remaining Enchilada Sauce and heavy cream; mix well and pour over filled tortillas. Top with queso blanco and bake at 350°F for 25–35 minutes or until hot and bubbly.

Seafood Grilling Times

Shrimp and seafood take only a few minutes to cook on the grill, so watch them carefully. Seafood fillets and steaks cook for about 10 minutes per inch of thickness, while small and medium shrimp and scallops can cook in 1–2 minutes. Large shrimp and sea scallops cook in about 4 minutes.

Chapter Nine

Poultry

Chicken Enchiladas Verdes

Serves 8

3 whole chicken breasts
2 tablespoons vegetable oil
1 teaspoon salt
⅛ teaspoon white pepper
2 poblano chiles
2 green bell peppers
1 cup tomatillos, husks
    removed
½ cup heavy cream
2 jalapeño peppers, diced
1 onion, chopped
3 cloves garlic, minced
1 (8-ounce) package cream
    cheese, softened
2 green onions, chopped
2 cups shredded Monterey
    jack cheese
12 (6") corn tortillas
¼ cup chopped cilantro

*Enchiladas verdes are green enchiladas, made with
roasted poblano chiles, green bell peppers, and tomatillos.
Chicken adds a delicious rich flavor and mellow texture to this dish.*

1. Preheat oven to 375°F. Place chicken breasts on cookie sheet and drizzle with olive oil; sprinkle with salt and pepper. Bake at 375°F for 25–30 minutes or until chicken is thoroughly cooked. Remove from oven and set aside until cool enough to handle. Shred chicken, discarding skin and bones.

2. Set oven to broil. Place poblano chiles and green bell peppers on baking sheet and broil 4" from heat source until blackened, turning frequently. Remove from oven and place in a paper bag; seal bag and let stand for 10 minutes. Remove skin from peppers by gently rubbing with paper towel; cut open and remove membranes and seeds.

3. Place roasted chiles and peppers in blender or food processor along with tomatillos, cream, jalapeño pepper, onion, and garlic. Blend or process until smooth.

4. In medium bowl, combine shredded chicken with cream cheese, green onion, 1 cup Monterey jack cheese, the cilantro, and 1 cup of the blended pepper sauce. Fill corn tortillas with this mixture and place in 13" x 9" baking dish. Pour remaining green sauce over all and sprinkle with remaining Monterey jack cheese. Bake at 375°F for 35–45 minutes or until sauce is bubbling and cheese melts and begins to brown.

Make Your Own Chicken Broth

You can freeze the skin and bones of cooked chicken breasts to make broth. When you accumulate a few pounds of the skin and bones, place in cold water to cover with onion, garlic, and celery and simmer for 2–3 hours. Freeze broth in ice cube trays and use as desired.

King Ranch Chicken Casserole

This famous recipe is pure Tex-Mex comfort food. You can make it ahead of time and refrigerate until it's time to eat. Then add 15–20 minutes to the baking time; make sure the casserole is bubbling and thoroughly heated.

∩

1. Preheat oven to 350°F. In heavy skillet, cook onions and garlic in butter and olive oil until crisp-tender. Add bell pepper and frozen corn; cook and stir for 2–3 minutes until corn is thawed. Remove from heat and top with chopped tomatoes. Set aside to cool.

2. In medium bowl, combine chicken, black beans, soups, green chiles, and light cream; stir to combine. Cut tortillas into 1" strips. In small bowl, combine chili powder, cumin, salt, and cayenne peppers and mix well. Sprinkle over tortillas and toss to coat.

3. Coat 9" x 13" baking dish with nonstick cooking spray. In the prepared dish, layer half of the chicken mixture, half of the tortillas, half of the bell pepper mixture, and half of the cheese. Repeat layers, ending with cheese.

4. Bake casserole at 350°F for 40–50 minutes or until sauce is bubbling and cheese is melted and beginning to brown. Serve with salsa, sour cream, and guacamole.

King Ranch: Fact or Fiction?

There really was a King Ranch, an actual working farm. In the 1800s, Richard King bought more than 800,000 acres between Corpus Christi and Brownsville, Texas for his ranch. At the time it was the largest spread in Texas—and that's saying a lot!

Serves 8

1 onion, chopped
3 cloves garlic, minced
2 tablespoons butter
1 tablespoon olive oil
1 red bell pepper, chopped
1 cup frozen corn
1 cup chopped tomatoes
3 cups cooked, cubed chicken
1 (15-ounce) can black beans, rinsed
1 (14-ounce) can cream of chicken soup
1 (14-ounce) can cream of mushroom soup with roasted garlic
1 (4-ounce) can diced green chiles, drained
½ cup light cream
8 corn tortillas
2 tablespoons chili powder
½ teaspoon cumin
½ teaspoon salt
⅛ teaspoon cayenne pepper
2½ cups shredded Cheddar cheese

Shredded Chicken for Tacos

Makes about 3 cups

2 pounds boneless, skinless
   chicken breasts
2 tablespoons chili powder
½ teaspoon cumin
½ teaspoon dried oregano
   leaves
1 teaspoon salt
⅛ teaspoon pepper
1 onion, finely chopped
½ cup chicken broth

Cooking chicken breasts in the crockpot makes them extra tender and juicy. Freeze this cooked meat in meal-sized portions and you can have chicken quesadillas, enchiladas, or tacos ready to eat in minutes.

1. In small bowl, combine chili powder, cumin, oregano, salt, and pepper and mix well. Rub this mixture into the chicken breasts and place them in a 4- to 6-quart crockpot along with the chopped onions. Pour chicken broth over all. Cover crockpot and cook on low for 4–6 hours, until chicken is completely cooked.

2. Remove chicken from crockpot, shred with forks, and return to crockpot. Mix well and use immediately or refrigerate or freeze for later use.

Chicken Tacos

Serves 4–6

1 ancho chile
2 tomatoes, seeded
2 cups Shredded Chicken for
   Tacos (above)
½ cup salsa
8 taco shells
3 cups shredded lettuce
2 cups shredded Colby cheese
½ cup Taco Sauce (page 101)

These delicious tacos should be served with guacamole, sour cream, extra salsa, and chopped raw onions if you like food with a nice kick.

1. Preheat oven to 375°F. Roast and peel ancho chile and dice. Combine in heavy skillet with tomatoes, chicken, and salsa and cook over medium heat until warm.

2. Heat taco shells in the oven for 5–10 minutes until hot. Make tacos with chicken mixture and remaining ingredients.

Chicken with Peppers

This colorful dish has a wonderful rich sauce.
Serve it with fresh or warmed tortillas and chopped avocados.

1. Preheat oven to 350°F. Drizzle chicken with 2 tablespoons olive oil and sprinkle with salt and garlic pepper. Bake at 350°F for 30–40 minutes until chicken is thoroughly cooked. Let cool until easy to handle, then discard skin and pull meat off the bone. Set aside.

2. In heavy skillet, heat 2 tablespoons olive oil and add onions and garlic. Cook over medium heat for 5–6 minutes until crisp-tender. Add peppers and chiles; cook and stir for 3–4 minutes until crisp-tender.

3. Cut cream cheese into cubes and add to skillet along with prepared chicken. Cook and stir until cream cheese begins to melt. Stir in sour cream and heat thoroughly, stirring gently. Season to taste with salt and pepper and serve with warmed tortillas.

Serves 6

6 chicken breast halves
2 tablespoons olive oil
1 teaspoon salt
½ teaspoon garlic pepper
2 tablespoons olive oil
2 onions, chopped
4 cloves garlic, minced
1 red bell pepper, sliced
1 yellow bell pepper, sliced
1 green bell pepper, sliced
2 jalapeño chiles, minced
1 (3-ounce) package cream cheese
1½ cups sour cream
Salt and pepper to taste

Serves 6

1½ cups Mole Sauce (page 95)
6 chicken breasts

Grilled Chicken in Mole Sauce

*This simple recipe can be made with pork tenderloin,
turkey tenderloins, or chicken thighs. You can also substitute
a canned Mole Sauce for the homemade variety.*

1. Loosen skin from chicken breasts, leaving attached at one side. Spread some Mole Sauce between the skin and flesh, then smooth skin back over chicken.

2. Prepare and heat grill and place chicken, skin side down, on grill over medium coals. Cover and grill for 20–30 minutes, turning once, or until chicken is thoroughly cooked. Brush with Mole Sauce halfway through cooking time, and at the end of cooking. Bring remaining sauce to a boil, boil for 2 minutes, and serve with chicken.

Serves 6

1 (4-pound) roasting chicken
12-ounce can beer
1 tablespoon red chile
    powder
½ teaspoon hot salt
2 teaspoons cumin
2 tablespoons adobo sauce
2 teaspoons chile paste
⅛ teaspoon cayenne pepper
⅛ teaspoon white pepper

Beer-Can Chicken

*This famous recipe is usually made with grill seasoning,
a blend of salt, pepper, and spices including garlic and cumin.
Using Tex-Mex ingredients gives it a real kick!*

1. Prepare and preheat grill. Wash chicken and dry thoroughly. Pour off (or drink) about half of the beer and set remainder aside. In small bowl, combine remaining ingredients. Rub ½ on the outside of the chicken, rub ¼ on the inside of the chicken, and add ¼ to the beer. Place chicken on can, using legs to hold chicken upright.

2. Cook chicken on grill, covered, over indirect heat for 1 to 1½ hours until chicken is deep golden brown and thoroughly cooked.

Crockpot Chicken Verde

Use a crockpot and your chicken will always be tender and perfectly cooked. This delicious dish can be served with different colors of corn tortillas, salsa, and Guacamole (page 20).

Ω

1. In blender container or food processor, combine onions, garlic, chipotle chile, cilantro, serrano chile, and drained tomatillos. Blend or process until mixture is smooth; set aside.

2. Sprinkle chicken with salt and garlic pepper. Heat lard or oil in heavy skillet and brown chicken, skin side down. As chicken browns, remove it to a 4- to 5-quart crockpot. When all chicken is browned, add onion sauce to skillet. Cook and stir to remove browned bits from bottom of skillet. Pour over chicken, cover crockpot, and cook on low for 8–9 hours until chicken is tender and thoroughly cooked.

Serves 4

2 onions, chopped
4 cloves garlic, chopped
1 chipotle chile in adobo sauce
1 cup chopped cilantro
1 serrano chile, seeded
1 (10-ounce) can tomatillos, drained
3-pound frying chicken, cut up
1 teaspoon salt
1 teaspoon garlic pepper
2 tablespoons lard or vegetable oil

Tequila Lime Chicken

Chicken should marinate for only a few hours in the refrigerator; any longer and the flesh will become too soft. This simple marinade can be used with turkey or pork, too.

Ω

1. In large bowl, combine all ingredients except chicken breasts and mix well. Add chicken and turn to coat. Cover and refrigerate for 2–4 hours.

2. Prepare and heat grill. Remove chicken from marinade and place, skin side down, on grill. Cover and cook for 10 minutes. Turn chicken, cover again, and cook for 10–20 minutes or until chicken is thoroughly cooked. Discard remaining marinade.

Serves 4

¼ cup tequila
¼ cup lime juice
2 tablespoons adobo sauce
1 teaspoon sugar
1 teaspoon salt
⅛ teaspoon cayenne pepper
4 cloves garlic, minced
4 chicken breasts

Chicken Tamales

Yields 16

16 corn husks
1 batch dough from Plain
Tamales (page 119)
1 cup Shredded Chicken for
Tacos (page 150)

Tamales are a treat and perfect for a celebration. Have your guests
help you in the kitchen; that cuts down the work and doubles the fun!

1. Soak corn husks in hot water for 1 hour. Meanwhile, prepare Plain Tamale dough.

2. Drain husks and spread tamale dough on husks to within 1" of edges. Place 1 tablespoon chicken filling in center of dough. Fold sides of husks to the middle so edges meet, then fold up bottom and fold down top to enclose filling. Tie with kitchen string. Place in colander and steam for about 1 hour until corn husks peel away easily from tamales. Serve with Tamale Sauce (page 99).

Steaming Tamales

You can buy tamale steamers, but a metal colander or Chinese bamboo steamer will work just as well. Start water boiling in a heavy skillet and place tortillas, in a single layer, in the colander or steamer. Set on the skillet, making sure the water doesn't touch the colander, cover, and steam until done.

Chicken Fajitas

Tender chicken is coated with Tex-Mex spices and cooked with onions and bell peppers in this fabulous recipe, then served in warm tortillas with an avocado spread.

Serves 4

4 boneless, skinless chicken
   breasts
2 tablespoons Taco
   Seasoning Mix (page 93)
4 flour tortillas
2 tablespoons vegetable oil
1 onion, sliced
3 cloves garlic, minced
1 red bell pepper, sliced
1 yellow bell pepper, sliced
2 jalapeño peppers, minced
1 tablespoon lime juice
½ cup sour cream
½ cup chunky salsa
1 avocado, peeled and diced

1. Sprinkle Taco Seasoning Mix over chicken breasts and rub into flesh. Cover and refrigerate for 1–2 hours. When ready to cook, preheat oven to 350°F. Wrap tortillas in foil and set aside.

2. Place vegetable oil in heavy skillet over medium heat. Cook chicken breasts, turning once, for 10–12 minutes until thoroughly cooked.

3. Remove chicken from pan. Add onion and garlic to pan; cook and stir for 4 minutes until crisp-tender. Add bell peppers and jalapeño peppers; cook for 2–3 minutes and remove from heat.

4. Cut chicken into thin strips and add to pan along with lime juice; stir gently. Cover pan and let stand for 4–5 minutes. In small bowl, combine sour cream, salsa, and avocado and mix well. Place chicken mixture in warmed tortillas and top with avocado mixture; roll up and serve.

What's a Fajita?

In Tex-Mex cooking, fajitas refer to meats such as steak or chicken breasts that have been quickly cooked, sliced, and served with vegetables and condiments in warmed soft tortillas. Use your favorite vegetables in this easy recipe; summer squash or zucchini would be a good substitute.

Turkey con Queso Casserole

Serves 4–6

2 tablespoons butter
1 onion, chopped
4 cloves garlic, minced
2 jalapeño chiles, minced
2 cups chopped cooked
    turkey
2 (15-ounce) cans pinto
    beans, rinsed
1 green bell pepper, chopped
1 cup diced pepper jack
    cheese
1 cup sour cream
1 avocado, mashed
1 tablespoon lime juice
2 cups Chili Gravy (page 98)
3 cups tortilla chips
2 cups shredded Cheddar
    cheese

Two kinds of cheese make this hearty casserole very rich and creamy. You could substitute canned enchilada sauce for the Chili Gravy if you'd like.

1. Preheat oven to 350°F. In heavy skillet, melt butter over medium heat and cook onion, garlic, and jalapeños until crisp-tender. Stir in turkey and well-drained pinto beans. Add green bell pepper and cook for 2–3 minutes longer. Remove from heat and stir in pepper jack cheese. In small bowl, combine sour cream, avocado, and lime juice; mix well.

2. Pour ½ cup Chili Gravy into 2-quart baking dish. Top with half of the tortilla chips, half of the turkey mixture, and half of the sour cream mixture. Repeat layers and top with Cheddar cheese. Cover and bake at 350°F for 30–40 minutes or until cheese is melted and casserole bubbles around the edges. Uncover and bake another 5–10 minutes until cheese begins to brown.

Recipe Substitutions and Tips

Get some thickly sliced cooked turkey from your deli, and cut it into chunks for this easy recipe. You could also substitute ½ cup frozen guacamole for the avocado and lime juice. And think about using flavored tortilla chips for even more spice.

Crockpot Ranch Casserole

Since this casserole cooks for such a long time in the moist environment of the crockpot, the tortillas are fried until crisp before being layered. They will keep their shape and a tiny bit of crunch when the casserole is finished.

∩

1. Heat vegetable oil in large skillet. Cut corn tortillas into eighths and fry, in batches, in oil until crisp and golden. Remove to paper towel to drain; sprinkle fried tortillas with chili powder. Set aside.

2. In same skillet, in same oil, cook onion and garlic until crisp-tender. Stir in red bell peppers and chicken; remove from heat. In large bowl, combine soups, diced tomatoes, green chiles, chili powder, cumin, and cayenne pepper and mix well.

3. In 4-quart crockpot, layer half of chicken mixture, fried tortillas, and soup mixture; repeat layers. Cover and cook on low for 8–9 hours or until casserole is bubbling around edges. Sprinkle with cheese, cover, and let stand for 10 minutes before serving.

Mild or Spicy?

Substitute canned green chiles for the pickled jalapeños and Monterey jack or Muenster cheese for the pepper jack for a milder taste. If you like your food really spicy, add minced serrano peppers or use pickled serrano peppers instead of the pickled jalapeños.

Serves 6–8

¼ cup vegetable oil
12 corn tortillas
1 tablespoon chili powder
1 onion, chopped
4 cloves garlic, minced
2 red bell peppers, chopped
3 cups cooked chopped chicken
1 (10-ounce) can cream of chicken soup
1 (10-ounce) can condensed nacho cheese soup
1 (14-ounce) can diced tomatoes, undrained
1 (4-ounce) can chopped green chiles
1 tablespoon chili powder
½ teaspoon cumin
⅛ teaspoon cayenne pepper
1 cup shredded Cheddar cheese
1 cup shredded pepper jack cheese

Chicken Chimichangas

*These crisp stuffed tortillas can be served with Pico de Gallo (page 91)
or Guacamole (page 20) or both!*

1. In heavy skillet, heat butter and add onion and garlic; cook and stir over medium heat until crisp-tender. Add bell pepper, serrano chile, chicken, and tomatoes; season with cumin, salt, and pepper. Cook and stir for 2–3 minutes. Cool for 30 minutes.

2. Place ¼ cup filling on each tortilla and fold tortilla around filling, tucking in sides. Heat oil in heavy skillet over medium heat to 375°F and fry chimichangas, two at a time, for 2–4 minutes on each side until brown and crisp. Drain well on paper towels before serving.

Chicken Taquitos

*A taquito is a cross between a taco and a burrito. Filled tortillas are rolled up
and fried until crisp; the open ends are reminiscent of tacos. Be sure to carefully
tip them from side to side to drain well when you remove them from the oil.*

1. Cut chicken into 1" chunks and brown in butter for 4–5 minutes. Add onion, garlic, and chipotle chile; cook and stir until chicken is thoroughly cooked, about 5 minutes longer. Season with salt and pepper and stir in cilantro. Using 2 forks, shred chicken finely and stir filling well.

2. Place 2 tablespoons chicken filling on each tortilla and top with some cheese. Roll up tightly and fasten with toothpicks. In heavy skillet, heat oil to 375°F and fry taquitos, two or three at a time, until very crisp. Drain on paper towels and serve.

Arroz con Pollo

Rice with chicken is a classic Mexican recipe given a Tex-Mex twist with Taco Seasoning Mix, cumin, jalapenos, and Cheddar cheese.

Serves 6

6 boneless, skinless chicken
   breasts
2 tablespoons Taco
   Seasoning Mix (page 93)
1 teaspoon salt
½ teaspoon cumin
⅛ teaspoon cayenne pepper
2 tablespoons butter
1 tablespoon vegetable oil
1 onion, sliced
4 cloves garlic, minced
2 jalapeño peppers, minced
1½ cups Texmati rice
½ teaspoon turmeric
1 (14-ounce) can ready-to-
   serve chicken broth
¼ cup tequila
1 (14-ounce) can diced
   tomatoes with green
   chiles
2 green bell peppers, sliced
1 cup shredded Cheddar
   cheese

1. Cut chicken breasts into strips. In small bowl, combine Taco Seasoning Mix, salt, cumin, and cayenne pepper; sprinkle over chicken and toss to coat.

2. In large skillet, melt butter with oil and sauté chicken strips over medium heat, stirring frequently, until chicken is browned, about 8-10 minutes. Remove from pan and reserve. Add onion, garlic, and jalapeño peppers to pan; cook and stir until crisp-tender. Add rice and turmeric; cook and stir for 3–4 minutes until rice is opaque.

3. Stir in chicken broth, tequila, and tomatoes, and stir well. Cover and simmer for 10 minutes. Return chicken to pan along with bell pepper strips, cover, and simmer for 10 minutes longer until rice is tender. Stir well, top with cheese, cover, and let stand for 5 minutes before serving.

About Turmeric

Turmeric is a ground spice made from the dried root of a plant in the ginger family. It is an ingredient in curry and is also used to provide a bright yellow color to many dishes. It is also a substitute for saffron, the world's most expensive spice.

Chicken-Fried Chicken
with Cream Gravy

Serves 6

2 eggs, beaten
2 tablespoons adobo sauce
1 teaspoon chile paste
⅓ cup whole milk
1 cup flour
½ cup masa harina
1 teaspoon ground red chile
  powder
½ teaspoon ground cumin
1 teaspoon salt
¼ teaspoon cayenne pepper
6 boneless, skinless chicken
  breasts
2 cups vegetable oil
1 cup milk
½ cup chicken broth

*Adobo sauce, masa harina, and ground red chile powder
make this chicken-fried chicken spicier than classic recipes.
You could leave them all out if you wish, but why would you?*

♫

1. In shallow bowl, combine eggs, adobo sauce, chile paste, and ⅓ cup milk and beat well. On shallow plate, combine flour, masa harina, chile powder, cumin, salt, and cayenne pepper.

2. Preheat oven to 350°F. Dip chicken breasts into flour mixture, then dip into egg mixture and back into flour mixture. Place on a wire rack and let dry for 15 minutes. Place oil in a large heavy skillet to within 1" of top of pan; heat to 375°F.

3. Fry chicken breasts, three at a time, turning once, just until golden. Remove from skillet and place onto baking sheet. When all the chicken is fried, bake at 350°F for 15–25 minutes or until chicken is thoroughly cooked.

4. Meanwhile, make cream gravy. Pour off all but 2 tablespoons of the vegetable oil, keeping the drippings and browned bits in the skillet. Add 2 tablespoons of leftover chicken coating mixture; cook and stir until bubbly, about 3–4 minutes. Add 1 cup milk and ½ cup chicken broth; cook and stir with wire whisk until mixture comes to a boil. Let simmer for 5–10 minutes until thickened; taste for seasoning. Serve chicken with gravy.

Crispy Cornmeal Chicken

*Flour, cornmeal, and nacho cheese tortilla chips form the very crisp
and flavorful coating on these chicken breasts.*

∩

1. Preheat oven to 350°F. On shallow plate, combine flour, salt, cayenne pepper, cornmeal, and crushed chips and mix well. Dip chicken breasts in Chile Puree, then dredge in flour mixture, patting to thoroughly coat chicken. Place on wire rack to dry for 20 minutes.

2. Heat oil to 375°F in a large heavy skillet. Fry chicken breasts, three at a time, turning once, just until golden. Remove from skillet and place onto baking sheet. When all the chicken is fried, bake at 350°F for 15–25 minutes or until chicken is thoroughly cooked.

Serves 6

½ cup flour
½ teaspoon salt
⅛ teaspoon cayenne pepper
¼ cup cornmeal
½ cup finely crushed nacho cheese tortilla chips
½ cup Chile Puree (page 105)
6 boneless, skinless chicken breasts
½ cup vegetable oil

Grilled Turkey Tenderloins

*This easy grilled recipe is wonderful for a summer evening dinner.
Serve it with corn on the cob and a fruit salad.*

∩

1. Rub turkey tenderloins with olive oil. Sprinkle Chile Rub over tenderloins, rub into flesh. Cover and refrigerate for at least 8 hours or overnight.

2. When ready to eat, prepare and heat grill. Grill tenderloins, 4–6" from medium coals for 20–30 minutes, or until turkey reaches 170°F on a meat thermometer. During last 10 minutes of cooking time, brush Rib Mopping Sauce on tenderloins; turn frequently. Discard any remaining Mopping Sauce.

Serves 6

2 turkey tenderloins
2 tablespoons olive oil
2 tablespoons Three-Chile Rub (page 93)
1 cup Rib Mopping Sauce (page 100)

Chicken Flautas

Serves 8

1 cup Shredded Chicken for
   Tacos (page 150)
1 cup shredded Cheddar
   cheese
16 corn tortillas
1 cup vegetable oil

Serve these crisp and flavorful little deep-fried treats with Pico de Gallo (page 91) or Salsa Fresca (page 29) and lots of cold sour cream for dipping.

∩

1. Drain Shredded Chicken well and mix with cheese in a medium bowl. Soften corn tortillas by wrapping them in microwave-safe paper towels and heating in the microwave on low for about 1 minute.

2. Place 2 tablespoons filling mixture on each tortilla and roll up as tightly as possible; fasten edge with toothpick. Heat vegetable oil in heavy skillet to 375°F.

3. Fry flautas, four at a time, for about 2–4 minutes or until golden brown and crisp. As flautas finish cooking, remove with tongs and gently tip the flautas back and forth over the hot oil to drain. Then finish draining on paper or kitchen towels.

Deep-Frying Temperature

When you're deep-frying, use a thermometer made for the process. Heat the oil to the temperature directed in the recipe, then add just a few items at one time to keep temperature as constant as possible. If you add too many items the oil temperature will drop too much, and the food will absorb grease, becoming soggy instead of crisp.

Chicken Chile Rellenos

These stuffed chiles are a real treat. Serve them as soon as they are cooked with Spanish Rice (page 79) and Three-Tomato Salad (page 49).

∩

1. Roast poblano chiles under a broiler or over a gas flame until skin is charred. Place chiles in a paper bag and let steam for 10 minutes. Remove skin with your fingers. Cut a slit in the side of each chile and carefully remove seeds and membranes.

2. In medium skillet, heat vegetable oil over medium heat and cook onion, garlic, jalapeño pepper, and pine nuts until vegetables are crisp-tender and pine nuts are golden, stirring frequently. Place in medium bowl and let cool for 20 minutes. Stir in chicken and cheese and mix well.

3. Stuff chicken mixture into each of the peeled chiles. In medium bowl, combine flour, masa harina, milk, and egg yolks. In small bowl, beat egg whites until stiff peaks form. Fold into egg yolk mixture.

4. In large heavy skillet, heat vegetable oil to 375°F. One at a time, dip the stuffed chiles into the batter, let excess batter drip off for a few seconds, and carefully lower into the oil. Deep-fry chiles until batter is golden brown; let drain on paper towels for a few minutes. When all the chiles are fried, serve with Enchilada Sauce.

Deep-Frying Safety

Be careful when deep-frying! Make sure that the oil doesn't completely fill the pan; there should be about 1" of space between the top of the oil and the top of the pan to avoid spillover. Use long-handled tongs to handle the food, and stand back when putting food into the oil. Turn off the heat when frying is finished, and let oil cool completely before discarding.

Serves 6-8

8 poblano chiles
1 tablespoon vegetable oil
1 onion, chopped
3 cloves garlic, minced
1 jalapeño pepper, minced
½ cup pine nuts
2 cups chopped cooked
    chicken breast
2 cups shredded Monterey
    jack cheese
½ cup flour
¼ cup masa harina
½ cup milk
2 eggs, separated
3 cups vegetable oil
1 cup Enchilada Sauce (page
    94), heated

Tex-Mex Turkey Pot Pie

Serves 8

2 tablespoons vegetable oil

1 onion, chopped

4 cloves garlic, minced

1 (15-ounce) can black beans, drained

2 cups frozen corn, thawed

2 cups chopped cooked turkey

1 (14-ounce) can diced tomatoes, undrained

2 tablespoons chili powder

1 cup Enchilada Sauce (page 94)

1 (8-ounce) package corn bread mix

½ cup shredded pepper jack cheese

½ cup milk

1 egg, beaten

3 tablespoons butter, melted

1½ cups shredded Cheddar cheese

*Substitute canned enchilada sauce for the homemade version if you like.
Serve this hearty pot pie with a green salad: that's really all it needs!*

1. Preheat oven to 400°F. Heat oil in large skillet over medium heat and cook onion and garlic until crisp-tender. Add black beans, corn, and turkey; cook and stir for 5 minutes. Then add tomatoes, chili powder, and Enchilada Sauce. Bring to a simmer and cook for 10 minutes.

2. In large bowl, combine corn bread mix and pepper jack cheese. In small bowl, combine milk, egg, and melted butter and beat well. Add to corn bread mixture and stir just until combined.

3. Pour turkey mixture into 13" x 9" glass baking dish and top with Cheddar cheese. Pour corn bread mixture over all. Bake at 400°F for 20–30 minutes or until topping is golden brown and set and casserole is bubbly.

Chapter Ten

Beef

Beef Chimichangas

Serves 8–10

2 pounds beef sirloin tip
1 onion, chopped
3 cloves garlic, minced
1 cup beef broth
2 tablespoons chili powder
½ teaspoon salt
1 cup Tomato Salsa (page 97)
¼ cup sliced green olives
1 (16-ounce) can refried
    beans
2 cups shredded Cheddar
    cheese
16 (8") flour tortillas
Vegetable oil

The filling for these excellent little deep-fried filled tortillas is cooked in the crockpot, making it tender and succulent. It cooks all day; when you get home, just form the chimichangas and fry until crisp.

∩

1. Cut beef into 2" cubes and place in a 4- to 6-quart crockpot along with onion, garlic, and beef broth. Cover and cook on low for 7–9 hours until beef is very tender. Using slotted spoon, remove beef and vegetables from broth. Shred meat, using 2 forks.

2. In large bowl, combine shredded beef and vegetables with chili powder, salt, Tomato Salsa, and green olives. Open can of refried beans and mash slightly.

3. Spread refried beans onto each tortilla. Top each with about ¼ cup of beef mixture, then 1 tablespoon of cheese. Fold tortillas around filling, tucking in sides; use toothpicks if necessary to hold together. Freeze any remaining filling.

4. Heat 1" of vegetable oil in heavy deep skillet to 375°F. Fry chimichangas, two at a time, for 2–4 minutes on each side, removing from oil when brown and crisp. Drain well on paper towels before serving. If necessary, keep warm in 250°F oven until all are cooked.

Serving Suggestions

Serve these spicy and crisp chimichangas with sour cream, tomatillo salsa, red tomato salsa, and fresh Guacamole (page 20) for dipping. Be sure to let them cool on paper towels or kitchen towels for at least five minutes before serving; they're very hot!

Picadillo

Picadillo is a spicy beef mixture made with ground beef, raisins, olives, and almonds. Use it as a filling for tacos or enchiladas or stuffed peppers, or as an appetizer dip with tortilla chips.

1. In heavy skillet, brown ground beef with onion and garlic until beef is no longer pink, stirring frequently to break up meat. Drain well.

2. Add remaining ingredients, stir, and simmer over low heat for 15–20 minutes to blend flavors. Serve with soft tacos, warmed tortillas, or hot cooked rice.

Serves 8

1 pound ground beef
1 onion, chopped
3 cloves garlic, minced
1 (14-ounce) can diced
    tomatoes with green
    chiles, undrained
3 tablespoons tomato paste
½ cup beef broth
⅓ cup raisins
1 tablespoon chili powder
½ teaspoon salt
⅛ teaspoon cayenne pepper
1 tablespoon vinegar
⅛ teaspoon cinnamon
¼ cup sliced pimento-stuffed
    green olives
¼ cup slivered almonds

Frito Pie

This unusual recipe may seem strange to you, but it's a Texas favorite. Attend any high school football game in Texas, and you'll see Frito Pie being enjoyed in the stands during halftime.

Split open the corn chip bags along the side. Pour heated chili and onion into the bags and sprinkle with cheese and jalapeño slices. Eat it right out of the bag with a plastic spoon.

Serves 2

2 (1.75-ounce) bags Fritos
    corn chips
1 cup canned chili con carne,
    heated
3 tablespoons chopped onion
½ cup shredded Cheddar
    cheese
4 pickled jalapeño slices, if
    desired

Who Invented Frito Pie?

The origins of this unique treat remain open to dispute. It may have been invented at a Woolworth's store lunch counter, or it could have been created by Mrs. Daisy Doolin, the mother of the man who bought the rights to the original corn chip recipe and founded the Frito-Lay Company.

Frito Pie for a Crowd

Serves 6

5 cups Fritos corn chips
3 cups chili con carne, canned
    or homemade
½ cup chopped onion
2 cups shredded Cheddar
    cheese

Use leftover Classic Chili (page 67) to make this comforting and filling main dish in the middle of winter. Don't try to use another brand of corn chips; the result just won't be the same.

Preheat oven to 350°F. In 2-quart baking dish, place half of the corn chips. Pour over half of the chili, onion, and Cheddar cheese; repeat layers. Bake at 350°F for 20–25 minutes or until cheese is melted and chili is bubbling.

Cheese Enchiladas in Chili Gravy

Serves 6

¼ cup vegetable oil
12 flour tortillas
3 cups shredded Cheddar
    cheese
1 onion, chopped
2 jalapeño chiles, minced
2 cups Chili Gravy (page 98)

Enchiladas were first folded, not rolled. This classic recipe can also be made with any brand of canned chili. Serve with sour cream, guacamole, and salsa.

1. Preheat oven to 375°F. Heat oil in large saucepan over medium heat. Place each tortilla in the hot oil for a few seconds, then place on work surface.

2. Top each tortilla with cheese, onions, and chiles and fold in half. Place in 13" x 9" glass baking dish. When all tortillas are filled, pour Chili Gravy over all. Bake at 375°F for 15–20 minutes until thoroughly heated.

Tex-Mex Meatloaf

You can use plain or flavored tortilla chips in this easy meatloaf as you'd like. If you don't have a meat thermometer, bake until the juices run clear and the meatloaf is no longer pink in the center.

∩

1. Preheat oven to 350°F. In large bowl, combine crushed tortilla chips, chili powder, oregano, pepper, buttermilk, egg, salsa, and cilantro and mix well until blended.

2. Add beef and sausage to buttermilk mixture and mix gently using hands. Do not overwork! Shape into oval loaf and place on broiler pan. In small bowl, combine ketchup, mustard, and Tabasco sauce and spread over loaf.

3. Bake at 350°F for 55–65 minutes or until meat thermometer inserted in center registers 165°F. Remove from oven, cover with foil, and let stand for 10 minutes before slicing.

Meatloaf Tips

The critical steps to making meatloaf are to make sure you do not overwork the meat, as this compacts the mixture and makes the meatloaf tough, and to let the meatloaf stand, covered with foil, for about 10 minutes after cooking so the juices can redistribute.

Serves 6

1 cup finely crushed tortilla chips
1 tablespoon chili powder
½ teaspoon dried oregano
⅛ teaspoon pepper
¼ cup buttermilk
1 egg
¼ cup salsa
2 tablespoons chopped cilantro
1 pound ground beef
½ pound pork sausage
¼ cup ketchup
1 tablespoon mustard
½ teaspoon Tabasco sauce

Beef and Bean Enchiladas

Serves 6–8

1½ pounds ground beef
1 onion, chopped
4 cloves garlic, minced
1 jalapeño pepper, minced
1 green bell pepper, chopped
1 (16-ounce) can refried
   beans
½ cup green salsa
½ teaspoon salt
⅛ teaspoon cayenne pepper
3 cups Enchilada Sauce
   (page 94)
½ cup vegetable oil
12 corn tortillas
2 cups shredded Cheddar
   cheese
1½ cups crumbled queso
   blanco
1 cup sour cream

Refried beans add smoothness and richness to the filling in these delectable enchiladas. Serve with a large green salad and some melon balls, and an ice cream sundae buffet for dessert.

1. Preheat oven to 350°F. In large skillet, cook ground beef with onion and garlic, stirring to break up meat, until beef is brown. Add jalapeño and green peppers and cook, stirring, for another 3–4 minutes. Drain well if necessary. Stir in refried beans, green salsa, salt, and cayenne pepper.

2. Pour 1 cup of Enchilada Sauce in a 13" x 9" baking dish. In heavy skillet, heat vegetable oil until hot. Dip corn tortillas, one at a time, into the oil, then dip into remaining Enchilada Sauce. Place on work surface and top with about ⅓ cup beef mixture and 1 tablespoon Cheddar cheese; roll up and place in baking dish.

3. Pour remaining Enchilada Sauce over rolled enchiladas and top with remaining cheeses. Bake at 350°F for 30–40 minutes or until sauce bubbles around edges and enchiladas are hot. Serve with sour cream, salsa, and chopped lettuce.

Homemade Refried Beans

Make your own refried beans by mashing about a pound of cooked or canned beans and frying in a few tablespoons of vegetable oil or lard. Add any spices you'd like and stir the mixture frequently, until the beans absorb the fat and are smooth and creamy.

Mexicali Rice and Beef

This hearty and rich casserole is perfect for a cold winter night.
Serve it with some warmed flour tortillas, a green salad with a mild ranch
salad dressing, and Pineapple Cake (page 269) for dessert.

∩

1. In heavy saucepan, combine rice with 2 cups beef broth, chili powder, and cumin, and bring to a boil. Cover, reduce heat, and simmer for 15–20 minutes until rice is tender and liquid is absorbed. Meanwhile, in heavy saucepan cook ground beef with onion and garlic until beef is browned. Add bell peppers and chipotle pepper; cook and stir for 2 minutes longer. Drain well.

2. Preheat oven to 375°F. Add tomato sauce, paste, adobo sauce, beef broth, and pepper to ground beef mixture. Cook over medium heat, stirring frequently, for 15 minutes. Combine cooked rice and beef mixture in 2-quart casserole and mix thoroughly. Top with cheese and bake at 375°F for 20–25 minutes until cheese melts.

How to Cook Rice

To cook fluffy rice, use double the amount of liquid as rice, do not uncover while rice is cooking, and let rice stand off the heat for 5 minutes before using, then fluff and serve. Use a fork to fluff rice; a spoon will crush the grains.

Serves 6

1 cup long-grain rice
2 cups beef broth
1 tablespoon chili powder
½ teaspoon cumin
1 pound ground beef
1 onion, chopped
3 cloves garlic, minced
2 green bell peppers, chopped
2 chipotle peppers in adobo sauce, minced
1 (8-ounce) can tomato sauce
1 (6-ounce) can tomato paste
2 tablespoons adobo sauce
1 cup beef broth
¼ teaspoon pepper
1½ cups shredded Colby cheese

Beef and Potato Burritos

Serves 6–8

1 Anaheim chile
1 pound ground beef
1 sweet potato, peeled and
    chopped
1 onion, chopped
3 cloves garlic, minced
2 chipotle chiles in adobo
    sauce, chopped
1 (15-ounce) can pinto beans,
    rinsed
⅓ cup taco sauce
½ teaspoon salt
⅛ teaspoon cayenne pepper
15 flour tortillas
1½ cups shredded pepper
    jack cheese
3 cups vegetable oil

Sweet potatoes are a common Tex-Mex ingredient with a honeylike flavor and tender texture. They hold together the filling in these sweet and spicy burritos and add a Southern touch.

Ω

1. Roast Anaheim chile under broiler or over a gas flame until blackened. Place in paper bag to steam, then peel, seed, and chop. Set aside.

2. In heavy skillet, crumble ground beef and add sweet potato, onion, and garlic. Sauté these ingredients, stirring frequently, until beef is brown and vegetables are tender. Drain well if necessary. Add Anaheim chile, chipotle chiles, pinto beans, taco sauce, salt, and pepper, and mix well.

3. Place 3 tablespoons beef mixture on each tortilla and top with 1 tablespoon grated cheese. Roll up tortillas, folding in ends.

4. Heat vegetable oil in a deep skillet to 375°F. Fry burritos, two at a time, until crisp and golden brown, about 2–3 minutes on each side. Drain on paper towels, let cool about 5 minutes, and serve.

About Sweet Potatoes

There are sweet potatoes and there are yams, and the two are not the same. Sweet potatoes (genus Ipomoea), with their yellow or orange flesh, are what Americans call yams. Technically, yams are a different variety of plant (genus Dioscore) with a white flesh that is not at all sweet.

Chicken-Fried Steak

*A little bit of masa harina is mixed in with the flour used to coat
the steaks (and to make the gravy) in this easy recipe;
it adds a bit more crunch and some subtle corn flavor.*

∩

1. Place cube steaks on waxed paper. On shallow plate, mix flour, masa harina, 1 teaspoon salt, ¼ teaspoon pepper, and chili powder; stir until combined.

2. In shallow bowl, beat eggs with ½ cup cream, ½ teaspoon salt, and cayenne pepper until smooth.

3. Dredge steaks in flour mixture, then dip into egg mixture and back into flour mixture. Place on wire rack and let stand for 15 minutes to dry.

4. Preheat oven to 200°F. In deep heavy skillet, heat oil to 375°F. Fry steaks, two or three at a time, for 8 minutes, then turn and fry for 4–5 minutes longer until crisp and golden. As steaks are cooked, remove to warm oven.

5. When all steaks are cooked, carefully remove most of the oil from the pan, leaving the drippings and brown bits behind in about 2 tablespoons of the oil. Add 3 tablespoons of the flour mixture used to dredge steaks and cook and stir over medium heat until light brown. Add milk, ½ cup heavy cream, and beef broth; cook over medium heat, stirring constantly, until mixture simmers and thickens. Serve gravy over steaks.

Menu Suggestions

This old-fashioned and classic Tex-Mex recipe is delicious served with mashed potatoes, a green salad, and a bakery cake for dessert. Be sure to serve the steaks as soon as the gravy is done so your guests get to enjoy the crisp crust and tender and melting interior.

Serves 6

6 (6-ounce) cube steaks
1 cup flour
½ cup masa harina
1 teaspoon salt
¼ teaspoon pepper
1 tablespoon chili powder
2 eggs
½ cup heavy cream
½ teaspoon salt
⅛ teaspoon cayenne pepper
3 cups vegetable oil
1 cup milk
½ cup heavy cream
½ cup beef broth

Chili Mac

Serves 4

1 pound ground beef
1 onion, chopped
2 cloves garlic, minced
1 green bell pepper, chopped
1 cup uncooked elbow
    macaroni
1 (14-ounce) can tomatoes
    with green chiles,
    undrained
1 (10-ounce) can condensed
    tomato soup
2 tablespoons Taco
    Seasoning Mix (page 93)
1 teaspoon ground red chile
    powder
⅛ teaspoon pepper
⅛ teaspoon cayenne pepper
1 (15-ounce) can kidney
    beans, drained
¾ cup water
1 cup grated Cheddar cheese

Chili Mac is a definite Mexican-American hybrid. Ground beef, kidney beans, and macaroni are all simmered together in a spicy tomato sauce to make a hearty and easy dinner ready in about 30 minutes.

∩

1. In large skillet, brown ground beef with onion and garlic; drain well if necessary. Add green pepper and cook for another 2–3 minutes. Stir in remaining ingredients except cheese and bring to a boil. Cover pan, reduce heat, and simmer for 15–20 minutes until macaroni is tender.

2. Leave in skillet and sprinkle with Cheddar cheese; cover pan and let stand for 3–4 minutes until cheese melts. Serve with sour cream, salsa, and guacamole.

Tone It Down for Kids

If you're serving this recipe to kids, you may want to cut down on the amount of chile powder and pepper. Serve some crushed red pepper flakes or ground red chile powder on the side for those who want to make their dinner spicier.

Beef Migas

*Corn chips are a classic Texas treat not common in Mexico.
In this layered casserole, they are used in place of pasta; the chips will soften
slightly as the casserole bakes but will retain a bit of crunch.*

∩

1. Preheat oven to 375°F. In heavy skillet, cook ground beef, onion, and garlic until beef is browned, stirring to break up meat. Drain well if necessary. Stir in tomato sauce, diced tomatoes, and Taco Seasoning Mix; stir well. Simmer over medium heat for 5 minutes.

2. Stir in corn, pinto beans, jalapeño pepper, and olives. In 2-quart casserole, layer one-third beef mixture with one-third of the chips. Repeat layers, ending with beef mixture. Sprinkle cheese over the top.

3. Bake at 375°F for 25–35 minutes or until cheese melts and casserole bubbles around the edge. Top with sour cream, salsa, and chopped avocado and serve.

More Toppings

You can put out more toppings if you'd like. Shredded lettuce, chopped fresh tomatoes, different types of shredded cheese, minced jalapeño or serrano chiles, or Pico de Gallo (page 91) and Salsa Verde (page 92) are all good with the bean and beef combination in this dish.

Serves 4–6

1 pound ground beef
1 onion, chopped
2 cloves garlic, minced
1 (8-ounce) can tomato sauce
1 (14-ounce) can diced
  tomatoes with green
  chiles, undrained
2 tablespoons Taco
  Seasoning Mix (page 93)
2 cups frozen corn
1 (15-ounce) can pinto beans,
  drained
2 jalapeño peppers, minced
½ cup garlic-stuffed green
  olive slices
1 (8-ounce) bag corn chips
1½ cups shredded Colby
  cheese

Rib-Eye Steak

This simple recipe can be used with just about any cut of steak.
Porterhouse steaks, T-bones, and sirloin steaks are all good choices.

Serves 6

¼ cup Three-Chile Rub
   (page 93)
6 rib-eye beef steaks
2 cups mesquite chips
3 tablespoons adobo sauce

1. Sprinkle the Three-Chile Rub over the steaks on both sides. Cover steaks and place in refrigerator for at least 2 hours. Soak mesquite chips in water for 2 hours.

2. When ready to cook, prepare and preheat grill. Sprinkle mesquite chips over coals and place steaks on grill. Cover and cook for 5 minutes. Turn steaks, brush each with adobo sauce, and cook until desired doneness. Let stand for 5 minutes before serving.

Beef Tamales

Make the dough for the tamales using beef broth instead of chicken broth
for more flavor. You can substitute cooked, drained ground beef
for the shredded beef in this classic recipe.

Yields 16

16 corn husks
1 tablespoon butter
½ cup onion, chopped
3 cloves garlic, minced
1 jalapeño pepper, minced
¼ cup Tamale Sauce
   (page 99)
½ cup shredded roast beef
1¾ cups Tamale Sauce
   (page 99)
1 batch dough from Plain
   Tamales (page 119)

1. Soak corn husks in hot water for 1 hour. Meanwhile, heat butter in heavy skillet and cook onion, garlic, and jalapeño pepper until crisp-tender. Add ¼ cup Tamale Sauce and beef; simmer for 4–5 minutes. Let cool for 30 minutes.

2. Drain husks and spread tamale dough on husks to within 1" of edges. Place 1 tablespoon beef filling in center of dough. Fold sides of husks to the middle so edges meet, then fold up bottom and fold down top to enclose filling. Tie with kitchen string. Place in colander and steam over simmering water for 1 hour or until corn husk peels away easily from tamales.

3. In medium saucepan, heat 1¾ cups Tamale Sauce over low heat and serve with tamales.

Oven-Barbecued Beef Brisket

You can use Brisket Mopping Sauce (page 103) instead of the recipe below if you'd like. Slice the brisket across the grain and serve with warmed flour tortillas, a variety of salsas, and some shredded cheese.

Serves 8–10

1 (5-pound) beef brisket
1 teaspoon garlic pepper
1 teaspoon onion salt
2 tablespoons chili powder
1 teaspoon cumin
¼ teaspoon cayenne pepper
1 (12-ounce) can beer
1 (18-ounce) bottle barbecue
    sauce
2 chipotle peppers in adobo
    sauce
3 tablespoons adobo sauce

1. Preheat oven to 300°F. Place beef brisket, fat side up, in a large baking pan. Sprinkle with garlic pepper, onion salt, chili powder, cumin, and cayenne pepper and rub into meat. Pour half of beer over meat, cover pan with foil, and bake at 300°F for 2 hours.

2. In heavy saucepan, combine remaining beer, barbecue sauce, chipotle peppers, and adobo sauce and bring to a simmer. Cook for 15–20 minutes until thickened.

3. Pour over meat in baking pan and bake, uncovered, 60–75 minutes longer until meat is tender. Remove from oven and let stand, covered, for 15 minutes before slicing.

Make-Ahead Tips

This barbecued meat can be frozen for up to 3 months. Slice it across the grain and pack into plastic food-storage containers along with some of the sauce. Cover, label, and freeze. To thaw and reheat, place in saucepan and cook over low heat, stirring frequently, until meat is hot and sauce bubbles.

Beef Empanadas

Serves 6–8

1 cup lard or solid shortening
¼ cup hot water
1 tablespoon milk
2½ cups flour
½ teaspoon salt
⅛ teaspoon cayenne pepper
1½ cups shredded Cheddar
   cheese
½ pound ground beef
1 onion, chopped
3 cloves garlic, minced
1 cup frozen hash brown
   potatoes
2 teaspoons chile paste
1 (4-ounce) can diced green
   chiles, drained
1 egg, beaten

*These little pastries can be partially made ahead of time.
Make the dough, cover, and chill. Make the ground beef filling,
cover, and chill. Then assemble and bake just before serving.*

1. In large bowl, place lard and top with hot water and milk. Beat mixture, using a fork, until fat absorbs the liquid and is fluffy. Add flour, salt, cayenne pepper, and cheese and mix well until a dough forms. Cover and chill while preparing filling.

2. In heavy skillet, cook ground beef with onion and garlic until beef is browned, stirring often to break up beef. Drain well; stir in potatoes, chile paste, and chiles; cook and stir until mixture is hot and thickens. Let cool for 30 minutes, then chill for 30 minutes.

3. Preheat oven to 375°F. Divide dough into 16 portions and roll or press out, on cornmeal-dusted surface, to 5" rounds. Place 2 tablespoons beef mixture in center of each dough circle; fold over and press edges with fork to seal. Place on baking sheet and brush with beaten egg. Bake at 375°F for 20–30 minutes or until pastries are golden and crisp.

Healthier Shortening

You can now buy solid vegetable shortening in a version that has zero grams of trans fat. Look for the specially marked packages in your grocer's baking aisle. Substitute it, measure for measure, for ordinary solid shortening, butter, margarine, or lard.

Beef Taco Salad

Processed cheese food, a classic Tex-Mex ingredient, is made with emulsifiers so it melts perfectly, every time. There's really no substitute.

∩

Serves 6–8

1 pound ground beef
1 onion, chopped
3 cloves garlic, minced
1 serrano chile, minced
2 tablespoons chili powder
½ teaspoon cumin
1 tablespoon Worcestershire
   sauce
1 (14-ounce) can tomatoes
   with green chiles,
   undrained
1 (16-ounce) package
   processed cheese food
1 (10-ounce) bag romaine
   lettuce
1 green bell pepper, chopped
1 red bell pepper, chopped
3 cups corn chips
2 cups shredded Cheddar
   cheese

1. In heavy skillet, cook ground beef, onion, garlic, and serrano chile until beef is browned, stirring to break up meat. Drain if necessary, then add chili powder, cumin, Worcestershire sauce, and tomatoes. Bring to a boil, then reduce heat and simmer for 20 minutes.

2. Cut processed cheese food into ½" pieces and stir into beef mixture; cover and let stand off the heat for 5 minutes.

3. In serving bowl, combine lettuce with bell peppers and corn chips. Top with beef mixture and sprinkle with Cheddar cheese; serve immediately.

Make-Ahead Tips

Ground beef, processed cheese food, tomatoes with green chiles, and corn chips are the "authentic" Tex-Mex ingredients in this yummy salad. You can make the beef mixture ahead of time, but don't add the cheese. Refrigerate until you're ready to eat, then reheat beef mixture, add cheese, and proceed with the recipe.

Shredded Beef Tacos

Serves 8–10

2 pounds beef top round
    steak
1 onion, chopped
3 cloves garlic, minced
½ cup water
1 cup salsa
2 tablespoons chili powder
3 cups torn lettuce
3 tomatoes, seeded and
    chopped
2 cups shredded Cheddar
    cheese
1 cup sour cream
¼ cup mayonnaise
2 avocados, peeled and diced
2 chipotle chiles in adobo
    sauce, minced
16 flour tortillas
2 cups vegetable oil

The meat for these delicious tacos cooks in the crockpot,
so when you come home from work or school,
all you have to do is assemble the tacos and eat them!

1. Place beef, onion, and garlic in 4-quart crockpot and pour water over all. Cover and cook on low for 8–10 hours until beef is very tender. Remove meat and vegetables from crockpot. Using 2 forks, shred meat, mixing onion and garlic into the meat.

2. Combine meat mixture, salsa, and chili powder in a large bowl. In another large bowl, combine lettuce, tomatoes, and cheese. In medium bowl, combine sour cream, mayonnaise, avocados, and chipotle chiles. Soften tortillas by wrapping in microwave-safe paper towels and heating on medium for 2–3 minutes.

3. Heat vegetable oil to 375°F in large skillet. Working with one at a time, place ¼ cup beef filling on a flour tortilla and fold in half; seal edges with toothpick. Immediately place in hot oil and cook until tortilla is golden and crisp, about 2–4 minutes. Remove from oil, tipping carefully to drain out any hot oil. Let drain on paper or kitchen towels for 2–3 minutes, then remove toothpicks, carefully pry open the tortilla and add lettuce mixture and sour cream mixture. Serve immediately.

A Simpler Method

You can also make these tacos in the usual way: heat purchased crisp taco shells and serve with meat mixture, lettuce mixture, sour cream mixture, and any other condiments you'd like. But at least once, try the fried tortilla method. The combination of hot crisp tortilla, tender, hot meat filling, and cold vegetables and sour cream is fabulous.

Tex-Mex Smoked Brisket

*As with any tough cut of meat, brisket becomes meltingly tender
when slowly cooked and sliced across the grain.*

∩

Serves 18–20

*5- to 6-pound beef brisket,
  well trimmed
5 cloves garlic, slivered
½ cup Three-Chile Rub
  (page 93)
6 cups mesquite chips
Brisket Mopping Sauce
  (page 103)*

1. Trim brisket well of any excess fat. Sliver garlic and, using a knife, cut a deep hole in the meat for each sliver of garlic; insert garlic. Sprinkle Three-Chile Rub over meat, rub in well, cover, and refrigerate overnight.

2. The next day, prepare grill for indirect cooking or prepare a smoker. Soak mesquite chips in water for a couple of hours and place on the coals. Put the brisket, fat side down, on the grill or smoker rack. Smoke for 1¼ hours per pound of meat, adding more charcoal to the grill or smoker about every hour. During last hour of cooking, spread Mopping Sauce over brisket several times.

3. When beef is tender, remove from smoker, cover with foil, and let stand for 15 minutes, then slice across the grain and serve.

Freeze Leftovers

Freeze the leftover meat to use in Shredded Beef Tacos (page 180) or Beef Chimichangas (page 166). Slice meat and place in freezer containers with a spoonful of the sauce. Seal, label, and freeze for up to 3 months. To thaw, let stand in refrigerator overnight, then reheat in microwave or top of a double boiler over simmering water.

Beef-Stuffed Chiles

Serves 6

6 poblano chiles
1½ cups shredded Oven-
   Barbecued Beef Brisket
   (page 177)
2 tablespoons vegetable oil
1 onion, chopped
1 green bell pepper, chopped
2 chipotle peppers in adobo
   sauce, minced
1 tomato, seeded and
   chopped
½ cup Red Chile Sauce
   (page 104)
1½ cups shredded Muenster
   cheese
2 tablespoons flour
4 eggs, separated
¼ cup flour
1 teaspoon salt
⅛ teaspoon pepper
2 cups vegetable oil

*When you gently lower the stuffed chiles into the oil,
keep the slit side up. The heat will seal the slit with the egg batter
so the filling stays inside while it cooks.*

∩

1. Roast poblano chiles under a broiler or over a gas flame until skin is charred. Place in paper bag and let steam for 10 minutes. Peel peppers, cut a slit in the side, and remove membranes and seeds.

2. Shred beef and set aside. In heavy skillet, heat vegetable oil over medium heat and cook onion and green bell pepper until crisp-tender. Add chipotle chiles and tomato along with shredded beef and Red Chile Sauce; cook and stir for 4–5 minutes. Remove from heat and let cool for 30 minutes.

3. Stuff peppers with beef mixture and 2 tablespoons Muenster cheese. Sprinkle with 2 tablespoons flour and shake off excess. In medium bowl, beat egg whites until stiff. In another medium bowl, beat egg yolks with ¼ cup flour, salt, and pepper; fold into egg whites.

4. Heat vegetable oil to 350°F in deep heavy skillet. Dip stuffed chiles, one at a time, into egg batter and gently lower into oil. Fry for 2–4 minutes on each side until golden brown. Drain on kitchen or paper towels and serve with salsa.

Fajitas with Soft Tortillas

If you make your own tortillas for this delicious dish, you probably won't need to warm them before rolling because they will stay soft for a day or two. If you purchase tortillas, warm them before serving.

∩

Serves 4

1 pound flank steak
2 tablespoons Taco
    Seasoning Mix (page 93)
1 tablespoon lime juice
2 tablespoons vegetable oil
2 tablespoons adobo sauce
1 tablespoon butter
1 onion, chopped
3 cloves garlic, minced
1 (4-ounce) can minced green
    chiles, drained
8 Flour Tortillas (page125)
1 cup shredded Cheddar
    cheese
Tomatillo Chutney (page 91)

1. Lightly score flank steak with the tip of a knife. Place in large zip-lock bag and add Taco Seasoning Mix, lime juice, vegetable oil, and adobo sauce. Seal bag and massage to rub the seasonings into the meat. Refrigerate at least 8 hours or overnight.

2. The next day, prepare and preheat grill. In heavy skillet, melt butter over medium heat and sauté onion, garlic, and green chiles until onion is crisp-tender; set aside. Remove flank steak from marinade; discard marinade.

3. Grill steak for 3–6 minutes on each side until desired doneness. Remove steak from grill, cover with foil, and let stand for 5 minutes. Slice steak thinly across the grain and serve with onion mixture, cheese, and Tomatillo Chutney in tortillas.

History of the Fajita

The Spanish word fajita means "belt" or "girdle" and refers to the skirt steak, a cheap cut of meat around the belly of the cow that ranch workers were given for their own use. These tough cuts were marinated, grilled, sliced against the grain, and served in warmed tortillas.

Chapter Eleven

Pork and Sausage

Carnitas

Serves 8–10

4-pound pork roast
2 teaspoons salt
¼ teaspoon pepper
1 teaspoon cumin
1 onion, chopped
5 cloves garlic, chopped
½ cup chicken broth

*Carnitas is slowly roasted pork that is then cooked in dry heat until crisp.
Serve with heated flour tortillas, chopped vegetables, and Jalapeño Pesto
(page 96) and let your guests make their own sandwiches at the table.*

1. Sprinkle roast with salt, pepper, and cumin, and place in a 4- to 6-quart crockpot. Surround with onions and garlic and pour chicken broth over all. Cover and cook on low for 8–9 hours until pork is very tender.

2. Preheat oven to 400°F. Remove pork from crockpot and place in large baking pan. Using 2 forks, shred meat. Take 1 cup of pan juices from the crockpot and mix into pork.

3. Bake at 400°F for 15–20 minutes or until pork is crisp on top. Stir pork mixture thoroughly and bake for 15–20 minutes longer or until pork is again crisp on top. Serve with crisp tacos, flour or corn tortillas, and lots of salsa.

Make It Spicy

Traditionally, carnitas is cooked without chili powder or fresh or dried chiles. However, you can certainly add some to the crockpot to help flavor the pork as it cooks. A chipotle pepper packed in adobo sauce, minced, would be delicious.

Baby Back Ribs

Ribs are an ideal entrée to serve for dinner on the porch. Make sure you provide lots of wet wipes and napkins, and offer cold beer and soda pop. Coleslaw is the traditional accompaniment; serve ice cream sundaes for a cooling dessert.

Serves 6–8

1 cup ketchup
½ cup chicken broth
2 tablespoons lime juice
2 tablespoons Worcestershire sauce
3 tablespoons brown sugar
½ cup diced onion
1 teaspoon salt
2 tablespoons chile powder
½ teaspoon celery salt
¼ teaspoon cayenne pepper
4 pounds pork baby back ribs

1. In heavy saucepan, combine all ingredients except ribs and bring to a boil. Reduce heat and simmer for 20 minutes to blend flavors. Let cool completely. Place ribs on large rectangles of heavy-duty foil and pour half of sauce over them. Wrap ribs in foil and refrigerate overnight.

2. Preheat oven to 300°F. Place ribs, still wrapped in foil, in baking pan and bake at 300°F for 2 hours. Uncover, add more sauce, and bake for 30–45 minutes longer until ribs are very tender. Serve with additional reheated sauce.

3. To grill ribs, first bake them as directed for 2 hours. Then place over medium coals and grill, covered, for 30–45 minutes, basting with sauce, until very tender.

Cookout Safety

After you're done grilling with charcoal, let the coals cool completely. Do not transfer warm or hot coals to another container or you risk starting a fire. Place the grill on a nonflammable surface, such as concrete or asphalt, and keep an eye on it until everything has completely cooled.

Tex-Mex Pork Casserole

*Serve this spicy casserole with warmed flour or corn tortillas,
hot cooked rice, guacamole, and sour cream.*

Serves 8

2 pounds pork loin
1 tablespoon chili powder
½ teaspoon cumin
1 teaspoon salt
⅛ teaspoon cayenne pepper
2 tablespoons olive oil
1 tablespoon butter
1 onion, chopped
2 cloves garlic, minced
1 serrano pepper, minced
½ cup chicken broth
½ cup Taco Sauce (page 101)
2 (16-ounce) cans black
    beans

1. Cut pork into 1" cubes. In small bowl, combine chili powder, cumin, salt, and cayenne pepper and mix well. Add to pork cubes and toss to coat well. In heavy skillet, cook coated pork cubes in olive oil and butter until browned, about 5–6 minutes.

2. Meanwhile, place onion, garlic, and serrano pepper in a 4- to 6-quart crockpot. Add browned pork cubes and pour chicken broth over all. Top with Taco Sauce and rinsed and drained black beans; mix well. Cover and cook on low for 8–10 hours or until pork is very tender.

Chorizo con Huevos

*Serve this spicy pork and egg mixture for a hearty breakfast with warmed flour
tortillas, sour cream, and guacamole. It also makes a filling late night supper,
served with a fresh fruit salad for a cool contrast.*

Serves 6

1 pound Chorizo (page 194)
1 onion, chopped
12 eggs
⅓ cup sour cream
½ teaspoon salt
⅛ teaspoon pepper
1 avocado, peeled and diced

1. In heavy skillet over medium heat, cook Chorizo until browned, stirring frequently to break up meat. Remove sausage from skillet and reserve. Cook onions in drippings until crisp-tender.

2. Meanwhile, in large bowl beat eggs with sour cream, salt, and pepper. When onions are done, add egg mixture to skillet along with reserved Chorizo. Cook and stir over medium heat until eggs are set. Fold in avocado and serve.

Pork and Beans

Slab bacon adds lots of flavor to this hearty bean dish. You could substitute the same amount of ham if you'd like.

∩

1. Cover pinto beans with water, bring to a boil, and boil for 1 minute. Remove from heat, cover, and let stand for 1 hour. Meanwhile, cut slashes in bacon almost to the rind. Add to beans along with chicken broth and water, garlic, and onion. Bring to a boil, then reduce heat, cover, and simmer for 1½ hours until beans are almost tender.

2. Add diced tomatoes, celery, serrano chile, chili powder, brown sugar, and oregano. Cover and simmer for 1½ hours longer. Stir well, add salt and pepper, remove bacon slab, and serve.

Serves 8

2¼ cups dried pinto beans
½ pound slab bacon
3 cups chicken broth
3 cups water
3 cloves garlic, minced
1 onion, chopped
1 (14-ounce) can diced
    tomatoes with green
    chiles, undrained
2 stalks celery, diced
1 serrano chile, minced
2 tablespoons chili powder
2 tablespoons brown sugar
½ teaspoon dried oregano
    leaves
1 teaspoon salt
⅛ teaspoon cayenne pepper

Chorizo Tacos

These soft tacos should be assembled at the table;
place all the ingredients in front of your guests and stand back!

∩

1. In heavy skillet, cook Chorizo and onion, stirring frequently, until Chorizo is thoroughly cooked. Drain well, then add jalapeños, bell peppers, and onion salt; cook and stir for 4–5 minutes until peppers are crisp-tender.

2. Wrap tortillas in microwave-safe paper towels and heat on low for 1–2 minutes until warm. Top tortillas with Chorizo mixture, Nacho Cheese Sauce, Pico de Gallo, and Jalapeño Pesto; roll up and serve.

Serves 4

1 pound Chorizo (page 194)
1 onion, chopped
2 jalapeño peppers, minced
1 green bell pepper, sliced
1 red bell pepper, sliced
½ teaspoon onion salt
8 flour tortillas
1 cup Nacho Cheese Sauce
    (page 99)
1 cup Pico de Gallo (page 91)
½ cup Jalapeño Pesto
    (page 96)

Chorizo Tamales

Yields 16

16 corn husks
½ cup Chorizo (page 194)
½ cup onion, chopped
1 serrano chile, minced
½ teaspoon celery salt
1½ cups Tamale Sauce
(page 99)
1 batch dough from Plain
Tamales (page 119)

You can substitute purchased chorizo sausage for the homemade Chorizo in this easy recipe. Serve with cold beer and lots of fresh fruit.

1. Soak corn husks in hot water for 1 hour. Meanwhile, in heavy skillet over medium heat, cook Chorizo, onion, and serrano chile until crisp-tender; drain well. Add celery salt and ¼ cup Tamale Sauce; simmer for 4–5 minutes. Let cool for 30 minutes.

2. Drain husks and spread Tamale dough on husks to within 1" of edges. Place 1 tablespoon Chorizo filling in center of dough. Fold sides of husks to the middle so edges meet, then fold up bottom and fold down top to enclose filling. Tie with kitchen string. Place in colander and steam over simmering water for 1 hour or until corn husks peel away easily from tamales. Serve with remaining heated Tamale Sauce.

Flavored Salts

There are many different kinds of flavored salts you can use in your cooking and at the table. Celery salt, garlic salt, and onion salt are the most common, but you can also find salt mixed with herbs, and even different varieties of sea salts.

Pork Tamales

*Have a tamale party! Make triple the recipe of Plain Tamales and
2 or 3 kinds of filling. Let your guests create their own tamales
and eat appetizers while the tamales steam.*

∩

1. Soak corn husks in hot water for 1 hour. Meanwhile, prepare Tamale
   dough and set aside. In medium bowl, combine Carnitas, cilantro, chili
   powder, adobo sauce, and jalapeño pepper and mix well.

2. Drain husks and spread Tamale dough on husks to within 1" of edges.
   Place 1 tablespoon Carnitas filling in center of dough. Fold sides of
   husks to the middle so edges meet, then fold up bottom and fold down
   top to enclose filling. Tie with kitchen string. Place in colander or
   tamale steamer and steam for about 1 hour until corn husks peel away
   easily from tamales. Serve with Tamale Sauce (page 99).

Cilantro Substitutions

*If you aren't a cilantro fan, you can use a combination of flat leaf parsley
and thyme as a substitute. To chop, wash parsley and tear the leaves
from the stems. Chop using a chef's knife until pieces are uniform.
Remove thyme leaves by running your finger along the stem to remove
the leaves, then chop.*

Yields 16

*16 corn husks
1 recipe Plain Tamales
   (page 119)
1 cup Carnitas (page 186)
2 tablespoons chopped
   cilantro
1 tablespoon chili powder
2 tablespoons adobo sauce
1 jalapeño pepper, minced*

BBQ Ribs

Serves 4–6

4 pounds meaty short pork
    ribs
1 teaspoon salt
½ teaspoon pepper
1 tablespoon vegetable oil
1 onion, chopped
5 cloves garlic, chopped
⅓ cup honey
1 (14-ounce) can diced
    tomatoes with green
    chiles, undrained
1 (6-ounce) can tomato paste
½ cup ketchup
3 tablespoons adobo sauce
1 tablespoon mustard
1 cup chicken broth
½ teaspoon dried oregano
    leaves
½ teaspoon salt
⅛ teaspoon cayenne pepper

Roasting the ribs plain before adding the barbecue sauce removes some of the fat and also makes the ribs crisper. Serve them with Tex-Mex Slaw (page 41) and warmed flour tortillas with Guacamole (page 20).

1. Preheat oven to 400°F. Sprinkle ribs with salt and pepper and place in heavy baking pan. Roast ribs, uncovered, for 1 hour. Drain fat from pan.

2. While ribs are roasting, in heavy saucepan sauté onions and garlic in vegetable oil until tender. Add remaining ingredients and bring to a boil. Reduce heat and simmer for 20–25 minutes, stirring frequently, until sauce is slightly thickened. Pour over ribs in baking pan. Reduce oven temperature to 350°F and roast ribs for 80–95 minutes, basting occasionally with sauce, until ribs are very tender.

Grill 'Em!

You can finish these ribs on the grill. Prepare the grill and, after ribs have roasted in the oven for 1 hour, place them over medium coals. Cover and grill ribs, turning frequently, for about 1 hour. Prepare sauce as directed and baste ribs with sauce. Continue grilling for 20–25 minutes, basting frequently with sauce, until ribs are done.

Stacked Tortas

The word torta technically means "sandwich," but it can also mean crisp tortillas stacked with a rich meaty filling and baked until crisp. Eat these with a knife and fork.

∩

1. Preheat oven to 350°F. In heavy skillet, cook pork sausage with onion and jalapeño pepper until pork is thoroughly cooked; drain well. Add red bell pepper, Colorado Sauce, and refried beans; mix well and remove from heat.

2. Heat oil in heavy skillet to 375°F. Fry corn tortillas, one at a time, until crisp, about 3 minutes apiece; drain on paper or kitchen towels. On 2 large baking sheets, place 6 crisp tortillas, 3 per sheet. Spread with half of the pork sausage mixture and top with some Taco Sauce and half the cheese. Repeat layers, making stacks three tortillas high, ending with a tortilla. Spread the top with some Taco Sauce and sprinkle with remaining cheese.

3. Bake tortas at 350°F for 15–20 minutes or until cheese is melted and stacks are thoroughly heated. Serve with a selection of fresh salsas and sour cream.

Serves 6

1 pound spicy pork sausage
1 onion, chopped
1 jalapeño pepper, minced
1 red bell pepper, chopped
½ cup Colorado Sauce (page 101)
1 (16-ounce) can refried beans
1 cup vegetable oil
18 corn tortillas
½ cup Taco Sauce (page 101)
2 cups shredded Cheddar cheese

Pork Fajitas

Serves 4–6

4 boneless pork chops
1 tablespoon Taco Seasoning
    Mix (page 93)
1 teaspoon salt
⅛ teaspoon cayenne pepper
2 tablespoons vegetable oil
1 onion, sliced
2 green bell peppers, sliced
1 cup shredded Cheddar
    cheese
6 (10") flour tortillas
½ cup Cilantro Pesto
    (page 90)

*Instead of being slowly cooked, the pork in this simple recipe is stir-fried,
so the fajitas are ready to eat in about 30 minutes.*

1. Cut pork chops into thin strips and place in medium bowl. Sprinkle with Taco Seasoning Mix, salt, and cayenne pepper; let stand for 15 minutes.

2. In heavy skillet, heat vegetable oil over medium heat. Stir-fry pork strips for 4–6 minutes until pork is cooked; remove from pan. Add onion and bell peppers; stir-fry until crisp-tender, about 4 minutes. Return pork to pan and remove from heat.

3. Fill the tortillas with the pork mixture, Cheddar cheese, and Cilantro Pesto and serve.

Chorizo

Makes 1 pound

1 pound ground pork butt
1 tablespoon red chile
    powder
1 teaspoon chile paste
1 teaspoon salt
¼ teaspoon pepper
½ teaspoon dried oregano
3 cloves garlic, minced
1 teaspoon smoked paprika
½ teaspoon cumin
⅛ teaspoon cayenne pepper
2 tablespoons vinegar

*Making your own chorizo is easy, and you can control
the amount of salt you use. It freezes very well too, for up to 3 months.*

1. Combine all ingredients in medium bowl and mix gently but thoroughly with hands. Cover and refrigerate for 2 days before using.

2. Form into patties and fry until thoroughly cooked, or brown in a skillet, drain, and use as directed in recipes.

Mexican Pizzas

These little pizzas are like tostadas, but they aren't topped with lettuce and tomatoes. Top them with a dollop of Guacamole (page 20) or a drizzle of Jalapeño Pesto (page 96).

∩

1. Preheat oven to 400°F. In heavy skillet, cook pork sausage with onion and garlic until pork is thoroughly cooked, stirring to break up meat. Drain well. Add pinto beans, refried beans, salsa, and Taco Sauce and mix well. Bring to a simmer and cook for 5 minutes.

2. In another heavy skillet, heat vegetable oil until a drop of water sizzles when dropped into the pan (about 350°F). Fry tortillas, turning once, about 2 minutes until crisp. Place tortillas on baking sheets.

3. Divide pork mixture among the fried tortillas and top with cheese. Bake pizzas at 400°F for 10–15 minutes or until cheese melts and begins to brown.

Go Vegetarian

You can make this recipe vegetarian by omitting the pork sausage and using vegetarian refried beans instead of regular. Vegetarian refried beans are fried in vegetable oil instead of lard.

Serves 6

1 pound spicy pork sausage
1 onion, chopped
3 cloves garlic, minced
1 (15-ounce) can pinto beans, drained
1 (16-ounce) can refried beans
1 cup chunky salsa
½ cup Taco Sauce (page 101)
¼ cup vegetable oil
6 flour tortillas
3 cups shredded Cheddar cheese

BBQ Pork Loin

Thinly carve the cooked loin and serve with additional BBQ Sauce, heated, on the side, along with warm Corn Tortillas (page 115), and Pico de Gallo (page 91).

1. Preheat oven to 350°F. Sprinkle roast with salt and cayenne pepper and place into roasting pan. Roast at 350°F for 1 hour.

2. Spoon BBQ Sauce over pork and roast for another hour, spooning sauce over meat occasionally. Remove from oven, cover, and let stand for 10 minutes before slicing.

Crockpot BBQ Shredded Pork

You can use any tomato-based sauce as a substitute for the Taco Sauce and Crockpot BBQ Sauce in this easy recipe.

Serves 6

1 onion, chopped
4 cloves garlic, minced
2 chipotle chiles in adobo
    sauce, minced
1 cup Taco Sauce (page 101)
½ cup Crockpot BBQ Sauce
    (page 102)
1 tablespoon chili powder
2-pound boneless pork loin
    roast
1 teaspoon salt
⅛ teaspoon cayenne pepper

1. In a 4- to 5-quart crockpot, combine all ingredients. Cover and cook on low for 8–10 hours or until pork is very tender.

2. Remove pork and shred with 2 forks; return to crockpot and cook on high for another 30 minutes. Serve over rice, or with warmed corn or flour tortillas and guacamole.

Make-Ahead Tip

This shredded pork mixture freezes very well. Cool it completely, then pack into hard-sided freezer containers, label well, cover, and freeze up to 3 months. To thaw, let stand in the refrigerator overnight, and then reheat in saucepan over low heat, stirring gently, until hot.

Tex-Mex Pork Kabobs

You can use metal or wood skewers to make these easy kabobs. If you choose wood, soak the skewers in water for 30 minutes before use so they don't burn on the grill.

∩

1. Cut tenderloin into 1" cubes and place in zip-lock bag. Sprinkle Three-Chile Rub, lime juice, and oil into bag; seal, and massage to work marinade into pork. Refrigerate for 4–6 hours.

2. Prepare and preheat grill. Thread pork cubes onto metal skewers, alternating with onion wedges, bell pepper slices, squash slices, and whole mushrooms. Grill over medium coals for 8–12 minutes until meat is thoroughly cooked, basting once during cooking with Colorado Sauce or purchased taco sauce. Or you can broil the kabobs for 8–12 minutes, 4–6" from heat source, turning once.

3. In small bowl, combine sour cream and Salsa Verde; serve with kabobs.

About Pork Loin

Pork loin is a wonderfully flavored cut of meat and is very tender. You can also grill the roast for about 1½ hours over medium coals, until internal temperature registers 160°F, basting with sauce only during the last half-hour of cooking time.

Serves 4

1½-pound pork tenderloin
2 tablespoons Three-Chile Rub (page 93)
1 tablespoon lime juice
1 tablespoon oil
1 sweet onion, cut into wedges
1 red bell pepper, sliced
1 yellow squash, sliced
12 button mushrooms
½ cup Colorado Sauce (page 101)
1 cup sour cream
½ cup Salsa Verde (page 92)

Pork Adobo

Serves 8

2-pound boneless pork
    shoulder roast
¼ cup apple cider vinegar
¼ cup soy sauce
¼ cup adobo sauce
½ cup tomato sauce
1 cup water
1 onion, chopped
3 garlic cloves, minced
1 jalapeño pepper, minced
¼ teaspoon crushed red
    pepper flakes
3 chipotle chiles in adobo
    sauce, minced
3 tablespoons olive oil
3 cups cooked Texmati rice

*In this hearty main dish recipe, pork is first simmered until tender, then sautéed
to add some crisp edges and caramelization, similar to Carnitas (page 186).*

1. Trim excess fat from pork and cut into 2" cubes. Combine in large bowl
   with vinegar, soy sauce, adobo sauce, and tomato sauce, and refrigerate overnight.

2. The next day, pour pork and marinade into heavy saucepan and add
   water, onion, garlic, jalapeño pepper, red pepper flakes, and chipotle
   chiles; bring to a boil. Reduce heat, cover, and simmer pork for 35–45
   minutes until pork and onions are very tender.

3. In heavy skillet, heat olive oil over medium heat. With a slotted spoon
   or strainer, remove pork from adobo sauce and add to pan. Cook until
   cubes are brown, about 10 minutes, stirring frequently. Add sauce to
   skillet with pork and bring to a simmer. Serve immediately with hot
   cooked rice.

Texmati and Basmati Rice

*Texmati rice is a long-grain rice grown in Texas that is a variety of the
Basmati rice used in Indian cooking. It has a tender texture and smells
like popcorn when it's cooking. Let it stand, covered, for 5 minutes after
it has finished cooking so the grains will be separate and fluffy.*

Chorizo Enchiladas

*Substitute any flavorful pork sausage for the Chorizo if you'd like.
If you can't find queso enchilada, substitute Monterey jack cheese along with 1
teaspoon ground red chile powder.*

∩

Serves 8

1 pound Chorizo (page 194)
1 onion, chopped
3 cloves garlic, minced
1 green bell pepper, chopped
1 jalapeño pepper, minced
1 cup Salsa Verde (page 92)
1 (8-ounce) package cream
  cheese
2 cups purchased enchilada
  sauce
12 flour tortillas
1½ cups shredded queso
  enchilada
1 cup shredded Monterey jack
  cheese

1. Preheat oven to 350°F. In heavy skillet over medium heat, cook Chorizo with onion and garlic until meat is thoroughly cooked. Drain well, then add bell pepper and jalapeño to skillet along with Salsa Verde. Bring to a simmer; add cream cheese and stir until melted.

2. Heat ½ cup enchilada sauce in small saucepan. Place a tortilla on work surface and spread thinly with enchilada sauce. Fill with pork mixture, top with some cheese, and roll up. Place in 13" x 9" glass baking dish. Continue with remaining tortillas, filling, and cheese.

3. When all tortillas are filled, pour remaining enchilada sauce over tortillas in casserole and top with Monterey jack cheese. Bake at 350°F for 30–35 minutes or until sauce is bubbling and cheese is melted.

Enchilada-Making Tip

Most Mexican and Tex-Mex enchiladas are made by dipping tortillas briefly in hot oil and then dipping into enchilada sauce before stuffing and rolling. Spreading the tortillas with a thin amount of warm sauce accomplishes the same thing and is much less messy.

Pork con Queso

Serves 4–6

1 pasilla chile
2 pounds pork tenderloin
2 tablespoons chili powder
1 teaspoon cumin
1 teaspoon salt
1 tablespoon butter
1 tablespoon vegetable oil
1 onion, chopped
3 cloves garlic, minced
1 jalapeño pepper, minced
1 (14-ounce) can tomatoes,
    undrained
¼ cup water
½ pound pasteurized
    processed cheese spread
1 cup sour cream

This rich dish could be served as an appetizer at an open house, or serve it over Green Rice (page 78) or plain Texmati rice cooked with an onion.

1. Cover pasilla chile with boiling water and let stand for 30 minutes. Puree in food processor with ¼ cup soaking water, strain, and set aside. Cut tenderloin into 1" cubes and toss with chili powder, cumin, and salt. In heavy skillet over medium heat, melt butter with oil and sauté pork, stirring frequently, until browned, about 4–5 minutes. Remove from skillet and set aside.

2. In drippings remaining in skillet, cook onion and garlic until crisp-tender, 4–5 minutes. Add jalapeño pepper, tomatoes, water, and pasilla chile puree and mix well. Add pork and bring to a simmer. Simmer over medium heat for 15–20 minutes or until pork is thoroughly cooked.

3. Cut cheese spread into cubes and add to pork mixture along with sour cream. Cook over medium heat until cheese melts and sauce is smooth, stirring occasionally; do not boil.

Chapter Twelve

Sandwiches

Texas Toast Grilled Sandwiches

Serves 4

¼ cup butter, softened
1 tablespoon chili powder
¼ teaspoon ground cumin
8 slices ½" thick bread
4 slices Muenster cheese
1 avocado, thinly sliced
8 slices tomato
¾ cup queso blanco, crumbled

This new take on grilled cheese sandwiches is really delicious.
Make sure that you soften the butter well so it spreads easily.
Use your favorite cheeses in this easy recipe.

1. In small bowl, combine butter, chili powder, and cumin and mix well. Spread on one side of each piece of bread. Make sandwiches with bread and remaining ingredients, placing cheese, avocado, and tomato on unbuttered sides of bread.

2. Grill sandwiches on griddle or in large skillet over medium heat, turning once, until cheese is melted and bread is golden brown, about 3 minutes on each side. Cover sandwiches while they are cooking to help the cheese melt. Or cook on a dual-contact indoor grill until bread is toasted and cheese melts, about 3–4 minutes.

Double-Bean Wrap Sandwiches

Serves 6–8

1 (15-ounce) can refried beans
1 (15-ounce) can black beans, rinsed
2 tomatoes, seeded and chopped
½ cup chopped jicama
1 yellow bell pepper, thinly sliced
1 cup shredded pepper jack cheese
1 avocado, peeled
½ cup sour cream
1 tablespoon lime juice
¼ cup chunky salsa
8 (8") flour tortillas

Two kinds of beans add special richness to these easy wrap sandwiches.
Serve them with a fresh fruit salad and some sparkling water
or orange juice for a delicious and nutritious lunch.

1. In medium bowl, place refried beans and mix until softened. Add black beans and tomatoes and mix gently.

2. Prepare jicama, yellow pepper, and cheese and set aside. In small bowl, place avocado and mash, leaving some pieces for a chunky texture. Add sour cream, lime juice, and salsa, and mix well until blended.

3. Place tortillas on work surface and spread with bean mixture. Top with vegetables and shredded cheese, then top with avocado mixture. Roll up tortillas, folding in ends, and serve.

Pimento Cheese Quesadillas

Traditional Southern pimento cheese is dressed up with a bit of spice for a Tex-Mex variation. Spread this delicious cheese mixture on tortillas and simply roll up, or use it as a sandwich spread.

∩

1. Drain pimentos and chop coarsely. In medium bowl, combine cream cheese and mayonnaise and beat until smooth and fluffy. Add pimentos, Cheddar cheese, Worcestershire sauce, jalapeño pepper, chili powder, and cayenne pepper and mix by hand until blended.

2. Spread a thin layer of butter on one side of each tortilla. Make sandwiches, buttered side outside, with the tortillas and pimento cheese mixture. Cook, uncovered, on griddle or skillet over medium heat until tortillas are toasted and cheese mixture melts, 3–4 minutes per side, turning once. (Or cook on dual-contact grill for 3–4 minutes until cheese melts.)

3. Let stand for 3–4 minutes before slicing into wedges and serving.

About Pimentos

Pimentos are large sweet red bell peppers that have been roasted and skinned. They add a sweet and smoky flavor to any recipe. You can buy them whole, sliced, or chopped in cans or bottles on the condiment aisle of the grocery market.

Serves 6

1 (7-ounce) jar pimentos, drained
1 (3-ounce) package cream cheese, softened
⅓ cup mayonnaise
2 cups shredded Cheddar cheese
1 teaspoon Worcestershire sauce
1 jalapeño pepper, minced
2 teaspoons chili powder
⅛ teaspoon cayenne pepper
3 tablespoons butter
12 flour tortillas

Cheese Quesadillas

Any combination of cheese can be used in this super-easy recipe.
Use jalapeño chiles or even canned chopped green chiles for a milder taste;
they can be omitted from the recipe if you're serving kids.

1. In medium bowl, toss together cheeses, chili powder, and serrano chile until well mixed.

2. Make sandwiches using cheese mixture and tortillas. Butter the outside of each sandwich. Heat griddle or skillet over medium high heat and cook quesadillas, turning once, about 3–4 minutes per side until tortillas are toasted and cheese mixture is melted. Let stand for 3–4 minutes before cutting into wedges.

Gordita Sandwiches

You can substitute chopped roast beef from the deli
for the Beef Brisket in this delicious sandwich recipe,
or use pita breads or corn tortillas instead of the Gorditas.

1. In medium bowl, combine beef, peppers, green onions, salsa, and cheese and blend well.

2. Spread refried beans evenly inside each Gordita bread and top with salad mix. Tuck beef mixture into each bread and serve.

Tex-Mex Burgers

These burgers could also be served in warmed flour tortillas with salsa,
sour cream, and guacamole, if you shape them into ovals instead of rounds.

∩

Serves 6

2 Anaheim chiles
1½ pounds ground beef
½ cup tortilla chip crumbs
¼ cup chopped sweet onion
¼ teaspoon cayenne pepper
6 slices pepper jack cheese
6 toasted whole wheat
    hamburger buns
1 cup salsa
½ cup sour cream

1. Broil Anaheim chiles 4–6" from heat, turning frequently, until charred all over. Place in paper bag and let steam for 10 minutes. Remove skin using paper towel or kitchen towel. Chop one of the peppers and slice the other.

2. In large bowl, combine chopped pepper, ground beef, tortilla chip crumbs, onion, and cayenne pepper; mix gently but thoroughly. Form into 6 hamburgers.

3. Grill hamburgers for 10–14 minutes, turning once, until meat is thoroughly cooked and instant-read thermometer registers 165°F. Top with pepper jack cheese and a few pepper slices, cover grill, and heat for 2–3 minutes to melt cheese. Serve on toasted buns with salsa and sour cream.

Ingredient Substitution

Just about any burger recipe can be made with ground turkey. There are two kinds of ground turkey: regular, which contains dark and white meat, and ground turkey breast, which is just white meat. Use regular for most burgers because it has a bit more fat and the burgers will be moister.

Soft and Crunchy Tacos

Serves 8

1 pound ground beef
1 onion, chopped
2 cloves garlic, minced
1 serrano pepper, minced
1 tablespoon chili powder
½ teaspoon cumin
½ teaspoon salt
⅛ teaspoon cayenne pepper
1 (8-ounce) can tomato sauce
¼ cup salsa
8 (8") flour tortillas
8 crisp corn taco shells
1 (16-ounce) can refried
    beans
2 cups shredded Cheddar
    cheese
4 tomatoes, seeded and
    chopped
1 cup sour cream
1 cup chunky salsa
2 cups shredded lettuce
1 avocado, chopped

This is a real American take on classic tacos.
A soft flour tortilla is spread with refried beans, then wrapped around a crisp
corn taco shell filled with seasoned beef and cheese.

1. Preheat oven to 325°F. In heavy skillet, cook ground beef with onion and garlic until ground beef is browned, stirring to break up meat. Drain well, then add serrano pepper, chili powder, cumin, salt, cayenne pepper, tomato sauce, and salsa. Cook over medium heat for 7–8 minutes, stirring frequently, until flavors are blended.

2. Meanwhile, wrap flour tortillas in heavy-duty foil and place on baking sheet. Place taco shells on baking sheet. Heat both at 325°F for 8–10 minutes until taco shells are hot and crisp and flour tortillas are warm and soft. Heat refried beans in medium saucepan over medium low heat, stirring frequently.

3. Unwrap flour tortillas and spread with refried beans. Wrap each one around a heated taco shell and fill with ground beef mixture, cheese, and tomatoes. Serve with sour cream, salsa, shredded lettuce, and chopped avocados.

Serving Suggestion

Set out a buffet and let your guests assemble their own soft and crisp tacos. Keep the flour tortillas covered in a bread or tortilla warmer. Set the refried beans and ground beef filling on warmers or keep them warm in crockpots or in chafing dishes.

Refried Bean Burgers

Refried beans add their rich smooth taste and texture to hamburgers cooked on the grill. This recipe takes a little bit of organization; read it through a few times before you begin.

∩

Serves 8

½ cup minced onion
½ cup tortilla chips crumbs
1 tablespoon Taco Seasoning Mix (page 93)
3 tablespoons adobo sauce
1 (16-ounce) can refried beans
2 pounds lean ground beef
8 whole wheat hamburger buns
½ cup purchased taco sauce
16 slices American cheese

1. In large bowl, combine onion, tortilla chip crumbs, Taco Seasoning Mix, adobo sauce, and half of the refried beans; mix well. Add ground beef; mix gently with your hands until blended. Form into 8 hamburger patties and refrigerate.

2. Prepare and preheat grill, using mesquite or apple wood chips if you'd like. Cut hamburger buns in half and toast, cut side down, on grill until crisp. Remove from grill. Add hamburgers to grill, cover, and cook for 5 minutes on first side.

3. Meanwhile, combine remaining refried beans and taco sauce in an ovenproof saucepan; place on grill and heat. Turn hamburgers and cover again. Place 1 slice of cheese on each hamburger bun half; place cheese side up on grill to melt. Remove hamburgers when internal temperature reaches 165°F, about 5 minutes longer.

4. Assemble hamburgers by spreading heated refried bean mixture onto each cheese-topped hamburger bun half; top with cooked hamburgers and second half of bun. Serve immediately.

Burger Tips

All ground meat recipes must be cooked until well done—that is, 165°F on an instant-read thermometer. For moist and tender burgers, handle the meat as little as possible and don't press down on the burgers while they are cooking.

Mexicali Tuna Melts

Serves 4

4 slices Texas Toast (page 109)
1 (12-ounce) can chunk tuna,
    drained
⅓ cup sour cream
⅓ cup Picante Sauce
    (page 100)
2 green onions, chopped
½ cup shredded Monterey
    jack cheese
4 slices pepper jack cheese

*This easy and delicious recipe can be made with canned chicken or shrimp
if you'd like. Serve with some fresh fruit and iced tea.*

1. Prepare Texas Toast. In medium bowl, combine tuna, sour cream,
   Picante Sauce, green onions, shredded cheese, and jalapeño pepper and mix well. Spread on Texas Toast and top with pepper jack
   cheese slices.

2. Broil 4–6" from heat source for 3–5 minutes until cheese melts and
   begins to brown. Serve immediately.

Tex-Mex Veggie Wraps

Yields 6

1 (15-ounce) can pinto beans,
    drained
1 red bell pepper, thinly sliced
1 yellow bell pepper, thinly
    sliced
1 jalapeño pepper, minced
4 green onions, chopped
¾ cup Nacho Cheese Sauce
    (page 99)
6 lettuce leaves
6 (10") spinach flour tortillas

*The fresh filling in these wraps is very good for you. Colorful bell peppers
contain a lot of vitamins A and C, and pinto beans are high in protein and fiber.*

1. In medium bowl, combine drained pinto beans, bell peppers, jalapeño
   peppers, and green onions; mix well. Spread 2 tablespoons Nacho
   Cheese Sauce on each flour tortilla, then top with lettuce and bell pepper mixture.

2. Roll up and serve immediately.

Packing the Lunch Box

*Most wrap sandwiches should be served right away so the tortillas don't
get soggy. For lunchboxes, put filling in a plastic container and let your
kids roll their own. Or spread tortillas with a thin layer of butter and top
with lettuce so the filling is enclosed; pack into insulated lunch boxes.*

Spicy Turkey Burgers

Add a few crisp lettuce leaves and some thinly sliced
red ripe tomatoes to these easy burgers if you'd like.

Ω

1. Prepare and heat grill. In large bowl, combine crushed chips, egg, chipotle chile, adobo sauce, salt, and pepper and mix well. Add turkey and mix gently with hands. Form into 4 patties.

2. In small bowl, combine salsa, mayonnaise, and cumin and mix well. Cook hamburgers, covered, over medium coals for five minutes. Meanwhile, cut hamburger buns in half and spread cut sides with butter. Turn hamburgers, cover grill, and cook for 3 minutes longer.

3. Uncover, place cheese on burgers, and add hamburger buns to the grill, cut side down. Cook until buns are toasted and hamburgers are thoroughly cooked, about 2 minutes longer. Serve with salsa mixture on hamburger buns.

What Is Indirect Grilling?

For indirect grilling, set up your grill so briquettes are on each side of an empty space in the middle. Place a drip pan in the empty space, then light the grill. Cook the food centered over the drip pan. Every 45 minutes, add a few briquettes to each side of the pan to maintain an even heat.

Serves 4

½ cup crushed nacho cheese
    tortilla chips
1 egg, beaten
1 chipotle chile in adobo
    sauce, minced
1 tablespoon adobo sauce
½ teaspoon salt
⅛ teaspoon pepper
1 pound ground turkey
¼ cup salsa
¼ cup mayonnaise
¼ teaspoon cumin
4 whole wheat hamburger
    buns
2 tablespoons butter
4 slices American cheese

Tex-Mex Grilled Cheese

These quick and easy sandwiches are nice for lunch on a busy day.
Serve them with apple and pear slices and a root beer float.

∩

Serves 4

8 slices whole wheat bread
¼ cup butter
4 slices American cheese
¼ cup salsa
2 pickled jalapeños, sliced
4 slices pepper jack cheese

1. Place bread on work surface. Spread one side of each piece with butter. Turn bread slices over. Place American cheese on half of the slices. Top with salsa and pickled jalapeño slices. Cover salsa with pepper jack cheese. Top with other half of bread slices, buttered side up.

2. Cook sandwiches for 4–5 minutes on each side on heated griddle, turning once, or in dual-contact grill for 4–5 minutes total until bread is brown and crisp and cheeses are melted.

Ground Beef Tacos

This is an old family recipe that is pure comfort food.
Spice it up if you'd like by adding some minced jalapeño or
serrano peppers to the beef filling—or a habanero if you're really brave!

∩

Serves 4–6

1 pound ground beef
1 onion, chopped
2 cloves garlic, minced
1 (4-ounce) can diced chiles,
   drained
1 (8-ounce) can tomato sauce
2 tablespoons chili powder
½ cup salsa
1 (16-ounce) can refried
   beans
2 cups shredded Colby cheese
8 taco shells
½ cup sour cream
1 cup Guacamole (page 20)

1. In heavy skillet over medium heat, cook ground beef with onion and garlic until beef is browned, stirring to break up beef. Drain well. Add chiles, tomato sauce, chili powder, and salsa; bring to a simmer, then simmer for 10 minutes, stirring frequently.

2. Meanwhile, heat refried beans in medium saucepan over medium low heat, stirring frequently. Heat taco shells as directed on package. Let family members and guests make their own tacos, offering the ground beef mixture, refried beans, cheese, sour cream, and Guacamole.

Chicken Avocado Sandwiches

Letting meat sit, covered, for a few minutes after cooking allows the juices to redistribute inside the flesh, so the juice doesn't run out when you cut into the meat.

∩

1. Place chicken breasts between pieces of waxed paper and flatten slightly with rolling pin. In small bowl, combine adobo sauce, chili powder, salt, and cayenne pepper; rub over both sides of chicken breasts. Heat dual-contact grill; cook chicken, one at a time, for 4–5 minutes or until thoroughly cooked. Cover and set aside.

2. Peel avocados; slice one thinly, sprinkle with half of lime juice, and set aside. Mash second avocado with remaining lime juice and mayonnaise. Toast bread and top half of bread with cheese. Spread mayonnaise mixture on one side of remaining bread slices. Slice chicken breasts into thin strips and add to sandwich; top with sliced avocados and remaining toast; serve immediately.

Serves 4

4 boneless, skinless chicken breasts
1 tablespoon adobo sauce
1 tablespoon chili powder
½ teaspoon salt
⅛ teaspoon cayenne pepper
2 avocados
2 tablespoons lime juice
¼ cup mayonnaise
8 slices whole wheat bread, toasted
4 slices Monterey jack cheese

Tex-Mex BLT

If you chop the lettuce and tomato and crumble the bacon, you could make BLT wrap sandwiches by combining all the sandwich filling ingredients and rolling it up in a warmed flour tortilla.

∩

1. In heavy skillet, cook bacon until crisp; drain on paper towels. Pour off almost all of the bacon fat; cook onion in remaining fat until tender. Remove from heat and place into small bowl. Add mayonnaise, taco sauce, jalapeño pepper, and lime juice to onion. Peel and chop avocado and add to mayonnaise mixture; mix well with fork, mashing avocado, until blended.

2. Toast bread and spread one side of each slice with butter. Make sandwiches using the toast, avocado spread, crisp bacon, lettuce, and tomato slices. Serve immediately.

Serves 4

8 slices bacon
½ cup minced onion
⅓ cup mayonnaise
2 tablespoons taco sauce
1 jalapeño pepper, minced
1 tablespoon lime juice
1 avocado
4 pieces romaine lettuce
4 thick slices tomato
8 slices whole wheat bread
2 tablespoons butter

Crockpot BBQ Beef Sandwiches

This hearty sandwich filling is great for a winter party.
Let the mixture cook all day and your home will smell wonderful;
plus, the filling for the sandwiches is ready whenever you are.

Serves 8

2-pound beef chuck roast,
    trimmed
1 cup beef broth
¼ cup adobo sauce
1 onion, chopped
1 teaspoon salt
⅛ teaspoon pepper
4 cloves garlic, minced
2 tablespoons chili powder
1 teaspoon cumin
⅓ cup ketchup
1 (8-ounce) can tomato sauce
2 avocados
2 tablespoons lime juice
1 jalapeño pepper, minced
2 tomatoes, seeded and
    chopped
8 (10") flour tortillas or
    Bolillos (page 122)

1. Place beef, broth, adobo sauce, and onion in 4-quart crockpot. Cover and cook on low for 7–9 hours or until beef is very tender. Remove beef from crockpot and shred. Return to crockpot along with salt, pepper, garlic, chili powder, cumin, ketchup, and tomato sauce. Cover and cook on low for 1–2 hours longer.

2. Peel and dice avocados; sprinkle with lime juice. Place in small bowl along with jalapeño pepper and tomatoes; mix gently. Make sandwiches with tomato mixture, shredded beef mixture, and tortillas or Bolillos.

Shredding Beef

It's very easy to shred beef. Remove the beef from the liquid it cooks in and let stand for a few minutes on a large platter. Using 2 forks, pull the meat apart into long strands, returning the shredded meat to the cooking liquid as you work.

Chicken Quesadillas

These crisp little sandwiches should be served immediately, so make serving them an occasion. Bring an electric griddle to the table and make the sandwiches in front of your guests. Serve with Pico de Gallo (page 91).

∩

1. Cut chicken breasts into ½" cubes. Sprinkle with chili powder, salt, and pepper and toss to coat. In heavy skillet, heat vegetable oil and add chicken cubes. Cook and stir until chicken is thoroughly cooked, about 4–7 minutes, stirring frequently. Remove chicken from skillet.

2. In medium bowl, combine Muenster cheese, Cheddar cheese, and jalapeño peppers. Make sandwiches using flour tortillas, cheese mixture, and cooked chicken. Cook, one at a time, on heated griddle, turning once, until tortillas are crisp and cheese is melted, about 4-6 minutes. Cut into quarters and serve immediately.

Serves 4–6

2 boneless, skinless chicken breasts
1 tablespoon chili powder
½ teaspoon salt
⅛ teaspoon pepper
1 tablespoon vegetable oil
1½ cups shredded Muenster cheese
½ cup shredded Cheddar cheese
2 jalapeño peppers, minced
8 (10") flour tortillas

Tex-Mex Egg Salad Sandwiches

*Substitute any hard rolls or crusty buns for the Bolillos in this recipe.
Or place the egg salad between 2 slices of whole wheat bread,
or wrap up in corn or flour tortillas.*

∩

1. Place eggs in a heavy saucepan and cover with cold water. Bring to a rolling boil over high heat, then cover pan, remove from heat, and let stand for 15 minutes. Place pan in sink and run cold water into pan until eggs are cool. Crack eggs slightly against the side of the pan and let sit another 5 minutes in the cold water. Peel eggs and coarsely chop.

2. In medium bowl, combine eggs with bell pepper, jalapeño, green onion, sour cream, mayonnaise, salt, cayenne pepper, and cilantro; mix gently. Spread butter on cut side of Bolillos and make sandwiches with egg salad filling.

Serves 4

6 eggs
¼ cup minced red bell pepper
2 jalapeño peppers, minced
¼ cup chopped green onion
½ cup sour cream
¼ cup mayonnaise
½ teaspoon salt
¼ teaspoon cayenne pepper
2 tablespoons chopped cilantro
2 tablespoons butter, softened
4 Bolillos (page 122), cut in half

Tex-Mex Steak Sandwiches

Serves 6

1 pound flank steak
1 tablespoon Taco Seasoning
    Mix (page 93)
½ teaspoon cumin
1 teaspoon salt
⅛ teaspoon cayenne pepper
2 tablespoons adobo sauce
1 tablespoon vegetable oil
1 onion, finely chopped
3 cloves garlic, minced
1 jalapeño pepper, minced
¼ cup taco sauce
1 avocado
1 tablespoon lime juice
6 slices Muenster cheese
6 Bolillos (page 122), split

*Flank steak is a fairly tough cut of meat, but it has a lot of flavor.
By marinating it and then slicing thinly across the grain after it's cooked,
it becomes meltingly tender, perfect for these elegant little sandwiches.*

1. Place flank steak in a large zip-lock bag. Combine Taco Seasoning Mix, cumin, salt, cayenne pepper, and adobo sauce in small bowl; rub into steak. Seal bag and refrigerate at least 8 hours or overnight.

2. When ready to eat, heat vegetable oil in medium skillet and cook onion, garlic, and jalapeño pepper until tender; remove to small bowl. Add taco sauce and mix well; set aside. Peel and slice avocado; sprinkle with lime juice.

3. Heat dual-contact indoor grill. Grill flank steak for 4–6 minutes until desired doneness. Remove from grill, cover, and let stand for 10 minutes. Thinly slice steak across the grain, and make sandwiches with the split Bolillos, steak slices, taco sauce mixture, cheese, and avocado.

Steak Doneness Tests

All steaks should be cooked to at least 145°F, or medium rare. Medium steaks are done when temperature reaches 160°F, and well-done steaks are 170°F. You can also test doneness by pressing the steaks. A rare steak feels soft, while medium steaks have a springy give to them and well-done steaks feel firm.

Monte Cristo Sandwiches

*Monte Cristo sandwiches are usually deep-fried; this version is browned
in butter, then baked for a lower fat content with the same crunch.*

∩

1. Preheat oven to 425°F. In shallow bowl, combine eggs, cream, and chili powder; beat well. Make sandwiches using bread, layering pepper jack cheese, 1 or 2 strips of chile, a slice of chicken, and American cheese. Dip sandwiches into egg mixture, turning once to coat.

2. Heat butter in heavy skillet over medium heat. Brown sandwiches on both sides in skillet, then place on baking sheet. When all sandwiches are browned, bake at 425°F for 12–15 minutes or until sandwiches are golden brown and cheese is melted. In small bowl, combine sour cream and salsa; serve with sandwiches for dipping.

Ingredient Substitutions

Use thin slices of boiled ham, or cooked turkey breast, smoked turkey breast, or even slices of roast beef in these delicious sandwiches. Or use different cheese combinations: Muenster and Cheddar would be nice, as well as Colby and Monterey jack.

Serves 6

3 eggs, beaten
⅓ cup cream
1 tablespoon chili powder
12 slices cracked wheat bread
6 slices pepper jack cheese
1 (4-ounce) can whole green
    chiles, drained
6 thin slices cooked chicken
    breast
6 slices American cheese
¼ cup butter
½ cup sour cream
½ cup salsa

Spicy Salmon Wraps

Serves 6

1 (3-ounce) package cream
    cheese, softened
⅓ cup sour cream
1 (15-ounce) can red sockeye
    salmon
⅓ cup salsa
1 serrano pepper, minced
½ teaspoon dried oregano
    leaves
¼ cup minced green onion
1 green bell pepper, chopped
6 leaves lettuce
6 (8") flour tortillas

*You could substitute 1 cooked salmon steak for the canned salmon
if you'd like, or 1 (12-ounce) can of chunk tuna. Choose a variety of
colored tortillas for these easy and delicious sandwiches.*

1. In medium bowl, beat cream cheese until softened and stir in sour cream. Drain canned salmon and remove skin and bones. Flake salmon into the sour cream mixture and combine with remaining ingredients except lettuce and tortillas.

2. Place lettuce on each tortilla, top with filling, and roll up tortillas. Serve immediately.

Recipe Additions

Add cheese to this recipe for even more flavor. Good choices include pepper jack, Monterey jack, Colby, longhorn, or Muenster cheese. To make it easier to shred the softer cheeses, place them in the freezer for 15 minutes to firm, then shred immediately.

Chapter Thirteen

Vegetarian

Calcabacita

*Calcabacita is Mexican succotash—a combination of squash
(or in this case zucchini) and corn. Ginger is the surprise ingredient here; it adds
a wonderfully crisp flavor to this smooth and mellow vegetarian main dish.*

Serves 6

2 tablespoons olive oil
1 onion, chopped
3 cloves garlic, minced
2 zucchini, sliced thin
2 tomatoes, peeled and
   chopped
2 cups frozen corn
¼ teaspoon ground ginger
½ teaspoon salt
⅛ teaspoon pepper
½ cup vegetable broth

1. Heat oil in heavy skillet over medium heat. Add onion and garlic; cook until crisp-tender, about 3–4 minutes, stirring frequently. Add zucchini and tomatoes; cook and stir for 2–3 minutes.

2. Add frozen corn, ginger, salt, pepper, and vegetable broth and stir well. Cover pan and simmer for 4–6 minutes until mixture is thoroughly heated and flavors are blended. Serve with hot cooked rice.

Chile Cheese Quiche

*If you like your food a bit milder, omit the jalapeño pepper and
use just the chopped green chiles. Serve this delicious quiche with
a fruit salad and some Sweet Tea (page 241).*

Serves 6

9" unbaked pie shell
1 teaspoon chili powder
1 tablespoon cornmeal
1½ cups shredded Monterey
   jack cheese
1 cup shredded Cheddar
   cheese
1 (4-ounce) can chopped
   green chiles, drained
1 jalapeño pepper, minced
1 (3-ounce) package cream
   cheese, softened
1 cup half-and-half
3 eggs
1 tablespoon flour
½ teaspoon salt
⅛ teaspoon cayenne pepper
¼ cup grated Parmesan
   cheese

1. Preheat oven to 325°F. Sprinkle chili powder and cornmeal onto pie crust and press in gently. Sprinkle Monterey jack and Cheddar cheeses into pie shell and top with green chiles and jalapeño pepper.

2. In medium bowl, beat cream cheese until fluffy. Slowly add half-and-half, beating until smooth. Add eggs, flour, salt, and cayenne pepper and mix until blended. Pour slowly into pie shell. Sprinkle with Parmesan cheese and bake at 325°F for 40–50 minutes or until pie is light golden brown, puffed, and set.

Chile Risotto

This rich vegetarian dish is full of flavor and color.
You must use short-grain rice in this recipe since it contains more starch,
which cooks out of the rice and makes the sauce rich and creamy.

∩

Serves 4

1 Anaheim chile
1 onion, chopped
3 cloves garlic, minced
2 tablespoons olive oil
2 tablespoons butter
1 cup Arborio or short-grain
   rice
4 cups vegetable broth
1 tablespoon lime juice
1 tablespoon chili powder
2 tomatoes, seeded and
   chopped
½ cup grated Parmesan
   cheese
1 tablespoon butter

1. Roast the Anaheim chile over a gas flame or under the broiler until skin is blackened. Remove to paper bag and let steam for 10 minutes. Remove the skin with a paper towel; do NOT rinse chile. Remove seeds, chop, and set aside.

2. In heavy skillet, cook onion and garlic in olive oil and 2 tablespoons butter until onion is tender. Add rice; cook and stir for 2–3 minutes until rice is coated with butter mixture. In another saucepan, heat vegetable broth, lime juice, and chili powder until hot; turn off burner.

3. Add vegetable broth mixture, ½ cup at a time, to the rice mixture, cooking and stirring over medium heat. Continue until all the broth is absorbed and the mixture is creamy, about 20-25 minutes total. Add reserved chopped chile, tomatoes, cheese, and butter; cook and stir for 2–3 minutes to melt cheese and butter.

Menu Ideas

Risotto is a classic Italian dish given a Tex-Mex twist with chiles, chili powder, lime juice, and tomatoes. Serve it with some chewy breadsticks or toasted garlic bread, a cool fruit salad dressed with honey and lime juice, and a chocolate ice cream pie for dessert.

Tex-Mex Quiche

Serves 6

9" unbaked pie crust
1 tablespoon cornmeal
1 tablespoon olive oil
1 onion, chopped
3 cloves garlic, chopped
1 (4-ounce) can chopped
    green chilies
1 (15-ounce) can black beans,
    rinsed
1½ cups grated pepper jack
    cheese
2 tablespoons tomato paste
4 eggs
½ cup sour cream
2 tablespoons flour
½ teaspoon dried oregano
    leaves
½ cup grated cotija or
    Parmesan cheese

Black beans, green chiles, tomato paste, and pepper jack cheese add a Tex-Mex twist to this classic quiche. Serve topped with salsa and cold sour cream.

∩

1. Preheat oven to 375°F. Sprinkle cornmeal in bottom of pie crust and press in gently; set aside.

2. In heavy skillet, heat olive oil over medium heat and cook onions and garlic until crisp-tender, 3–4 minutes. Remove vegetables from pan with slotted spoon and place in pie crust. Sprinkle drained green chilies and black beans over vegetables in pie crust. Sprinkle pepper jack cheese over green chilies.

3. In medium bowl, combine tomato paste, eggs, sour cream, flour, and oregano, and beat to mix well. Pour over cheese in pie crust and sprinkle with cotija or Parmesan cheese. Bake at 375°F for 35–40 minutes or until quiche is set and puffed and top is light golden brown.

Tomato Paste Information

You can buy tomato paste in a metal tube with a twist top. That way it's easy to measure out small amounts of this rich ingredient without opening a whole can. It's also easy to freeze leftover tomato paste in spoonfuls; store in a freezer bag for up to 3 months.

Huevos Rancheros

*This hearty dish makes a perfect breakfast when you have
a busy day ahead; it will keep you going for hours!
Serve it with cold orange juice and some fresh fruit.*

Serves 4–6

1 cup Ranchero Sauce
 (page 97)
¼ cup vegetable oil
6 (6") corn tortillas
8 eggs
¼ cup heavy cream
½ teaspoon salt
⅛ teaspoon white pepper
3 green onions, chopped
1 cup vegetarian refried
 beans
1 chipotle chile in adobo
 sauce, minced
2 tablespoons adobo sauce
1½ cups shredded Cheddar
 cheese
1 avocado, peeled and sliced

1. Heat Ranchero Sauce in medium saucepan. Meanwhile, heat vegetable oil over medium heat in large skillet. Fry tortillas, turning once, until crisp, about 1 minute on each side. Remove to paper towels to drain. Drain off all but 1 tablespoon vegetable oil.

2. Beat eggs with cream, salt, and pepper until smooth; add green onion and pour into hot oil. Scramble eggs over medium heat, stirring occasionally, until eggs are cooked through. Meanwhile, combine beans, chipotle chile, and adobo sauce in another small saucepan and warm over medium heat.

3. When ready to eat, spread refried bean mixture over the crisp tortillas. Top with a spoonful of Ranchero Sauce and a generous portion of eggs. Top with more Ranchero Sauce, sprinkle with cheese, and top with avocado; serve immediately.

Egg Safety

This recipe for Huevos Rancheros is made with scrambled eggs for food safety reasons. Scrambled eggs, cooked until set, are safer than eggs fried or poached "easy," with a runny yolk. If you prefer eggs "over easy," use pasteurized eggs.

Quesadillas

Serve these crisp little cheese "sandwiches" with Pico de Gallo (page 91), cold sour cream, and some freshly made Guacamole (page 20).

Serves 4–6

1 cup shredded Cheddar
  cheese
1 cup shredded pepper jack
  cheese
2 oil-packed sun-dried
  tomatoes, drained
1 teaspoon red chile powder
½ teaspoon cumin
⅛ teaspoon cayenne pepper
2 teaspoons chili powder
8 flour tortillas
3 tablespoons vegetable oil

1. In small bowl, combine cheeses and finely chopped sun-dried tomatoes and toss. In small bowl, combine chile powder, cumin, pepper, and chili powder.

2. Place 4 tortillas on work surface. Brush with half of the vegetable oil and sprinkle with some of the chile powder mixture. Divide cheese mixture among tortillas and cover each with another tortilla.

3. Heat remaining vegetable oil in large skillet and cook quesadillas, one at a time, for 3–4 minutes on each side until tortillas are crisp and cheese melts.

Bean Burritos

Refried beans have a wonderful rich texture and a hearty, meaty taste; they add so much to this simple recipe. Serve with a fruit salad and some Orange Fizz (page 241).

Serves 6

2 tablespoons vegetable oil
1 onion, chopped
3 cloves garlic, minced
1 chipotle chile, minced
1 (15-ounce) can kidney
  beans, rinsed
1 (15-ounce) can pinto beans,
  rinsed
½ teaspoon cumin
2 cups Tamale Sauce
  (page 99)
12 corn tortillas
2 cups shredded Cheddar
  cheese

1. Preheat oven to 350°F. In heavy skillet, heat oil and cook onion and garlic over medium heat, stirring frequently, for 3–4 minutes. Add chile, kidney and pinto beans, cumin, and ½ cup Tamale Sauce; mash some of the beans and cook and stir mixture for 3–4 minutes.

2. Place a thin layer of Tamale Sauce in 13" x 9" glass baking dish. Dip each tortilla into more Tamale Sauce, top with ⅓ cup bean filling, roll up, and place in dish. Top with cheese; bake at 350°F for 20–30 minutes or until hot and bubbly.

Spinach Enchiladas

Frozen spinach is a good buy; it takes a lot of spinach to cook down to 10 ounces, and all the work is done for you. Be sure it's well drained before using in this or any recipe.

∩

Serves 6

2 (10-ounce) cans enchilada sauce or 2 cups Enchilada Sauce (page 94)
1 (10-ounce) package frozen spinach
2 tablespoons butter
1 onion, chopped
2 garlic cloves, minced
1 serrano chile, minced
4 green onions, chopped
1 (3-ounce) package cream cheese, softened
1 cup sour cream
2 cups shredded queso enchilada
12 flour tortillas

1. Bring enchilada sauce to a simmer in a small saucepan. Thaw spinach and drain in colander. Press down on the spinach to get rid of liquid. Place spinach in a kitchen towel and press again to dry. Set aside.

2. In heavy skillet, melt butter and add onion, garlic, serrano chile, and green onions. Cook and stir over medium heat for 4–5 minutes until onions are crisp-tender. Stir in drained spinach; cook and stir for 3–4 minutes. Remove from heat and stir in cream cheese and sour cream until cheese melts. Stir in 1 cup queso enchilada.

3. Preheat oven to 350°F. Coat bottom of 13" x 9" glass baking dish with a few spoonfuls of the enchilada sauce. Using tongs, dip each tortilla briefly into the hot enchilada sauce and place on work surface. Top with a spoonful of spinach filling and roll up; place in casserole. Repeat using remaining tortillas, sauce, and filling. Pour remaining enchilada sauce over all and sprinkle with remaining 1 cup cheese.

4. Bake at 350°F for 25–35 minutes until casserole is bubbly and cheese melts.

Veggie Taco Salad

Serves 6–8

2 tablespoons olive oil
1 onion, chopped
3 cloves garlic, minced
1 red bell pepper, chopped
1 yellow squash, chopped
2 jalapeño peppers, minced
1 teaspoon cumin
1 tablespoon chili powder
½ teaspoon Tabasco sauce
1 (14-ounce) can diced
   tomatoes with green
   chiles, undrained
2 (14-ounce) cans pinto
   beans, drained
1 cup diced Cheddar cheese
1 (10-ounce) bag mixed salad
   greens
2 cups slightly crushed tortilla
   chips
1 cup shredded pepper jack
   cheese
1 cup salsa
½ cup sour cream

This salad is a perfect choice for a luncheon or a Saturday lunch for company. The combination of the seasonings with the vegetables is so hearty that you will never miss the meat. Serve with a cold drink and a simple chocolate cake for dessert.

1. In heavy skillet, heat olive oil and add onion and garlic. Cook and stir for 4–5 minutes until crisp-tender. Add red pepper, yellow squash, and jalapeño; cook 2 minutes longer. Add cumin, chili powder, Tabasco sauce, tomatoes, and pinto beans. Simmer mixture, stirring occasionally, for 10 minutes. Remove from heat, sprinkle with Cheddar cheese, and set aside while preparing rest of salad.

2. Place salad greens and crushed tortilla chips on serving plates and top with vegetable mixture. Sprinkle with pepper jack cheese, garnish with salsa and sour cream, and serve.

Make-Ahead Tip

You can make the vegetable mixture ahead of time if you'd like. Prepare it up to the addition of the tomatoes and pinto beans, then cool, cover, and store in the refrigerator. Bring the mixture back to a simmer and continue with the recipe.

Mixed-Bean Lasagna

This lasagna is spectacular, and it's perfect for entertaining.
Serve it with Margarita Fruit Salad (page 49) or
Fruit and Avocado Salad (page 56) for a cooling complement.

∩

1. Roast Anaheim chile under broiler or over a gas flame until skin is blackened. Place in paper bag and let steam for 10 minutes. Remove skin and seeds, chop chile, and set aside.

2. In heavy skillet, heat vegetable oil and cook onion and garlic over medium heat until crisp-tender. Add diced tomatoes, tomato sauce, tomato paste, chili powder, oregano, salt, pepper, and chopped Anaheim chile. Bring to a simmer, cover pan, and cook for 10–12 minutes until flavors are blended.

3. Preheat oven to 375°F and spray a 13" x 9" glass baking dish with nonstick cooking spray; set aside. In large bowl, combine ricotta, cream cheese, masa harina, eggs, pepper jack cheese, and Cheddar cheese and blend well.

4. In prepared baking dish, place 1 cup of the tomato chile sauce. Cover with 3 uncooked lasagna noodles. Top with one half of the ricotta mixture. Top with 3 more uncooked lasagna noodles and pour more tomato sauce over the noodles. Spread with one half of remaining ricotta mixture and top with rinsed and drained black and pinto beans. Spread remaining ricotta mixture over beans and top with 3 uncooked lasagna noodles. Pour remaining tomato chile sauce over noodles and sprinkle with 2 cups shredded mozzarella cheese, Parmesan cheese, and paprika.

5. Cover casserole tightly with foil and bake at 375°F for 45–50 minutes or until noodles are soft when pierced with fork and casserole is bubbling. Uncover and bake 10–15 minutes longer or until cheese is melted and browned.

Serves 8–10

1 Anaheim chile
1 tablespoon vegetable oil
1 onion, chopped
4 cloves garlic, minced
1 (14-ounce) can diced
   tomatoes with green
   chiles, undrained
1 (8-ounce) can tomato sauce
1 (6-ounce) can tomato paste
1 tablespoon chili powder
½ teaspoon dried oregano
   leaves
½ teaspoon salt
¼ teaspoon pepper
1 cup ricotta cheese
1 (8-ounce) package cream
   cheese, softened
1 tablespoon masa harina
2 eggs, beaten
1 cup shredded pepper jack
   cheese
1 cup shredded Cheddar
   cheese
9 uncooked lasagna noodles
1 (14-ounce) can black beans,
   rinsed
1 (14-ounce) can pinto beans,
   rinsed
2 cups shredded mozzarella
   cheese
½ cup grated Parmesan
   cheese
1 teaspoon paprika

Spicy Filo Burritos

Serves 6

2 tablespoons butter
1 onion, chopped
1 green bell pepper, chopped
3 cloves garlic, minced
2 jalapeño peppers, minced
2 tablespoons Taco
   Seasoning Mix (page 93)
2 tablespoons adobo sauce
⅓ cup water
1 (16-ounce) can pinto beans,
   rinsed
⅓ cup salsa verde
9 sheets filo dough, thawed
⅓ cup melted butter
1 cup shredded Cheddar
   cheese
¼ cup grated Parmesan
   cheese

Filo dough, or Phyllo dough, is a very thin Middle Eastern pastry you can find in your grocer's freezer aisle. Follow the instructions for thawing and use carefully.

1. In heavy skillet over medium heat, melt butter and add onion, bell pepper, garlic, and jalapeño pepper; cook and stir until vegetables are crisp-tender. Stir in Taco Seasoning Mix, adobo sauce, water, and drained pinto beans and mix to blend. Simmer for 5 minutes, then add salsa verde; stir and remove from heat. Let cool for 30 minutes.

2. Preheat oven to 375°F. Place 1 sheet of filo dough on work surface and brush with butter, then top with another filo sheet and brush with butter. Add a third sheet, then cut the stack of sheets in half crosswise. Place a spoonful of the bean filling at one end of the filo stack and top with Cheddar cheese. Roll filling inside filo dough, folding in ends and sealing edges with butter. Repeat with second filo stack. Repeat with remaining filo sheets and butter, making six bundles altogether.

3. Brush bundles with remaining butter and sprinkle with Parmesan cheese. Place bundles on cookie sheet and bake at 375°F for 20–25 minutes or until filling is thoroughly heated, cheese is golden brown, and filo dough is browned and crisp. Serve with sour cream and salsa.

Working with Filo

Filo dough is a delicate pastry that has to be handled very carefully. Keep the sheets of dough covered with a very lightly dampened kitchen towel, and brush sheets with butter immediately after removing from the rest. Don't worry if it tears—just fix it with a patch of dough pasted onto the tear with melted butter.

Veggie Tacos

You could add just about any vegetable to this delicious recipe—for instance, use chopped yellow squash, zucchini, seeded and chopped tomatoes, mushrooms, or broccoli.

∩

1. Preheat oven to 350°F. Heat vegetable oil in heavy skillet over medium heat. Cook onion and garlic until tender. Add bell peppers, jalapeño peppers, textured vegetable protein, and salt; cook and stir for 4–5 minutes until mixture is hot. Add 1 cup Taco Sauce; simmer for 4 minutes.

2. Heat refried beans in small saucepan over low heat, stirring frequently. Heat taco shells in oven as directed on package. Let guests assemble their own tacos using refried beans, bell pepper mixture, Cheddar cheese, Taco Sauce, lettuce, tomatoes, sour cream, and Guacamole.

Textured Vegetable Protein

Textured vegetable protein (TVP) is a vegetarian product made from soy that is found in the frozen foods section of your supermarket. It looks and tastes just like ground beef; substitute it, still frozen, in place of ground beef to just about any recipe and heat thoroughly.

Serves 6

2 tablespoons vegetable oil
2 onions, chopped
4 cloves garlic, minced
1 green bell pepper, chopped
1 red bell pepper, chopped
2 jalapeño peppers, minced
2 cups frozen textured vegetable protein
½ teaspoon salt
1 cup Taco Sauce (page 101)
1 (16-ounce) can vegetarian refried beans
12 crisp taco shells
2 cups shredded Cheddar cheese
1 cup Taco Sauce (page 101)
1 cup shredded lettuce
2 tomatoes, seeded and chopped
1 cup sour cream
1 cup Guacamole (page 20)

Bean Quesadillas

Serves 6

1 (16-ounce) can vegetarian
   refried beans
2 tablespoons chili powder
¼ teaspoon Tabasco sauce
12 (10") flour tortillas
½ cup chopped sweet onion
1 cup shredded Cheddar
   cheese

*This versatile recipe can be served as an appetizer, or a light lunch with a fruit
salad and some Sweet Tea (page 241) or Mango Smoothies (page 245).*

1. In medium saucepan, heat beans, chili powder, and Tabasco sauce, stirring frequently, until hot. Place 6 tortillas on work surface and divide refried bean mixture among them. Sprinkle with onion and Cheddar cheese and top with remaining tortillas.

2. Heat comal or griddle and cook quesadillas, turning once, until crisp and golden brown. Cut into quarters and serve. Serve with Tomatillo Salsa (page 104) or Picante Sauce (page 100).

Spinach Quesadillas

Serves 8–10

1 (10-ounce) package frozen
   spinach
1 tablespoon vegetable oil
1 onion, chopped
2 jalapeño peppers, minced
½ cup Salsa Verde (page 92)
2 cups shredded pepper jack
   cheese
16 corn tortillas

*Serve a selection of quesadillas for lunch or an appetizer buffet;
keep them warm on a warming plate. Be sure to have a selection of fresh
salsas and other condiments ready so your guests can serve themselves.*

1. Thaw spinach and drain well in colander; press between paper or kitchen towels to dry. Heat vegetable oil in heavy skillet; add onion and jalapeños and cook until crisp-tender. Add spinach and stir to break up; cook for 2–3 minutes. Add Salsa Verde and remove from heat; let cool for 20 minutes.

2. Make sandwiches by spreading spinach filling and cheese on tortillas and topping with another tortilla. Cook on comal or griddle until golden brown and crisp, turning once during cooking. Cut into quarters and serve.

Chile Rellenos Casserole

*This easy recipe is a great way to serve Chile Rellenos to a crowd.
Make sure you have bowls of cold sour cream, different salsas,
and guacamole on the table so your guests can garnish as they like.*

∩

1. Grease bottom of 13" x 9" glass baking dish. Cut each green chile in half and place half the strips in a prepared dish. Sprinkle with the pepper jack cheese and sweet onion, and top with remaining green chile strips.

2. In large bowl, beat eggs until very thick and lemon colored. Add half-and-half, flour, chili powder, pepper, salt, and baking powder and mix until blended. Pour into baking dish and top with queso fresco. Bake casserole at 375°F for 25–35 minutes or until set and light golden brown.

Serves 8–10

3 (4-ounce) cans whole green chiles
2½ cups shredded pepper jack cheese
1 sweet onion, chopped
11 eggs
¾ cup half-and-half
⅓ cup flour
1 tablespoon chili powder
⅛ teaspoon pepper
½ teaspoon salt
1½ teaspoons baking powder
1 cup crumbled queso fresco

Potatoes Rancheros

*This hearty and delicious vegetarian main dish is perfect for a weekend
brunch, served with Churros (page 126) or Pan Dulce Rolls (page 127),
along with freshly squeezed orange juice.*

∩

1. Peel potatoes and cut into ½" cubes. Melt butter in heavy skillet and cook potatoes until almost tender. Add onion and garlic; cook and stir until onion is crisp-tender and potatoes are golden.

2. In medium bowl, beat together eggs, salt, pepper, and sour cream. Add to potato mixture in skillet and cook, stirring occasionally, until eggs are set. Sprinkle with cheese, cover, and remove from heat.

3. Heat Ranchero Sauce in small saucepan and peel and slice avocado; sprinkle with lime juice. For each serving, place Ranchero Sauce on a heated plate, top with potato mixture and avocado.

Serves 4

2 russet potatoes
2 tablespoons butter
1 onion, chopped
2 cloves garlic, minced
7 eggs
½ teaspoon salt
⅛ teaspoon cayenne pepper
⅓ cup sour cream
1 cup shredded Cheddar cheese
1 cup Ranchero Sauce (page 97)
1 avocado, sliced
1 tablespoon lime juice

Chile Soufflé

Serves 6

⅓ cup butter
½ cup minced onion
⅓ cup flour
2 tablespoons chili powder
½ teaspoon cumin
½ teaspoon salt
⅛ teaspoon cayenne pepper
1 cup whole milk
1 cup cream
2 cups shredded Cheddar
    cheese
1 (4-ounce) can diced green
    chiles, drained
6 eggs, separated
¼ teaspoon cream of tartar

*This elegant dish must be served the instant it comes out of the oven;
it can't wait for guests. So serve a first course of a fruit or spinach salad
while the soufflé bakes so everybody is ready to eat.*

1. Preheat oven to 300°F. In heavy saucepan, melt butter over medium heat. Add onion; cook and stir until tender. Add flour, chili powder, cumin, salt, and cayenne pepper; cook and stir until bubbly. Add milk and cream; cook and stir until mixture thickens. Add cheese and stir until melted. Remove pan from heat.

2. Add chiles and egg yolks to cheese mixture; beat well and set aside. Meanwhile, in clean bowl beat egg whites with cream of tartar until stiff peaks form. Stir a dollop of the beaten egg whites into cheese mixture, then fold in remaining egg white.

3. Pour mixture into 2-quart soufflé dish. Bake at 300°F for 65–75 minutes or until soufflé is puffed and golden brown. Serve immediately.

Ingredient Information

Cream of tartar is a dry powder found in the spice or baking aisle of your supermarket. It is NOT tartar sauce, or cream sauce. It is used to make the egg white foam more structurally sound and ensures that the soufflé will rise dramatically and perfectly.

Potato Chile Frittata

This rich frittata uses fresh and dried chiles for a wonderfully complex flavor that isn't too spicy. Serve it with mild salsa instead of the Jalapeño Pesto if you like.

Serves 4

1 Anaheim chile
1 ancho chile
2 russet potatoes
¼ cup olive oil
1 onion, chopped
3 cloves garlic, minced
6 eggs
¼ cup cream
1 teaspoon salt
⅛ teaspoon pepper
1 cup pepper jack cheese
½ cup Jalapeño Pesto
   (page 96)

1. Roast Anaheim chile under broiler or over gas flame until skin is charred. Place in paper bag for 10 minutes to steam. Remove skin and seed and chop flesh. Cover ancho chile with 1 cup boiling water and let stand for 15 minutes. Puree the chile with 3 tablespoons soaking water in food processor or blender and strain puree. Set aside.

2. Peel and dice potatoes. In heavy skillet or nonstick omelet pan, heat olive oil and add potatoes, onion, and garlic. Cook over medium heat, stirring frequently, until vegetables are golden. Add chopped Anaheim chile and ancho chile puree.

3. Beat eggs with cream, salt, and pepper, and add to skillet. Cook over medium heat, shaking the pan and lifting mixture with spatula so uncooked egg mixture flows underneath, until almost set. Sprinkle with cheese and place pan under broiler (cover handle with foil if not ovenproof). Broil for 2–4 minutes until cheese melts and eggs are cooked. Serve with Jalapeño Pesto.

Frittata or Omelet?

A frittata is Spanish, and an omelet is French. Beyond nationality, a frittata is generally served flat and has the ingredients cooked together with the eggs, while an omelet is usually filled with other ingredients and is served rolled. Frittatas are also finished by broiling for a crisp top, while omelets are cooked entirely on the stovetop.

Chile Rellenos

Serves 4

4 poblano chiles
2 cups shredded Muenster
    cheese
1 cup shredded Cheddar
    cheese
1 sweet onion, chopped
2 jalapeño peppers, minced
¼ cup heavy cream
3 eggs, separated
¼ teaspoon cream of tartar
2 cups vegetable oil
¼ cup flour
1½ cups Pico de Gallo
    (page 91)

*The whipped egg batter that coats these stuffed chiles is as light as air.
Serve them immediately so the contrast between the crisp coating
and the soft melted cheese is extreme.*

1. Roast poblano chiles under a broiler or over a gas flame until skins are charred. Place in paper bag and let steam for 10 minutes. Remove skin with fingers and cut slit in side of peppers. Remove seeds and membranes.

2. In medium bowl, combine cheeses, onion, and peppers. Stuff this mixture into the poblanos; set aside. In medium bowl, beat heavy cream with egg yolks until thick and lemon-colored. In small bowl, beat egg whites with cream of tartar until stiff peaks form. Fold into egg yolk mixture.

3. Heat vegetable oil in large skillet over medium heat until it reaches 375°F. Sprinkle each stuffed pepper with flour and shake off excess, then dip into the egg mixture and place in hot oil. Fry until golden brown, turning once, about 4–5 minutes. Drain on paper or kitchen towels and serve with Pico de Gallo.

Why Poblanos?

Poblano chiles are a bit hotter than Anaheims, but they are easier to work with because the flesh is thicker. Poblano chiles hold their shape better after being roasted and peeled. For a milder taste, just omit the jalapeños in the cheese filling, or use canned diced green chiles.

Chilequiles

This recipe is a bit like Matzo Brei, but with a Tex-Mex twist. The tortilla chips take the place of the matzos, and the seasoning is pure Southwest.

∩

1. In heavy skillet, melt butter over medium heat and cook onion and garlic until crisp-tender. In medium bowl, beat eggs with cream, oregano, and pepper flakes and add to skillet along with tortilla chips. Cook, stirring occasionally, until eggs are set.

2. Add tomato and Taco Sauce; cook and stir for 2–4 minutes until thickened. Sprinkle with cheese, cover pan, and remove from heat. Let stand for 4–5 minutes until cheese has melted, then serve.

Serves 4–6

2 tablespoons butter
1 onion, diced
2 cloves garlic, minced
8 eggs, beaten
½ cup heavy cream
½ teaspoon dried oregano
⅛ teaspoon crushed red
    pepper flakes
2 cups coarsely crushed
    tortilla chips
1 tomato, seeded and
    chopped
1 cup Taco Sauce (page 101)
1 cup shredded Cheddar
    cheese

Chapter Fourteen

Beverages

Blue Moon Margaritas

*Curaçao makes these delicious margaritas a delicate blue color.
They're refreshing and beautiful! Serve them for a special dinner
or a Tex-Mex theme party.*

1. Dip rim of margarita glasses in the ¼ cup of lime juice and dip into sugar to coat; set aside.

2. In blender or food processor, combine remaining ingredients, including leftover lime juice. Blend or process until mixture is thick and smooth. Pour into prepared glasses and serve.

Tex-Mex Hot Chocolate

*To top this deliciously rich drink, coat mini marshmallows in cinnamon sugar
to add even more flavor. Let them melt in the hot drink.*

1. In heavy saucepan, combine condensed milk, syrup, and chocolate chips over medium heat. Cook and stir until chocolate melts and mixture blends. Remove from heat and stir in remaining ingredients using a wire whisk.

2. Return saucepan to medium heat and cook, stirring constantly with wire whisk, until mixture begins to bubble around the edges. Serve hot topped with marshmallows.

Frozen Margaritas

*Dip the rims of margarita glasses in extra lime juice
and then dip in salt to coat.
That gives each sip of this frozen drink a bit of salty contrast.*

Serves 6

1 (6-ounce) can frozen
   limeade
2 tablespoons lime juice
¾ cup gold tequila
½ cup triple sec
2 drops bitters
3 cups ice cubes

1. Working with half of the ingredients at one time, place in a heavy-duty blender. Cover and blend until mixture is smooth. Repeat, using remaining ingredients. Pour into margarita glasses and serve.

2. You can make this drink ahead of time, then store it in the freezer. Because of the alcohol, it will not freeze completely solid. Stir well and serve in the salt-rimmed margarita glasses.

Ingredient Substitutions

Substitute frozen lemonade concentrate and lemon juice to make Lemon Margaritas, or use frozen concentrated orange juice and lemon juice for Orange Margaritas. Frozen cranberry juice concentrate and orange juice make Cranberry Margaritas. For the sweeter margaritas, dip the rims of the glasses into sugar instead of salt.

Tequila Sunrise

Serves 4

2 cups orange juice
1 tablespoon lemon juice
½ cup tequila
2 tablespoons grenadine
Ice cubes
Cracked ice

This cocktail is called a "sunrise" because the grenadine, tequila, and orange juice layer in the glass so the drink looks like a bright sky at sunrise.

In cocktail mixer, combine orange juice, lemon juice, and tequila. Add ice cubes and shake well. Strain into 4 cocktail glasses over cracked ice. Quickly pour grenadine syrup over each glass. Serve immediately.

Plain Margaritas

Serves 6

1 (6-ounce) can frozen
    limeade concentrate
2 tablespoons lemon juice
1 cup tequila
¼ cup beer
½ cup triple sec
¼ cup sugar
1 cup ice water

Beer adds smoothness and a bit of carbonation to these classic margaritas.

Combine all ingredients in blender and mix until thoroughly blended. Serve in margarita glasses with salted rims, over ice.

Consider Your Equipment

If you serve a lot of cocktails and drinks at your parties, it makes sense to invest in a good cocktail shaker, a few shot glasses, and a heavy-duty blender, along with an assortment of wine glasses, highball glasses, margarita glasses, and swizzle sticks.

Texas Tea

*This is one potent drink. Be sure to warn people
that they aren't really drinking tea, but a strong mixed drink!*

Serves 12

½ cup tequila
½ cup bourbon
½ cup rum
½ cup vodka
¼ cup lime juice
¼ cup sweet-and-sour mix
6 cups cola beverage

1. Combine all ingredients and stir briskly. Pour into cocktail glasses and add some crushed ice. Garnish with lime slices.

2. To make ahead of time, combine everything except cola beverage and mix well; cover and place in refrigerator up to 8 hours. When ready to serve, add cola beverage and mix gently, then pour over crushed ice.

White Sangria

*This recipe for Sangria uses tequila, for a Tex-Mex twist.
Serve it in a big punch bowl; with all the colorful fruits,
it makes a wonderful centerpiece for a buffet.*

Serves 12–14

1 bottle white wine
1 (6-ounce) can frozen
    limeade concentrate
¾ cup tequila
⅓ cup superfine sugar
¼ cup lime juice
2 cups frozen sliced peaches
1 cup green grapes
1 cup raspberries
3 cups chilled lemon-lime
    soda

1. In large punch bowl, combine wine, limeade, tequila, sugar, and lime juice; blend well until thoroughly mixed. Add peaches and grapes. Cover and chill at least 8 hours or overnight.

2. When ready to serve, add raspberries, stir, and then add lemon-lime soda, stirring to mix. Add chunks of ice or a frozen ice ring.

Make a Frozen Ice Ring

To make a frozen ice ring, arrange frozen fruits (cherries, peaches, strawberries, raspberries) in a ring mold. Prepare a 12-ounce can of frozen limeade according to package directions and pour into the mold. Freeze until solid, unmold, and float the ring in the punch.

Micheladas

Serves 2

1 (16-ounce) bottle beer
2 tablespoons lime juice
¼ teaspoon Tabasco sauce
2 teaspoons Worcestershire
   sauce
1 tablespoon soy sauce
½ teaspoon salt
2 cups crushed ice

You can vary the ingredients in this classic drink to your taste.
Try it with different kinds of beer too;
dark ale will make a more robust Michelada than a light beer.

In cocktail shaker, combine all ingredients except ice and shake to blend well. Strain over ice placed in 2 highball glasses.

In the Liquor Store

In some liquor stores or grocery stores, you may be able to find a Michelada mix to add to cold beer. Or you can use Clamato, a tomato based liquid that contains clam juice, instead of the Worcestershire sauce, soy sauce, and salt.

Tequila Slammer

Serves 1

1 measure tequila
1 measure lemon-lime
   beverage
Dash lime juice

This is less a recipe than a way of drinking!
Serve outdoors, or in a place where you don't care if some spilling occurs.

In small glass, mix all ingredients. Cover the top of the glass with your hand and slam it down on the bar or table (be careful!). This will make the drink very fizzy; drink it down immediately.

Orange Fizz

Orange soda pop is very popular in Mexican and Tex-Mex restaurants. This is a more nutritious version that's very simple to make.

In pitcher, combine orange juice, lemon juice, and ginger ale and mix gently. Divide ice among highball glasses and pour orange mixture over. Garnish with mint and serve immediately.

Serves 4

2 cups orange juice, chilled
2 tablespoons lemon juice
2 cups chilled ginger ale
4 cups crushed ice
4 sprigs fresh mint

Sweet Tea

Classic Sweet Tea is a must at every Tex-Mex gathering. The sugar is dissolved in hot water, making a simple syrup, and is added to the tea while still warm for the best flavor.

Serves 6–8

6 tablespoons loose tea
   leaves
3 cups cold water
1 cup sugar
1 gallon container
Lemon wedges

1. Place tea leaves in a tea ball or strainer. In medium saucepan, combine cold water and sugar and bring to a boil, stirring to dissolve the sugar. Add the tea ball and remove from heat. Let steep for 25–35 minutes, then remove tea ball.

2. Pour mixture into gallon container and add enough cold water to fill the container. Cover and refrigerate up to 2 days. Serve with lemon wedges.

How to Make Sun Tea

To make Sun Tea, place tea leaves in a tea ball and place in clear glass container; add 6 cups of cold water and stir well. Cover container and let the mixture stand in direct sunlight for 2 to 3 hours. Remove ball, stir, chill thoroughly, and serve.

Bloody Mary

Serves 2

¼ cup chile-flavored Bloody
    Mary mix
6 tablespoons tequila
1¼ cups vegetable tomato
    juice
1 tablespoon lime juice
½ teaspoon ground red chile
    powder
¼ teaspoon hot salt mix
1 cup crushed ice

*Tequila, once again, makes this drink a Tex-Mex favorite. You can find Bloody
Mary mixes flavored with chiles and other ingredients in any liquor store.*

Combine all ingredients in a cocktail shaker and shake well to blend.
Pour into 2 highball glasses and garnish with celery sticks.

About Hot Salt

*Some companies are beginning to make seasoned salt mixes flavored
with lots of peppers and ground chiles, most notably Morton's Hot Salt.
Look for them in the extract and spice section of your grocery store.
They are great for adding a nice kick to beverages.*

Mojito

Serves 2

½ cup fresh mint leaves
2 tablespoons sugar
3 tablespoons lime juice
6 tablespoons tequila
3 drops bitters
1 cup club soda
1 cup crushed ice

*Mojitos are actually a Cuban invention, made of fresh mint, rum, and sugar.
Using tequila instead of rum gives this fresh drink a Tex-Mex twist.*

1. In cocktail shaker, place mint leaves and sugar. Using a muddler or the
   back of a spoon, crush the leaves, using the sugar to help crush. Blend
   in lime juice, tequila, and bitters and mix well.

2. Stir in club soda. Strain into 2 highball glasses filled with crushed ice,
   garnish with more fresh mint, and serve.

Cucumber Margaritas

Cucumbers offer a mild and cooling contrast in these pretty light green drinks. Garnish them with a cucumber wheel: peel stripes from a cucumber, then slice the cucumber into rounds with a slit cut in the side.

Serves 6

2 cucumbers
⅓ cup lime juice
2 tablespoons superfine sugar
½ cup tequila
½ teaspoon salt
⅛ teaspoon cayenne pepper
1 cup crushed ice

1. Peel cucumber, cut in half, and remove seeds with a spoon. Cut into chunks and place in blender container or food processor with remaining ingredients. Cover and blend or process until mixture is smooth and thick.

2. Serve immediately, garnished with small chile peppers and cucumber slices.

Hot Spiced Cider

When it's cold outside, make this delicious hot drink and place it in a crockpot. It will stay hot on low for several hours. Serve with a punch or soup ladle.

Serves 6

2 quarts apple cider
1 cup orange juice
1 tablespoon lime juice
2 cinnamon sticks
¼ cup sugar
1 tablespoon Red Hots
    candies

Combine all ingredients in large saucepan and bring just to a simmer, stirring to dissolve sugar and candy. Serve immediately or pour into crockpot to keep warm. Discard cinnamon sticks before serving.

In the Candy Aisle

Really spicy and hot candies are becoming very popular. You can buy not only the simple round red hot candies, but jelly beans flavored with chiles, and hot hard candies. Browse through a candy store or the candy aisle of your supermarket to find new favorites.

Red Sangria

*Red wine sweetened with sugar and honey and
spiked with lots of citrus juice makes a wonderfully refreshing drink.*

Serves 8–10

2 oranges
1 grapefruit
2 limes
1 (750 ml) bottle red wine
⅓ cup sugar
⅓ cup honey
1 (5-ounce) can crushed
   pineapple
1 (16-ounce) bottle club soda,
   chilled

1. Juice 1 orange and cut the other into thin slices. Juice the grapefruit and 1 lime. Cut the other lime into thin slices. In large container, combine juices, red wine, sugar, honey, and undrained pineapple and mix well until sugar dissolves. Cover and chill for 2–4 hours.

2. When ready to serve, pour wine mixture into large pitcher or punch bowl. Slowly pour in the club soda and mix gently; serve immediately.

Strawberry Margaritas

*Cantaloupe is the secret ingredient in this fabulous margarita recipe.
It adds a smoothness, richness, and slight taste of honey to this delicious drink.*

Serves 4

½ cup tequila
⅓ cup triple sec
1 (8-ounce) package frozen
   strawberries
½ cup chopped cantaloupe
1 cup crushed ice
½ cup simple syrup (see
   sidebar)
2 tablespoons lime juice
2 tablespoons lemon juice

1. Combine all ingredients in blender or food processor and blend or process until mixture is smooth and thick. Pour into margarita glasses that have their rims dipped in water and sugar to coat.

How to Make Simple Syrup

To make simple syrup, combine 1 part water with 2 parts sugar in a heavy saucepan, stir well, and bring to a boil. Simmer mixture, stirring frequently, until sugar is completely dissolved. Store the syrup, covered, in the refrigerator up to 2 weeks and use in beverages such as lemonade or margaritas.

Café con Leche

Using sweetened condensed milk instead of sugar means that you don't have to dissolve sugar in the milk. Brew your coffee stronger or lighter depending on your tastes, but remember, Café con Leche is traditionally half coffee and half milk.

∩

1. Place coffee, cinnamon, and nutmeg in the top of a drip coffeemaker. Pour cold water into the machine and set it to brew.

2. Meanwhile, combine condensed milk and milk in a large saucepan. Place over medium heat and cook, stirring frequently, until steam rises from the surface.

3. Pour the brewed coffee into the hot milk and stir. Serve immediately.

Serves 6

½ cup dark-roast coffee grounds
½ teaspoon cinnamon
Dash nutmeg
3 cups cold water
½ cup sweetened condensed milk
2½ cups milk

Mango Smoothies

Make the mango cubes ahead of time; then whenever you want you can pull out your blender and whip up a smoothie or two.

∩

1. Peel the mangoes and slice the flesh away from the rounded pit. Place in blender or food processor along with frozen orange juice concentrate and lime juice. Blend or process until smooth. Divide among ice cube trays and freeze solid. When frozen solid, remove cubes from trays and pack into freezer bags; freeze up to 3 months.

2. For smoothies, place 6 cubes in blender or food processor and add undrained pineapple and milk. Blend or process until mixture is smooth and thick. Serve immediately.

Serves 4–6

4 ripe mangoes
½ cup frozen orange juice concentrate
2 tablespoons lime juice
1 (5-ounce) can crushed pineapple
2 cups milk

Mexican Coffee

*If you'd like to make this rich hot beverage alcoholic,
stir in a dollop of Kahlua or white tequila.*

Ω

Serves 4

½ cup dark-roast coffee
   grounds
1 teaspoon cinnamon
½ vanilla bean
4 cups cold water
¼ cup chocolate syrup
½ cup sweetened condensed
   milk
½ cup heavy cream
Dash cinnamon
2 tablespoons powdered
   sugar

1. In drip coffeemaker, place coffee grounds, cinnamon, and vanilla bean. Add 4 cups cold water and brew. Meanwhile, in small bowl combine chocolate syrup and condensed milk and mix well. Divide syrup mixture among 4 coffee mugs. In small bowl, combine cream, dash cinnamon, and sugar; beat until stiff peaks form.

2. When coffee has finished brewing, pour over syrup mixture in mugs and stir well. Top with flavored whipped cream and serve.

About Mexican-Grown Coffee

Coffee, especially organic coffee, has been a major crop in Mexico since coffee plants arrived from Jamaica in the nineteenth century. Varieties include Arabica and Altura. Most of the organic beans are grown on small farms with high standards, which helps ensure high quality.

Champurrado

*This unusual drink is traditional at Tex-Mex gatherings around Christmas time.
It's basically hot chocolate thickened with masa harina
and flavored with cinnamon. Try it!*

∩

Serves 6–8

¼ cup masa harina
1½ cups water
1 (12-ounce) can evaporated milk
1 cinnamon stick
¼ teaspoon cinnamon
¼ teaspoon salt
¼ cup sugar
¼ cup brown sugar
3 ounces Mexican chocolate
1 cup half-and-half
1 teaspoon vanilla
½ cup whipping cream
1 tablespoon powdered sugar
Freshly grated nutmeg

1. In heavy saucepan, bring masa harina, water, and evaporated milk to a boil. Cook, stirring, over medium heat for 4–5 minutes until mixture has thickened. At this point you can strain the mixture for a smoother drink.

2. Add cinnamon stick, cinnamon, salt, sugar, brown sugar, and Mexican chocolate and bring back to a simmer. Cook and stir with a wire whisk until chocolate has melted, sugar has dissolved, and mixture is blended. Stir in half-and-half and vanilla and bring just to a simmer; stir and remove from heat.

3. In small bowl, combine whipping cream and powdered sugar and beat until stiff peaks form. Pour chocolate mixture into mugs and top with cream. Sprinkle with nutmeg.

About Mexican Chocolate

Mexican chocolate is a specialty product you can find in the ethnic foods aisle of your supermarket. It's chocolate flavored with sugar, cinnamon, and ground nuts. If you can't find it, for 1 ounce substitute 1 ounce semisweet chocolate, a pinch of cinnamon, and 1 tablespoon of ground almonds.

Chapter Fifteen

Desserts

Caramel Bread Pudding

8 slices Pan Dulce Loaves
    (page 127), cubed
1 cup golden raisins
4 eggs, beaten
1 (13-ounce) can caramel-
    flavored sweetened
    condensed milk
1 cup whole milk
¼ cup brown sugar
¼ teaspoon cinnamon
2 tablespoons butter, melted
¼ teaspoon salt
2 teaspoons vanilla

This delicious and rich bread pudding is pure comfort food!
Serve it on a cold winter day to charm your guests. Substitute regular raisins,
dried cranberries, or chocolate chips for the golden raisins.

1. Preheat oven to 325°F. Place cubed bread in a 2-quart casserole dish and sprinkle with golden raisins; set aside.

2. In large bowl, combine eggs, condensed milk, whole milk, brown sugar, cinnamon, butter, salt, and vanilla and mix well with wire whisk. Pour into casserole over bread cubes.

3. Bake pudding at 325°F for 45–55 minutes or until pudding is set and top is light golden brown. Serve warm with heavy cream or vanilla ice cream.

Ingredient Substitution

You can usually find caramel-flavored sweetened condensed milk in the Hispanic or Tex-Mex section of your supermarket. If it's unavailable, substitute regular sweetened condensed milk (not evaporated), and increase the brown sugar amount by 1 tablespoon.

Chocolate Flan

Flan is a classic Tex-Mex dessert. Sugar is melted and used to coat a baking pan, then a rich egg and milk mixture is baked until set. Be sure to carefully follow the instructions for best results.

∩

Serves 8

¾ cup sugar
2 tablespoons water
1 cup whole milk
1 (14-ounce) can sweetened
   condensed milk
1 vanilla bean
⅓ cup chocolate syrup
2 tablespoons cocoa powder
½ cup semisweet chocolate
   chips
4 eggs
2 eggs yolks
¼ cup sugar

1. Preheat oven to 325°F. In small heavy saucepan, combine ¾ cup sugar and water. Cook over medium heat, stirring frequently, until sugar melts and turns golden. Watch carefully. When the sugar is completely melted, carefully pour mixture into 6 6-ounce custard cups or ramekins that you hold with oven mitts; swirl to coat bottom of cups. Set aside.

2. In heavy saucepan, combine milk, condensed milk, and vanilla bean; bring to a boil. Stir in chocolate syrup, cocoa, and chocolate chips and stir until blended; remove from heat and let stand for 10 minutes. Remove vanilla bean and dry off. Using sharp knife, split vanilla bean and scrape out seeds. Add to milk mixture along with eggs, egg yolks, and ¼ cup sugar. Beat well with wire whisk until blended.

3. Pour custard mixture through a sieve into another large bowl. Then divide mixture into prepared custard cups. Place cups in a large baking pan and place pan in oven. Carefully pour hot tap water around the cups to a depth of 1". Bake flans for 25–35 minutes or until a toothpick inserted in center comes out clean.

4. Remove cups from water bath and cool on wire rack to room temperature. Cover and chill flans for 3–4 hours. To remove from pans, run a knife around the inside edge of the custard cups and invert onto serving plate. Lift up the cup, and the flan will slide out, covered with the caramel.

The Smoothest Custard

Baked custard is strained to remove any cooked bits of egg yolk and to remove the chalazae, a thin ropy part of the egg white that holds the yolk in place inside the shell. This step, and baking in a water bath, makes custard as smooth as silk.

Ground-Up Puerco Cake

Yes, there really is pork sausage in this dessert. The sausage is a substitute for butter or shortening. The cake won't taste like pork; it is simply intensely spicy. Choose a mild or spicy sausage according to your tastes.

½ pound bulk pork sausage, crumbled

1½ cups sugar

¼ cup brown sugar

3 eggs

2½ cups flour

1½ teaspoons baking powder

½ teaspoon salt

½ teaspoon baking soda

1 teaspoon ground cinnamon

½ teaspoon nutmeg

¼ teaspoon cloves

1 cup buttermilk

1 cup grated peeled apple

1 cup chopped pecans

1. Preheat oven to 350°F. In large mixing bowl, combine sausage and sugars and beat well until fluffy. Add eggs and beat until combined. In medium bowl, combine flour, baking powder, salt, baking soda, and spices. Add to sausage mixture alternately with buttermilk, beating after each addition, beginning and ending with dry ingredients.

2. Fold in apples and pecans. Pour batter into a 10" tube pan. Bake at 350°F for 50–60 minutes, or until top springs back when lightly touched and sides of cake pull away from pan.

3. Cool in pan on rack for 15 minutes, then loosen edges and invert cake onto wire rack; serve while warm or cool completely and then serve.

Homemade Caramel Sauce

Serve this cake warm with homemade caramel sauce. Combine ½ cup purchased caramel fudge ice cream sauce and 2 tablespoons cream in a small microwave-safe bowl; microwave on high for 30–40 seconds until warm, stirring until well blended. Store any leftovers in the refrigerator.

Chocolate Buttermilk Bars

Chocolate and cinnamon are a classic Mexican flavor combination. These layered bars are delicious served with any flavored tea or coffee.

∩

1. Preheat oven to 350°F. In large bowl, combine flour, sugar, brown sugar, butter, and pecans and mix until crumbly. Press 2 cups of this mixture into a 13" x 9" pan and set aside.

2. To remaining crumbs in bowl, add baking soda, cinnamon, salt, buttermilk, ⅓ cup cocoa powder, ½ teaspoon vanilla, almond extract, and egg and beat well. Pour over crust in pan. Bake at 350°F for 20–25 minutes until bars are set and toothpick inserted in center comes out clean. Set pan on wire rack.

3. In medium bowl, combine powdered sugar, ¼ cup cocoa powder, melted butter, milk, and ½ teaspoon vanilla and mix thoroughly. Pour over warm bars and spread to cover. Let cool, then cut into bars.

Make Your Own Buttermilk

If you don't have buttermilk on hand, you can make your own! Place 1 tablespoon vinegar in a measuring cup and add enough sweet milk to make 1 cup. Let this mixture stand for about 5 minutes, then use as buttermilk in any recipe.

Makes about 36

2 cups flour
1 cup sugar
½ cup brown sugar
½ cup butter, softened
½ cup chopped pecans
1 teaspoon baking soda
½ teaspoon cinnamon
¼ teaspoon salt
1 cup buttermilk
⅓ cup cocoa powder
½ teaspoon vanilla
½ teaspoon almond extract
1 egg
3 cups powdered sugar
¼ cup cocoa powder
2 tablespoons butter, melted
¼ cup milk
½ teaspoon vanilla

Cherry Enchiladas

Serves 8

1 (16-ounce) can cherry pie
    filling
2 cups frozen Bing cherries,
    thawed
8 flour tortillas
¼ cup butter, softened
¼ cup sugar
1 tablespoon cinnamon
¼ cup butter
½ cup corn syrup
¼ cup water
1 cup brown sugar

You could use any flavor of canned pie filling in these sweet enchiladas. Make sure to add more of the same fruit or a complementary fruit to the filling. Top these enchiladas with whipped cream or chocolate cherry ice cream.

1. Preheat oven to 350°F. In medium bowl, combine cherry pie filling and thawed cherries; mix well and set aside. Place tortillas on work surface; spread each with some of the ¼ cup butter. Combine ¼ cup sugar and cinnamon and sprinkle over each tortilla.

2. Fill coated tortillas with the cherry mixture; roll up and place seam side down in 9" x 13" pan. In heavy saucepan, combine ¼ cup butter, corn syrup, water, and brown sugar and mix well. Bring to a boil; reduce heat and simmer for 1–2 minutes, stirring constantly, until mixture comes together and forms syrup.

3. Pour hot syrup over enchiladas. Bake at 350°F for 20–25 minutes until enchiladas are hot. Let cool 10–15 minutes before serving. Top with cinnamon-flavored whipped cream.

Cinnamon Whipped Cream

To make cinnamon whipped cream, combine 1 cup chilled heavy whipping cream, ¼ cup powdered sugar, and ½ teaspoon cinnamon in a medium bowl. Beat with mixer or eggbeater until stiff peaks form. Store the whipped cream, covered, in refrigerator for up to 3 days.

Fried Ice Cream

This is definitely a recipe to serve when you want to impress your guests!
The deep-frying must be done at the very last minute;
make sure the ice cream balls are frozen solid before frying.
Have the topping ingredients ready and waiting for the ice cream.

∩

1. Using ice cream scoop, make 8 (½-cup) scoops of ice cream; freeze until solid.

2. In shallow bowl, combine maple syrup, cinnamon, and corn syrup and mix well. Place crushed cereal on shallow plate. Dip ice cream balls into syrup mixture, then into cereal to coat well. Freeze again until solid. Repeat coating process; freeze for at least 3 hours.

3. When ready to serve, heat oil to 375°F. One at a time, fry the frozen ice cream balls for 10–15 seconds, just until coating is heated. Serve with whipped cream, ice cream toppings, and maraschino cherries.

Serves 8

1 quart vanilla ice cream
½ cup maple syrup
1 teaspoon cinnamon
1 tablespoon corn syrup
2 cups crushed nut and grain flake cereal
2 quarts vegetable oil
Whipped cream
Ice cream toppings
Maraschino cherries

Grilled Bananas

Serves 4

4 ripe but firm bananas
2 tablespoons butter
2 tablespoons brown sugar
2 cups strawberry sorbet
⅓ cup Butterscotch Caramel
    ice cream topping
½ cup chopped cashews

Any grilled fruit tastes rich because the heat caramelizes the sugars in the fruit and concentrates the taste. You can serve this with other flavors of ice cream sauces as well; pineapple and chocolate would be a wonderful combination.

∩

1. Prepare and preheat grill. Cut bananas in half but do not peel. Spread cut sides of bananas with butter and sprinkle with brown sugar. Place bananas on grill over medium coals, skin side up, cover grill, and cook for 5–8 minutes until butter and brown sugar are melted and bananas are heated through.

2. Place 2 banana halves on each plate and top with sorbet, ice cream topping, and cashews.

About Ice Cream Toppings

Look for specialty ice cream toppings in jars and squeeze bottles near the ice cream in your grocer's freezer section. There are many unique varieties, including some Tex-Mex flavors such as Dulce con Leche, and gourmet flavors such as caramel fudge and butterscotch fudge.

Mango Cream Pie

This pie is easy to make with bottled mango slices, which have the taste of fresh mango but not the texture. If you have leftover puree, just freeze it in ice cube trays, then place in a freezer bag for longer storage. Use in Mango Smoothies (page 245) or in other recipes.

∩

1. Preheat oven to 375°F. In medium bowl, combine cookie crumbs, coconut, and melted butter; mix well. Press into bottom and up sides of 9" pie plate. Bake at 375°F for 8–10 minutes until coconut begins to brown; watch carefully. Set aside to cool completely.

2. Drain mango slices, reserving ¼ cup juice; puree mango slices in blender; measure out 1 cup puree. Freeze any remaining puree. In large bowl, beat cream cheese until light and fluffy, then add condensed milk and 1 cup mango puree; beat until smooth.

3. In small microwave-safe bowl, combine reserved ¼ cup mango juice, lemon juice, and unflavored gelatin. Let stand for 5 minutes to soften, then microwave on high power for 20–30 seconds; stir until gelatin is completely dissolved. Fold into mango mixture along with salt. In small bowl, beat cream with vanilla and powdered sugar; fold into mango mixture.

4. Pour mango mixture into cooled pie crust. Cover and refrigerate for 3–4 hours until firm. Garnish with more whipped cream and mint leaves, if desired.

Serves 8

2 cups shortbread cookie crumbs
½ cup shredded coconut
⅓ cup butter, melted
1 (20-ounce) jar mango slices
1 (8-ounce) package cream cheese, softened
1 (14-ounce) can sweetened condensed milk
1 (1-ounce) envelope unflavored gelatin
¼ cup reserved mango juice
2 tablespoons lemon juice
¼ teaspoon salt
½ cup heavy cream
1 teaspoon vanilla
2 tablespoons powdered sugar

Using Fresh Mangoes

Fresh mangoes can be used in this pie. To prepare a mango, cut the fruit in half, avoiding the pit in the center. Score through the flesh in a checkerboard pattern and push on the skin so it turns inside out and the flesh is exposed. Use a knife to slice the cubes off the skin.

Pecan Pralines

Makes about 30

1 cup brown sugar
1 cup sugar
1 (12-ounce) can evaporated
   milk
¼ cup light corn syrup
¼ cup butter
½ teaspoon cinnamon
1 teaspoon vanilla
3 cups pecan halves

*Adding a bit of Mexican cinnamon to this traditional southern delight helps
cut down the sweetness a bit. You could use any kind of nuts you'd like in this
decadent candy; cashews or peanuts would also be good.*

1. In large heavy saucepan, combine brown sugar, sugar, milk, corn
    syrup, and butter. Place over medium heat and bring to a boil. Cover
    pan with lid for 5 minutes to let steam wash down sides of pan. Remove
    cover and clip a candy thermometer to the side of the pan, making sure
    it doesn't touch the bottom.

2. Reduce heat to medium low and cook candy until thermometer regis-
    ters 238°F or a small amount of candy dropped into cold water forms a
    soft ball that flattens when you pick it up. Remove pan from heat and
    stir in cinnamon, vanilla, and pecan halves.

3. Beat candy until mixture begins to lose its gloss and looks creamy.
    Then quickly drop onto parchment paper–lined cookie sheets by
    tablespoons. Let stand until set. Store in an airtight container in cool
    dry place.

Frozen Pumpkin Chocolate Bars

Pumpkins are squashes and are staples in Mexican and Tex-Mex cooking. When paired with a rich chocolate sauce that is scented with cinnamon, the combination is just fantastic. Top with cinnamon-flavored whipped cream and some toasted pumpkin seeds.

∩

1. In medium saucepan, combine powdered sugar, butter, evaporated milk, and chocolate chips. Bring to a boil, stirring frequently. Boil mixture for 6–7 minutes until mixture thickens. Remove from heat and stir in cinnamon and vanilla. Set aside to cool completely. Stir several times while the sauce is cooling.

2. Soften ice cream by letting it stand at room temperature for 20 minutes. Place 1 cup of the ice cream in a large mixing bowl and beat in pumpkin puree until smooth. Stir in remaining ice cream and beat until smooth. Fold in whipped topping. Place in 13" x 9" pan and place in freezer for 1 hour. Pour chocolate sauce over ice cream mixture. Freeze for 4–6 hours until firm.

Solid-Pack or Pie Filling?

There are several different kinds of canned pumpkin. Solid-pack pumpkin is cooked and pureed pumpkin with nothing added. Pumpkin pie filling often has sweeteners and spices added and has a much softer consistency. Use solid-pack pumpkin for this dessert recipe.

Serves 16

2 cups powdered sugar
⅓ cup butter
1 (12-ounce) can evaporated milk
1 (12-ounce) package semisweet chocolate chips
½ teaspoon cinnamon
1 teaspoon vanilla
½ gallon vanilla ice cream
1 cup canned pumpkin puree
1 cup frozen nondairy whipped topping, thawed

Mexican Fudge Bars

Yields 36

2 cups chocolate chips
¼ cup butter
¼ teaspoon cinnamon
1 (14-ounce) can sweetened
    condensed milk
2 cups flour
2 cups quick-cooking rolled
    oats
1 cup brown sugar
½ cup sugar
¼ cup cocoa powder
1 teaspoon baking soda
½ teaspoon cinnamon
¼ teaspoon salt
1 cup butter, melted
1 cup chopped pecans

These delicious bars have smooth fudge filling nestled between layers of crisp buttery chocolate oatmeal crumbs.

1. Preheat oven to 350°F. In microwave-safe bowl, combine chocolate chips, ¼ cup butter, ¼ teaspoon cinnamon, and condensed milk. Heat on medium power for 2–3 minutes until chips and butter are melted. Stir until smooth and set aside.

2. In large bowl, combine flour, oats, sugars, cocoa, baking soda, ½ teaspoon cinnamon, and salt. Pour melted butter over and mix until crumbs form. Stir in pecans. Press half of the crumb mixture into a 13" x 9" pan. Stir chocolate mixture again, and then pour over crust. Sprinkle remaining crumb mixture over chocolate filling.

3. Bake at 350°F for 25–30 minutes or until light golden brown. Let cool completely, and then cut into bars. Store covered at room temperature.

Condensed vs. Evaporated

Make sure you don't confuse sweetened condensed milk with evaporated milk; they are two very different products. Sweetened condensed milk is very sweet, is cooked with lots of sugar, and is much thicker than evaporated milk. It is used for desserts, drinks, and sauces.

Chocolate Cinnamon Ice Cream

*Using several different kinds of chocolate is the secret
to the depth of flavor in this easy recipe.*

Ω

1 (12-ounce) can evaporated
   milk
2 egg yolks, beaten
1 cup sugar
3 (1-ounce) squares
   unsweetened chocolate,
   chopped
¼ cup cocoa powder
½ cup chocolate syrup
1 teaspoon vanilla
1 cinnamon stick
½ teaspoon ground
   cinnamon
⅛ teaspoon salt
1½ cups heavy cream

1. In heavy saucepan, combine milk, egg yolks, and sugar and beat well. Place over medium heat and cook, stirring constantly, until mixture comes to a boil. Boil and stir for 3 minutes.

2. Add chopped chocolate; cook and stir until chocolate melts. Add cocoa and chocolate syrup; stir until blended and smooth. Remove from heat and stir in vanilla, cinnamon stick, ground cinnamon, and salt. Let cool for 30 minutes.

3. Remove cinnamon stick, stir in heavy cream, cover, and refrigerate until very cold. Freeze according to ice cream maker's instructions.

Get an Ice Cream Maker

There are many varieties of ice cream makers on the market. They range in price from a few dollars to hundreds of dollars for electric gelato machines. The separate insert hand-cranked machines are the best buy; you don't have to use salt and ice to freeze, and kids think it's fun to turn the crank!

Unfried Ice Cream Balls

*When you don't feel like going through all the work of Fried Ice Cream
(page 255), this easy recipe fits the bill.*

∩

Serves 8

½ cup coconut
½ cup chopped pecans
½ cup chopped almonds
1 cup frosted cornflake cereal
4 cups vanilla ice cream
½ cup chocolate ice cream
    topping
1 cup whipped topping

1. In heavy skillet, place coconut. Toast over medium heat, stirring frequently, until coconut is evenly browned. Remove from pan. Add pecans and almonds to pan and toast them over medium heat, stirring frequently, until fragrant. Add to coconut and let cool.

2. Crush cereal and mix with coconut and nuts. Form ice cream into eight balls and roll in cereal mixture to coat. Freeze until solid, and then serve with ice cream topping and whipped topping.

Arroz con Leche

*Long-grain rice is the best to use for this pudding, as it doesn't release too
much starch and become too thick. Serve it warm from the stove, or cool it
and serve with warmed caramel or chocolate ice cream topping.*

∩

Serves 8

1½ cups cooked long-grain
    rice
1 cup milk
1 (14-ounce) can sweetened
    condensed milk
¼ cup sugar
1 teaspoon grated lime peel
¼ teaspoon salt
1 egg yolk
1 egg
1 teaspoon vanilla
½ teaspoon cinnamon

1. In heavy saucepan, combine rice, milk, condensed milk, sugar, lime peel, and salt. Bring to a boil, then reduce heat to low and simmer for 20–25 minutes until thick.

2. Beat egg yolk and egg in small bowl and add ½ cup of the warm mixture; beat, then return all to saucepan. Cook for 4–6 minutes longer until thick. Remove from heat and stir in vanilla and cinnamon. Serve warm or cold.

Tex-Mex Brownies

A tiny bit of cayenne pepper gives these brownies a bit of a kick.
They're topped with a cinnamon sugar mixture that gives them a crisp crust,
while the brownies stay moist and chewy.

Ω

Makes 36

¾ cup butter
½ cup cocoa powder
1¾ cups sugar
4 eggs
1 teaspoon vanilla
1 cup flour
1 teaspoon cinnamon
⅛ teaspoon cayenne pepper
1 teaspoon baking powder
1 cup chocolate chips
3 tablespoons sugar
½ teaspoon cinnamon

1. Preheat oven to 350°F. Spray 13" x 9" pan with nonstick cooking spray and set aside. In large saucepan, melt butter. Stir in cocoa powder until smooth. Add 1¾ cups sugar and mix thoroughly. Remove pan from heat and stir in eggs and vanilla, beating until smooth. Add flour, 1 teaspoon cinnamon, cayenne pepper, and baking powder and mix well.

2. Stir in chocolate chips and pour into prepared pan. In small bowl, combine 3 tablespoons sugar and ½ teaspoon cinnamon and mix well. Sprinkle evenly over brownie batter. Bake at 350°F for 25–35 minutes or until brownies are just set. Cool completely and cut into bars.

Brownie Frosting

If you'd rather frost these brownies, omit the cinnamon sugar. In a microwave-safe small bowl, combine 2 cups of semisweet chocolate chips with ⅓ cup peanut butter and heat for 2 minutes at 50% power until chips are almost melted. Mix well with wire whisk until blended and smooth, and pour over brownies.

Peach Daiquiri Pie

Serves 8

1½ cups crushed pretzels
½ cup chopped pecans
½ cup melted butter
⅓ cup brown sugar
1 (8-ounce) package cream
   cheese, softened
1 (14-ounce) can sweetened
   condensed milk
⅓ cup daiquiri mix
2 cups frozen peaches in
   syrup, thawed and
   chopped
2 tablespoons lime juice
1 cup heavy cream
2 tablespoons powdered
   sugar

*This pie is delicious for summer or holiday entertaining. The pretzel crust,
daiquiri mix, and lime juice give it the flavor of a daiquiri drink.*

1. In small bowl, combine pretzels, pecans, melted butter, and sugar and blend well. Press into bottom and up sides of 9" pie plate and set aside.

2. In large bowl, beat cream cheese until fluffy; gradually add condensed milk and daiquiri mix; beat until smooth and well blended. Add peaches with syrup and lime juice and mix well. In small bowl, beat cream with powdered sugar until stiff peaks form; fold into peach mixture until blended. Pour into prepared pie shell. Cover and freeze until firm. To serve, let pie stand at room temperature for 20 minutes before slicing.

How to Toast Nuts

Toast nuts to bring out their flavor. Spread any variety in single layer on a baking sheet. Bake in a preheated 400°F for 4–9 minutes, shaking pan frequently and watching carefully, until nuts deepen in color and become fragrant. Cool before using.

Pecan Bars

A crust made out of cinnamon graham crackers and pecans is topped with a wonderfully chewy filling. If you can't find cinnamon graham crackers, use regular and add ½ teaspoon cinnamon to the crust mixture.

Ω

1. Preheat oven to 350°F. In large bowl, combine graham cracker crumbs, ½ cup pecans, and ½ cup melted butter and mix until crumbly. Press into the bottom of a 13" x 9" pan and set aside.

2. In same bowl, cream ¾ cup butter with brown sugar and sugar until light and fluffy. Beat in corn syrup, eggs, and vanilla until well blended. Stir in flour, then pecans. Pour over graham cracker crust.

3. Bake bars at 350°F for 30–40 minutes or until filling is just set. Cool for 30 minutes on wire rack. In small microwave-safe bowl, melt chocolate chips and oil together, about 1 minute at medium power; stir until smooth. Drizzle over bars. Cool completely and cut into bars.

The Ubiquitous Pecan

Pecans are used in many Mexican and Tex-Mex desserts because they are so inexpensive—and for people with pecan trees in their backyard, free. The cuisine was originally peasant food, based on what people could harvest or collect themselves, so pecans are a popular ingredient.

Yields 36

2 cups cinnamon graham cracker crumbs
½ cup ground pecans
½ cup butter, melted
¾ cup butter, softened
1 cup brown sugar
¾ cup sugar
¼ cup corn syrup
3 eggs, beaten
1 teaspoon vanilla
1¼ cups flour
2 cups chopped pecans
½ cup semisweet chocolate chips
½ teaspoon vegetable oil

Caramel Apple Flautas

Serves 6–8

3 Granny Smith apples,
    peeled and chopped
1 tablespoon lemon juice
3 tablespoons butter
¼ cup sugar
⅓ cup caramel fudge ice
    cream topping
8 flour tortillas
¼ cup butter, softened
½ cup sugar
1½ teaspoons cinnamon
Vegetable oil

Serve these delicious crisp flautas with ice cream and drizzle with more caramel fudge ice cream topping and chocolate ice cream topping.

1. Sprinkle apples with lemon juice. In a heavy saucepan, heat 3 table-spoons butter and ¼ cup sugar, stirring constantly, until sugar melts. Add apples; cook and stir for 6–8 minutes or until apples are just tender. Remove from heat and stir in ice cream topping.

2. Wrap flour tortillas in microwave-safe paper towels and microwave on high for about 1 minute until softened. Remove from oven and spread each tortilla with some of the ¼ cup softened butter. In small bowl, combine ½ cup sugar and 1½ teaspoons cinnamon. Sprinkle half of the cinnamon sugar mixture over tortillas.

3. Divide apple mixture among prepared tortillas and roll up tightly. Fasten closed with toothpicks. In heavy saucepan, heat 1" of vegetable oil until it reaches 375°F. Fry flautas, two at a time, until golden and crisp, about 2–3 minutes on each side, turning once. Remove from pan using tongs, tipping flautas carefully from side to side to drain off excess oil. Place on paper towels to drain and sprinkle with remaining cinnamon sugar mixture. Serve warm.

Caramel Pear Flautas

You can make flautas with peeled and chopped pears instead of apples. Choose firm but ripe Comice pears and peel just before you're ready to use them so they don't turn brown. Be sure to sprinkle them immediately with lemon juice to stop enzymatic browning.

Mexican Chocolate Caramel Pie

*Chocolate and caramel are a wonderfully decadent combination.
This pie will satisfy all chocolate lovers; the edges are chewy,
while the center is moist and gooey.*

∩

1. Preheat oven to 350°F. Let pie crust stand at room temperature for 20 minutes, then place into 9" pie plate and flute edges. Set aside.

2. In large saucepan, combine butter and chocolate; heat over medium heat until chocolate melts, stirring frequently. Add sugar and mix well. Remove from heat and beat in eggs. Add flour, baking powder, salt, cinnamon, and vanilla and mix just until blended.

3. Place caramels and heavy cream in microwave-safe bowl; microwave on medium power for 5–7 minutes, stirring twice during melting, until mixture is smooth.

4. Pour half of chocolate batter into prepared pie crust. Place caramel mixture in a ring on batter, leaving ½" space at edges and 1" hole in the center. Top carefully with remaining batter. Bake at 350°F for 40–55 minutes or until filling is just set and crust is golden brown. Cool completely.

How Do You Make a Pie Crust?

Combine 1¼ cups flour and a little salt; cut in 7 tablespoons shortening until small crumbs form. Sprinkle with ¼ cup cold water; stir until ball forms. Roll out between 2 sheets of waxed paper, peel off top paper and flip into pie pan. Peel off second sheet, press into pan, and flute.

Serves 8–10

1 refrigerated pie crust
½ cup butter
3 (1-ounce) squares
    unsweetened chocolate
1¾ cups sugar
4 eggs
1¼ cups flour
½ teaspoon baking powder
¼ teaspoon salt
½ teaspoon cinnamon
1 teaspoon vanilla
20 caramels, unwrapped
2 tablespoons heavy cream

Dulce con Leche Cake

Serves 8

1¼ cups flour
1¼ cups sugar
1½ teaspoons baking powder
¼ cup butter, softened
¼ teaspoon salt
6 tablespoons whole milk
1 teaspoon vanilla
2 egg whites
1 (14-ounce) can sweetened
    condensed milk
1 cup heavy whipping cream
½ cup whole milk
2 tablespoons rum, if desired

*Three kinds of milk are mixed together and poured over this light white cake
until absorbed. The result is a very moist, almost pudding-like texture.
Top with some toasted pecans or crusted peanut brittle for some crunch.*

∩

1. Preheat oven to 350°F. Grease and flour a 9" round baking pan and line bottom with waxed paper; set aside.

2. In large bowl, combine flour, sugar, and baking powder and mix well. Add butter, salt, milk, and vanilla and beat on low speed until combined. Then add unbeaten egg whites and beat for 2 minutes on medium speed. Pour batter into prepared pan. Bake at 350°F for 25–35 minutes or until cake is light golden brown and starts to pull away from sides of pan. Cool on wire rack for 15 minutes, then remove from pan, peel off waxed paper, and cool completely on wire rack.

3. Place cake in a deep serving dish with sides and pierce surface of cake with fork. In medium bowl, combine condensed milk, whipping cream, whole milk, and rum; beat well until combined. Slowly pour over cake. Cover and refrigerate cake for 2–4 hours until milk mixture is absorbed. Store covered in refrigerator.

Pineapple Cake

It's important to beat cake batter as long as the recipe specifies to allow the flour proteins to develop. That helps the cake structure trap air from the baking powder and results in a light cake with an even texture.

∩

1. Preheat oven to 325°F. Drain pineapple thoroughly, using small strainer, pressing on pineapple to extract juice. Reserve juice (there should be about ½ cup) and pineapple. Spray 13" x 9" cake pan with nonstick baking spray; set aside.

2. In large bowl, combine flour, sugar, baking powder, baking soda, salt, reserved pineapple juice, lime juice, buttermilk, vegetable oil, vanilla, eggs, and ground almonds; beat for 2 minutes on medium speed.

3. Pour batter into prepared pan. Bake at 325°F for 30–40 minutes or until toothpick inserted in center comes out clean and cake begins to pull away from pans. Remove to wire rack; cool completely.

4. In large bowl, combine cream cheese and butter; beat until fluffy. Add 2 cups powdered sugar and reserved pineapple and beat well. Beat in remaining powdered sugar. Add more powdered sugar or lime juice as needed for desired spreading consistency. Frost cooled cake; cover and store in refrigerator.

Serves 10–12

1 (5½-ounce) can crushed pineapple
2½ cups flour
1½ cups sugar
4½ teaspoons baking powder
½ teaspoon baking soda
¼ teaspoon salt
½ cup reserved pineapple juice
2 tablespoons lime juice
2 tablespoons buttermilk
¾ cup vegetable oil
1 teaspoon vanilla
4 eggs
½ cup ground almonds
1 (8-ounce) package cream cheese, softened
¼ cup butter
4 cups powdered sugar
1–2 tablespoons lime juice, if needed

Why Isn't Fresh Pineapple Used in Cooking?

Pineapple contains an enzyme called bromelin that breaks down protein molecules. This enzyme is denatured when pineapple is heated in the canning process; that's why it's necessary to use canned pineapple when making frostings, especially cooked frostings, and gelatin desserts.

Spicy Banana Pops

Yields 18

4 cups milk
2 (3-ounce) packages instant
    vanilla pudding mix
3 bananas
1 tablespoon lime juice
¼ teaspoon ground ancho
    chile powder
⅛ teaspoon cayenne pepper
1 cup frozen whipped
    topping, thawed
2 cups mini semisweet
    chocolate chips
18 paper drink cups
18 frozen-dessert sticks

One of the newest trends in ice cream is adding spices to make a cold treat "hot."
Change the amount of ground chiles and cayenne pepper to suit your tastes.

1. In large bowl, combine milk and pudding mixes and beat with wire whisk until thickened. In small bowl, mash bananas with lime juice and stir into pudding mixture. Add chile powder, cayenne pepper, and fold in whipped topping and mini chocolate chips. Divide mixture evenly among paper drink cups.

2. Place drink cups on baking sheet and freeze for 1–2 hours until just firm. Insert frozen-dessert sticks into banana mixture, return to freezer, and freeze for 3–4 hours until frozen solid. Peel away drink cups to serve.

Grilled Pineapple with Cinnamon

Serves 6

1 fresh pineapple
½ cup brown sugar
¼ cup orange juice
1 tablespoon rum, if desired
1 tablespoon butter, melted
½ teaspoon cinnamon
Pinch cayenne pepper, if
    desired

As the pineapple heats on the grill, the sugars in the fruit caramelize
and brown, adding a wonderful rich flavor. Serve it with ice cream
and caramel or pineapple ice cream topping.

1. Twist leaves off top of pineapple. Cut off skin, making sure to remove brown spots or eyes. Cut pineapple into ½" slices. In small bowl, combine remaining ingredients and mix well.

2. Prepare and preheat grill. Brush one side of each pineapple slice with some of the brown sugar mixture and place on grill, 4–6" from medium coals. Grill, uncovered, for 8–9 minutes, turning once and brushing frequently with brown sugar mixture, until pineapple is heated and grill marks are golden brown.

Tex-Mex Tea Cakes

These little melt-in-your-mouth teacakes are wrapped around
a dark chocolate kiss for an intense flavor sensation.
Serve them as part of a cookie tray; they're especially nice at Christmas.

∩

Yields 36

1 cup butter, softened
¾ cup powdered sugar
1 teaspoon vanilla
2 cups flour
¼ cup cocoa powder
¼ teaspoon salt
⅛ teaspoon nutmeg
1 cup finely chopped pecans
36 dark chocolate kiss
 candies, unwrapped
1 cup powdered sugar
2 tablespoons cocoa powder
1 teaspoon cinnamon

1. Preheat oven to 350°F. In large bowl, combine butter and powdered sugar; beat well until fluffy. Add vanilla and mix well. Stir in flour, ¼ cup cocoa powder, salt, and nutmeg and mix until a dough forms, then stir in pecans. Cover and chill several hours in the refrigerator.

2. Form dough into 36 balls. Wrap dough around unwrapped candies, completely covering the chocolate with dough. Place on baking sheet and bake at 350°F for 11–14 minutes or until just set.

3. While cookies are baking, combine 1 cup powdered sugar, 2 tablespoons cocoa powder, and cinnamon in a shallow bowl; mix well until combined. When cookies are done, remove from baking sheet and place directly into powdered sugar mixture; roll to coat. Then set cookies on wire rack to cool. When cool, roll in powdered sugar mixture again.

Tex-Mex Glossary

Adobo: A thick sauce made with tomatoes, vinegar, onions, cumin, and other spices used as a condiment or to can chipotle chiles.

Albóndigas: Mexican word for "meatballs."

Ancho chile: A dried poblano chile.

Arroz: Spanish word for "rice," almost always long-grain white rice.

Bolillos: Hard rounded rolls with pointed ends, used for sandwiches.

Burrito: Flour tortilla filled with meat and cheese, rolled up, then eaten as is or deep-fried until crisp.

Carne: Spanish word for "meat"; usually means beef.

Chalupas: Spanish word meaning "canoes," this crisp slightly folded tortilla is topped with beans, cheese, and other ingredients.

Chilequiles: A dish made of pieces or strips of tortillas and tortilla chips layered with other ingredients and a sauce, then baked.

Chimichangas: Rolled tortillas filled with meat and deep-fried until crisp. The name means "whatchamacallits." Also known as deep-fried burritos.

Chorizo: A pork sausage made from pork butt, seasoned with garlic, chiles, onions, and spices.

Churros: A Tex-Mex dessert made of corn or flour dough piped through a pastry bag into logs, then deep-fried and sprinkled with sugar.

Cilantro: Also called "Chinese parsley," a fresh herb used extensively in Mexican and Tex-Mex cooking.

Comal: A griddle or flat pan without sides.

Comino: The Spanish word for "cumin," a smoky spice popular in Tex-Mex cooking.

Con: Spanish word meaning "with," as in *Arroz con Pollo* or Rice with Chicken.

Coriander: The seeds of the cilantro plant, used whole or ground.

Corn husks: Also known as corn shucks, these are the outer leafy layer of an ear of corn minus all the silky strands. They are used as wrappers for tamales.

Cream gravy: Also called meat gravy, made from pan drippings, flour, seasonings, and a liquid, served with fried or grilled meats.

Dry ingredients: Flour, salt, baking powder, flavorings, herbs, and other ingredients that are low in water content.

Dry rub: A combination of herbs, salt, pepper, and spices that is rubbed into meats to help flavor and tenderize before cooking.

Empanadas: A flour pastry dough filled with everything from meat to beans to cooked fruit, folded, sealed, and deep-fried.

Enchiladas: An entrée made by dipping tortillas in sauce and filling them, then rolling them up and baking in more sauce.

Fajita: Spanish word for "belt," the diaphragm muscle of a cow. This tough meat is marinated, grilled, then sliced across the grain and served in flour tortillas.

Flan: A sweet egg custard, usually made in a dish coated with caramel.

Flautas: Word means "flute" in Spanish. It is a tightly rolled stuffed tortilla that is deep-fried. Has a long thin shape and looks like a flute.

Food safety: The steps and techniques used to prevent food poisoning. Perishable foods must be handled, stored, and cooked at certain temperatures and for certain times to ensure the safety of the food we eat.

Frijoles: The Spanish word for "beans," such as pinto beans or black beans. Frijoles refritas means "refried" beans, or beans mashed and cooked in fat and seasonings.

Fry: A dry-heat cooking method where the food is surrounded by hot cooking oil until it reaches a safe internal temperature.

Gorditas: A small thick tortilla baked or fried until puffy, then sliced in half and filled; the Tex-Mex version of pita bread.

Grate: To push hard, or firm, cheeses or vegetables against a grater with coarse, serrated holes to make long thin strands.

Grease: To coat the surface of a baking pan or sheet with shortening, butter, or oil before adding the batter, preventing the food from sticking after it is cooked.

Grill: A dry-heat cooking method where food is cooked on a rack over hot burning coals.

Herbs: The fragrant leaves of many deciduous plants used in cooking to provide flavor, aroma, and color. Herbs include basil, thyme, rosemary, chervil, dill, marjoram, oregano, sage, savory, tarragon, mint, and coriander.

Hominy: Corn treated with lime. The lime removes the tough outer skin of the corn.

Huevos: Spanish word for "eggs."

Lard: Rendered pork fat, used in cooking and baking, especially tamale dough.

Margarita: A popular Tex-Mex drink made with lime and tequila; also made sweet with the addition of pureed fruit or fruit juices.

Masa: Corn dough used to make tortillas and tamales. Made from corn treated with lime and ground to a powder.

Masa harina: Flour made from ground dried fresh masa used to make tortillas and tamales.

Mesquite: A scrub tree that grows wild in Texas and Mexico; its wood is used to flavor grilled foods and barbecue.

Migas: Spanish word meaning "crumbs," scrambled eggs or a casserole made with crumbs and bits of fresh or fried corn tortillas.

Molcajete: A mortar, or rough bowl, made out of volcanic rock, used to pound herbs and vegetables into a coarse puree. See Tejolote.

Nachos: Tortilla chips topped with meat or beans and cheese, then baked until bubbly.

Nopales: The pads of the prickly pear cactus, cleaned of large thorns and small stickers.

Pan dulce: Phrase meaning "sweet bread" in Spanish; sweet rolls or bread flavored with vanilla and lemon.

Peel: To remove the skin or outer covering of fruits and vegetables with a knife or swivel-bladed vegetable peeler.

Pinto Beans: A dried legume that is colored with a mixture of beige and pink; pinto means "painted" in Spanish.

Pollo: Spanish word meaning "chicken."

Puerco: Spanish word for "pork."

Puree: To blend, in a blender, food processor, or grinder, until all ingredients are very finely chopped and evenly mixed.

Quesadillas: Tortillas filled with cheese or meat then topped with another, or folded over, and fried until crisp.

Queso: Spanish word for "cheese." Queso blanco is white cheese, queso fresco is fresh uncured cheese.

Roux: A mixture of flour and fat, cooked until bubbly or until light golden brown, used to thicken sauces and gravies.

Salsa: Word means "sauce" in Spanish, usually a combination of tomatoes and peppers served as a garnish or an appetizer.

Salsa verde: Green sauce, made from tomatillos, peppers, onions, and garlic.

Taco: Crisp or soft flour or corn tortilla filled with meats, beans, cheeses, and salsa.

Tamales: Made with corn flour dough spread on corn husks, filled with meat or cheese, then folded up and steamed.

Tejolote: A round-end tool used with a molcajete as a pestle, to grind herbs and other foods into a paste.

Tomatillos: Small green round tart fruits covered with a papery husk, used to make salsas and cooked sauces.

Tortilla: Flat bread made of corn or flour, served at almost every Tex-Mex meal.

Tostada: Means "toasted" in Spanish, usually flour or corn tortillas fried or toasted until crisp, then topped with meats, beans, and cheeses.

Tostaditas: Tiny round or quartered tortillas fried or baked until very crisp; usually served with a dip as an appetizer.

Tuna: The fruit of the prickly pear cactus.

Menu Suggestions

Combination Platter I

Chicken Enchiladas Verdes
Refried Frijoles
Spanish Rice

Combination Platter II

Chile Rellenos
Beef and Bean Enchiladas
Green Rice
Refried Frijoles

Combination Platter III

Spinach Enchiladas
Tex-Mex Crockpot Rice
Drunken Beans

Appetizer Open House Buffet

Beverages

Sweet Tea
Red Sangria
Orange Fizz

Appetizers

Mexican Layered Dip
Fruit Salsa
Meatballs con Queso

Texas Caviar
Tortilla Chips
Queso con Chile
Jalapeño Poppers
Mini Tamales
Chicken Quesadillas

Desserts
Chocolate Buttermilk Bars
Tex-Mex Brownies
Pineapple Cake

Lunch on the Porch
Tex-Mex Pasta Salad
Cheese Quesadillas
Strawberry Margaritas
Peach Daiquiri Pie
Texas Tea

Birthday Celebration Dinner
Ceviche
Corn and Tomatillo Salad
Spicy Salmon Steaks
Bolillos
Asparagus with Avocado
Fried Ice Cream

Dinner for the Boss
Corn Tartlets
Pomegranate Green Salad
Rib-Eye Steaks
Arroz con Avocado
White Sangria
Mango Cream Pie

Summer Brunch

Huevos Rancheros
Tex-Mex Quiche
Glorified Rice
Guacamole Salad
Pan Dulce Rolls

Christmas Eve Feast

Appetizers

Fruit Salsa
Guacamole
Tortilla Chips
Fiery Pecans

Dinner

Christmas Eve Salad
Seafood Enchiladas
Pork Tamales
Chipotle Chile Corn Bread

Beverages

Champurrado
Red Sangria

Desserts

Tex-Mex Tea Cakes
Dulce con Leche Cake
Pecan Bars

Vegetarian Dinner

Bean Nachos
Greens with Cilantro Dressing
Margarita Fruit Salad
Spicy Filo Burritos
Chocolate Flan

Watching the Game

Cheese Quesadillas
Spicy Salmon Wraps
Tex-Mex Egg Rolls
Crockpot BBQ Beef Sandwiches
Queso con Chile
Tortilla Chips
Jalapeño Cheese Crackers
Queso Fundito
Plain Margaritas
Micheladas
Chocolate Buttermilk Bars
Pecan Pralines

Dinner on the Grill

Tex-Mex Shrimp and Scallop Cocktail
Frozen Margaritas
Grilled Corn on the Cob
Fajitas with Soft Tortillas
Fruit and Avocado Salad
Grilled Pineapple with Cinnamon

Index

Mexican oregano, 6
mole
    Grilled Chicken in Mole
        Sauce, 152
    Mole Sauce, 95
Muffins, Tex-Mex Corn, 121

N

nachos, 4
    Bean Nachos, 28
    Nacho Cheese Sauce, 99
    Plain Nachos, 26
nopales, 5
    Deep-Fried Nopales, 36
    Nopales Salad, 46
nuts and seeds
    toasting, 7

O-P

oregano, 6
pasta
    Chili Mac, 174
    Mixed-Bean Lasagna, 225
    Tex-Mex Pasta Salad, 52
Peach Daiquiri Pie, 264
pecans
    Fiery Pecans, 21
    Pecan Bars, 265
    Pecan Pralines, 258
peppers
    See also chiles
    Chicken with Peppers, 151
    roasted, 7
    Tex-Mex Veggie Wraps, 208

pesto
    Cilantro Pesto, 90
    Grilled Snapper with
        Cilantro Pesto, 143
    Grilled Tilapia with
        Avocado Pesto, 139
    Jalapeño Pesto, 96
Picadillo, 167
pies
    Frito Pie, 167
    Frito Pie for a Crowd, 168
    Mango Cream Pie, 257
    Mexican Chocolate Caramel
        Pie, 267
    Peach Daiquiri Pie, 264
    Shrimp and Corn Pot Pie,
        134
    Tex-Mex Shrimp Tart, 131
    Tex-Mex Turkey Pot Pie,
        164
Pimento Cheese Quesadillas,
    203
pineapple
    Grilled Pineapple with
        Cinnamon, 270
    Pineapple Cake, 269
pinto beans. *See* beans
Pizzas, Mexican, 195
Pomegranate Green Salad, 53
pork
    See also bacon; sausage
    Baby Back Ribs, 17
    BBQ Pork Loin, 196
    BBQ Ribs, 192
    Carnitas, 186
    Chili Colorado, 68
    Crockpot BBQ Shredded
        Pork, 196

Crockpot Pozole, 66
Mini Tamales, 22
Pork Adobo, 198
Pork and Beans, 189
Pork con Queso, 200
Pork Fajitas, 193
Pork Tamales, 191
Stacked Tortas, 192
Tex-Mex Meatloaf, 169
Tex-Mex Pork Casserole,
    188
Tex-Mex Pork Kabobs, 197
potatoes
    Beef and Potato Burritos,
        172
    Chipotle Potatoes, 86
    Potato Chile Frittata, 231
    Potatoes Rancheros, 229
    Roasted Sweet Potatoes, 85
    Tex-Mex Potato Salad, 42
pot pies. *See* pies
poultry. *See* chicken; turkey
prawns. *See* shrimp
puff pastry, 134
pumpkin
    Frozen Pumpkin Chocolate
        Bars, 259
    Pumpkin Bread, 118
    Pumpkin Corn Bread, 116
    Pumpkin Soup, 64

Q

quesadillas
    Bean Quesadillas, 228
    Cheese Quesadillas, 204
    Chicken Quesadillas, 213

THE EVERYTHING SERIES!

BUSINESS & PERSONAL FINANCE

Everything® Budgeting Book
Everything® Business Planning Book
Everything® Coaching and Mentoring Book
Everything® Fundraising Book
Everything® Get Out of Debt Book
Everything® Grant Writing Book
Everything® Home-Based Business Book, 2nd Ed.
Everything® Homebuying Book, 2nd Ed.
Everything® Homeselling Book, 2nd Ed.
Everything® Investing Book, 2nd Ed.
Everything® Landlording Book
Everything® Leadership Book
Everything® Managing People Book
Everything® Negotiating Book
Everything® Online Business Book
Everything® Personal Finance Book
Everything® Personal Finance in Your 20s and 30s Book
Everything® Project Management Book
Everything® Real Estate Investing Book
Everything® Robert's Rules Book, $7.95
Everything® Selling Book
Everything® Start Your Own Business Book
Everything® Wills & Estate Planning Book

COMPUTERS

Everything® Online Auctions Book
Everything® Blogging Book

COOKING

Everything® Barbecue Cookbook
Everything® Bartender's Book, $9.95
Everything® Chinese Cookbook
Everything® Cocktail Parties and Drinks Book
Everything® College Cookbook
Everything® Cookbook
Everything® Cooking for Two Cookbook
Everything® Diabetes Cookbook
Everything® Easy Gourmet Cookbook
Everything® Fondue Cookbook
Everything® Gluten-Free Cookbook
Everything® Glycemic Index Cookbook
Everything® Grilling Cookbook

Everything® Healthy Meals in Minutes Cookbook
Everything® Holiday Cookbook
Everything® Indian Cookbook
Everything® Italian Cookbook
Everything® Low-Carb Cookbook
Everything® Low-Fat High-Flavor Cookbook
Everything® Low-Salt Cookbook
Everything® Meals for a Month Cookbook
Everything® Mediterranean Cookbook
Everything® Mexican Cookbook
Everything® One-Pot Cookbook
Everything® Pasta Cookbook
Everything® Quick Meals Cookbook
Everything® Slow Cooker Cookbook
Everything® Slow Cooking for a Crowd Cookbook
Everything® Soup Cookbook
Everything® Tex-Mex Cookbook
Everything® Thai Cookbook
Everything® Vegetarian Cookbook
Everything® Wild Game Cookbook
Everything® Wine Book, 2nd Ed.

CRAFT SERIES

Everything® Crafts—Baby Scrapbooking
Everything® Crafts—Bead Your Own Jewelry
Everything® Crafts—Create Your Own Greeting Cards
Everything® Crafts—Easy Projects
Everything® Crafts—Polymer Clay for Beginners
Everything® Crafts—Rubber Stamping Made Easy
Everything® Crafts—Wedding Decorations and Keepsakes

HEALTH

Everything® Alzheimer's Book
Everything® Diabetes Book
Everything® Health Guide to Adult Bipolar Disorder
Everything® Health Guide to Controlling Anxiety
Everything® Health Guide to Fibromyalgia
Everything® Hypnosis Book

Everything® Low Cholesterol Book
Everything® Massage Book
Everything® Menopause Book
Everything® Nutrition Book
Everything® Reflexology Book
Everything® Stress Management Book

HISTORY

Everything® American Government Book
Everything® American History Book
Everything® Civil War Book
Everything® Irish History & Heritage Book
Everything® Middle East Book

GAMES

Everything® 15-Minute Sudoku Book, $9.95
Everything® 30-Minute Sudoku Book, $9.95
Everything® Blackjack Strategy Book
Everything® Brain Strain Book, $9.95
Everything® Bridge Book
Everything® Card Games Book
Everything® Card Tricks Book, $9.95
Everything® Casino Gambling Book, 2nd Ed.
Everything® Chess Basics Book
Everything® Craps Strategy Book
Everything® Crossword and Puzzle Book
Everything® Crossword Challenge Book
Everything® Cryptograms Book, $9.95
Everything® Easy Crosswords Book
Everything® Easy Kakuro Book, $9.95
Everything® Games Book, 2nd Ed.
Everything® Giant Sudoku Book, $9.95
Everything® Kakuro Challenge Book, $9.95
Everything® Large-Print Crosswords Book
Everything® Lateral Thinking Puzzles Book, $9.95
Everything® Pencil Puzzles Book, $9.95
Everything® Poker Strategy Book
Everything® Pool & Billiards Book
Everything® Test Your IQ Book, $9.95
Everything® Texas Hold 'Em Book, $9.95
Everything® Travel Crosswords Book, $9.95
Everything® Word Games Challenge Book
Everything® Word Search Book

Bolded titles are new additions to the series.
All Everything® books are priced at $12.95 or $14.95, unless otherwise stated. Prices subject to change without notice.

HOBBIES

Everything® Candlemaking Book
Everything® Cartooning Book
Everything® Drawing Book
Everything® Family Tree Book, 2nd Ed.
Everything® Knitting Book
Everything® Knots Book
Everything® Photography Book
Everything® Quilting Book
Everything® Scrapbooking Book
Everything® Sewing Book
Everything® Woodworking Book

HOME IMPROVEMENT

Everything® Feng Shui Book
Everything® Feng Shui Decluttering Book, $9.95
Everything® Fix-It Book
Everything® Home Decorating Book
Everything® Homebuilding Book
Everything® Lawn Care Book
Everything® Organize Your Home Book

KIDS' BOOKS

All titles are $7.95
Everything® Kids' Animal Puzzle &
    Activity Book
Everything® Kids' Baseball Book, 4th Ed.
Everything® Kids' Bible Trivia Book
Everything® Kids' Bugs Book
Everything® Kids' Christmas Puzzle
    & Activity Book
Everything® Kids' Cookbook
Everything® Kids' Crazy Puzzles Book
Everything® Kids' Dinosaurs Book
**Everything® Kids' Gross Hidden Pictures
    Book**
Everything® Kids' Gross Jokes Book
Everything® Kids' Gross Mazes Book
Everything® Kids' Gross Puzzle and
    Activity Book
Everything® Kids' Halloween Puzzle
    & Activity Book
Everything® Kids' Hidden Pictures Book
Everything® Kids' Horses Book
Everything® Kids' Joke Book
Everything® Kids' Knock Knock Book
Everything® Kids' Math Puzzles Book
Everything® Kids' Mazes Book
Everything® Kids' Money Book
Everything® Kids' Nature Book

Everything® Kids' Pirates Puzzle and
    Activity Book
Everything® Kids' Puzzle Book
Everything® Kids' Riddles & Brain Teasers Book
Everything® Kids' Science Experiments Book
Everything® Kids' Sharks Book
Everything® Kids' Soccer Book
Everything® Kids' Travel Activity Book

KIDS' STORY BOOKS

Everything® Fairy Tales Book

LANGUAGE

Everything® Conversational Japanese Book
    (with CD), $19.95
Everything® French Grammar Book
Everything® French Phrase Book, $9.95
Everything® French Verb Book, $9.95
**Everything® German Practice Book with
    CD, $19.95**
Everything® Inglés Book
Everything® Learning French Book
Everything® Learning German Book
Everything® Learning Italian Book
Everything® Learning Latin Book
Everything® Learning Spanish Book
Everything® Sign Language Book
Everything® Spanish Grammar Book
Everything® Spanish Phrase Book, $9.95
Everything® Spanish Practice Book
    (with CD), $19.95
Everything® Spanish Verb Book, $9.95

MUSIC

Everything® Drums Book (with CD), $19.95
Everything® Guitar Book
**Everything® Guitar Chords Book with CD,
    $19.95**
Everything® Home Recording Book
Everything® Playing Piano and Keyboards
    Book
Everything® Reading Music Book (with CD),
    $19.95
Everything® Rock & Blues Guitar Book
    (with CD), $19.95
Everything® Songwriting Book

NEW AGE

Everything® Astrology Book, 2nd Ed.
Everything® Dreams Book, 2nd Ed.
Everything® Love Signs Book, $9.95

Everything® Numerology Book
Everything® Paganism Book
Everything® Palmistry Book
Everything® Psychic Book
Everything® Reiki Book
Everything® Tarot Book
Everything® Wicca and Witchcraft Book

PARENTING

Everything® Baby Names Book, 2nd Ed.
Everything® Baby Shower Book
Everything® Baby's First Food Book
Everything® Baby's First Year Book
Everything® Birthing Book
Everything® Breastfeeding Book
Everything® Father-to-Be Book
Everything® Father's First Year Book
Everything® Get Ready for Baby Book
Everything® Get Your Baby to Sleep Book,
    $9.95
Everything® Getting Pregnant Book
Everything® Homeschooling Book
Everything® Mother's First Year Book
Everything® Parent's Guide to Children
    and Divorce
Everything® Parent's Guide to Children
    with ADD/ADHD
Everything® Parent's Guide to Children
    with Asperger's Syndrome
Everything® Parent's Guide to Children
    with Autism
Everything® Parent's Guide to Children with
    Bipolar Disorder
Everything® Parent's Guide to Children
    with Dyslexia
Everything® Parent's Guide to Positive
    Discipline
Everything® Parent's Guide to Raising a
    Successful Child
**Everything® Parent's Guide to Raising
    Boys**
**Everything® Parent's Guide to Raising
    Siblings**
Everything® Parent's Guide to Tantrums
Everything® Parent's Guide to the Overweight
    Child
Everything® Parent's Guide to the Strong-
    Willed Child
Everything® Parenting a Teenager Book
Everything® Potty Training Book, $9.95
Everything® Pregnancy Book, 2nd Ed.

Bolded titles are new additions to the series.
All Everything® books are priced at $12.95 or $14.95, unless otherwise stated. Prices subject to change without notice.

Everything® Pregnancy Fitness Book
Everything® Pregnancy Nutrition Book
Everything® Pregnancy Organizer, $15.00
Everything® Toddler Book
Everything® Toddler Activities Book
Everything® Tween Book
Everything® Twins, Triplets, and

PETS

Everything® Boxer Book
Everything® Cat Book, 2nd
Everything® Chihuahua Bo
Everything® Dachshund Book
Everything® Dog Book
Everything® Dog Health Bool
Everything® Dog Training and
Everything® German Shepher
Everything® Golden Retriever
Everything® Horse Book
Everything® Horse Care Bc
Everything® Horseback Riding
Everything® Labrador Retrieve
Everything® Poodle Book
Everything® Pug Book
Everything® Puppy Book
Everything® Rottweiler Book
Everything® Small Dogs Book
Everything® Tropical Fish Boc
Everything® Yorkshire Terrier

REFEREN

Everything® Car Care Book
Everything® Classical Mythol
Everything® Computer Book
Everything® Divorce Book
Everything® Einstein Book
Everything® Etiquette Book, 2
Everything® Inventions and P
Everything® Mafia Book
Everything® Mary Magdale
Everything® Philosophy Book
Everything® Psychology Book
Everything® Shakespeare Boc

RELIGIO

Everything® Angels Book
Everything® Bible Book
Everything® Buddhism Book
Everything® Catholicism Book

Everything® Christianity Book
Everything® Freemasons Book
Everything® History of the Bible Book
Everything® Jewish History & Heritage Book
Everything® Judaism Book
Everything® Kabbalah Book

Everything® Yoga Book

TRAVEL

Everything® Family Guide to Hawaii
Everything® Family Guide to Las Vegas,
    2nd Ed.
Everything® Family Guide to New York City,
    2nd Ed.
...erything® Family Guide to RV Travel &
    Campgrounds
...rything® Family Guide to the Walt Disney
    World Resort®, Universal Studios®,
    and Greater Orlando, 4th Ed.
...rything® Family Guide to Cruise Vacations
...rything® Family Guide to the Caribbean
...rything® Family Guide to Washington
    D.C., 2nd Ed.
...rything® Guide to New England
...rything® Travel Guide to the Disneyland
    Resort®, California Adventure®,
    Universal Studios®, and the
    Anaheim Area

WEDDINGS

...rything® Bachelorette Party Book, $9.95
...rything® Bridesmaid Book, $9.95
...rything® Elopement Book, $9.95
...rything® Father of the Bride Book, $9.95
...rything® Groom Book, $9.95
...rything® Mother of the Bride Book, $9.95
...rything® Outdoor Wedding Book
...rything® Wedding Book, 3rd Ed.
...rything® Wedding Checklist, $9.95
...thing® Wedding Etiquette Book, $9.95
...thing® Wedding Organizer, $15.00
...thing® Wedding Shower Book, $9.95
...thing® Wedding Vows Book, $9.95
...thing® Weddings on a Budget Book, $9.95

WRITING

...thing® Creative Writing Book
...ything® Get Published Book, 2nd Ed.
...thing® Grammar and Style Book
...thing® Guide to Writing a Book Proposal
...thing® Guide to Writing a Novel
...thing® Guide to Writing Children's Books
...thing® Guide to Writing Research Papers
...thing® Screenwriting Book
...thing® Writing Poetry Book
...thing® Writing Well Book

Available wherever books are sold!
To order, call 800-289-0963, or visit us at *www.everything.com*
Everything® and everything.com® are registered trademarks of F+W Publications, Inc.